Tips for the
Science
Teacher

Tips for the Science Teacher

Research-Based Strategies to Help Students Learn

Hope J. Hartman
Neal A. Glasgow

CORWIN PRESS, INC
A Sage Publications Company
2455 TellerRoad
Thousand Oaks, CA 91320-2218

e-mail: order@corwinpress.com
Call: (800) 818-7243 Fax: (800) 417-2486
www.corwinpress.com

Copyright © 2002 by Corwin Press, Inc.

For information:

Corwin Press, Inc.
A Sage Publications Company
2455 Teller Road
Thousand Oaks, California 91320
E-mail: order@corwinpress.com

Sage Publications Ltd.
6 Bonhill Street
London EC2A 4PU
United Kingdom

Sage Publications India Pvt. Ltd.
M-32 Market
Greater Kailash I
New Delhi 110 048 India

Printed in the United States of America

Library of Congress Cataloging-in-Publication Data

Hartman, Hope J.
    Tips for the science teacher: Research-based strategies to help students learn / by Hope J. Hartman and Neal A. Glasgow.
        p. cm.
    Includes bibliographical references and index.
    ISBN 0-7619-7588-8 (c) — ISBN 0-7619-7589-6 (p)
    1. Science—Study and teaching. 2. Science teachers—Training of. I. Glasgow, Neal A. II. Title.
    Q181 .H33 2001
    507′.1′273—dc21   2001002190

This book is printed on acid-free paper.

01   02   03   04   05   10   9   8   7   6   5   4   3   2   1

Acquiring Editor: Faye Zucker
Corwin Editorial Assistant: Julia Parnell
Production Editor: Diane S. Foster
Editorial Assistant: Cindy Bear
Typesetter/Designer: Hespenheide Design
Cover Designer: Michelle Lee

Contents

Introduction

Within the culture of science, especially science research, the mechanisms for dissemination of new knowledge are clear. Research is done, and scientists communicate various aspects of the research through a vast array of literature. This accomplishes two things. First, it provides an arena for peer review, a self-regulating feature that forms a basis for establishing the validity and importance of any new information. Second, it provides an avenue through which intermediary science writers and others can digest the new information, add a bit of social critique or opinion, and make it available to the more mainstream media and therefore the public in general. This begins a sort of "societal filtering process" in which the general public has an opportunity to assess and evaluate new science information. Ethical issues, potential applications, and general usefulness of the research then fall within the public and private arenas of discourse.

Unlike science research, educational research, conducted and published in a similar way, suffers a communication breakdown on its way to the public. Intermediary writers, of the kind so important in the preliminary sorting of science research, aren't as visible and available. Information is not as readily transferred to the public or, more important, to the professional educational practitioners in the trenches. The community of classroom teachers who could benefit enormously from the findings of educational investigators rarely learn about current research on teaching and learning.

It is our objective in this book to bring some of the more useful research findings to the classroom teacher. Rather than merely report the research findings, we attempt to present the information in an authentic and useful context, explaining how it can be applied in real classrooms with real students.

We present here a great range of tips based on educational, psychological, and sociological research studies and some critiques. This diversity provides teachers with many choices as they look for solutions to individual teaching and learning problems and also provides inspirational triggers, offering opportunities for teachers' professional growth. This book is designed to provide an easy way for the classroom teacher to benefit from the many ideas embedded in the academic literature.

The format of the book makes it an easy and ready reference for the science teacher. It consists of seven chapters, each with a theme representing one aspect of the typical instructional program: instructional strategies, developing students' scientific thinking and learning skills, emotional aspects of science learning, social aspects of science classrooms, using technology in science teaching, informal science learning, and assessment in the science classroom. Each chapter presents a collection of teaching tips, concisely presented in a user-friendly format:

- **THE TIP:** A simple, concise, or crisp statement of the teaching tip.

- **What the Research Says:** A brief discussion of the research that led to the tip. This section should simply give the teacher some confidence in, and a deeper understanding of, the principle being discussed as a "teaching tip."

- **Classroom Applications:** A description of how this teaching tip can be used in the science instructional program.

- **Precautions and Possible Pitfalls:** Caveats intended to make possible a reasonably flawless implementation of the teaching tip. In this section we present ways to help teachers avoid common difficulties before they occur.

- **Bibliographies:** These are provided so that the reader may refer to the original research to discover in more detail the processes and findings.

Each tip suggests ways to apply the findings from research and encourages teachers to develop their own applications so that their students learn science more deeply and with more appreciation. Students often consider science to be one of the most difficult subjects they take. Because of its perceived difficulty, many students even develop science phobias, much as some tend to do with mathematics. Our ultimate goal in this book is to help teachers develop in students the desire to be lifelong science learners, as well as the motivation and capability to apply what they have learned about science in diverse contexts.

We see this book as an important step in bringing educational research findings to the classroom, where they can do the most good. Perhaps teachers will see that there is much to be gained from reviewing educational research with an eye toward adapting and applying the findings to their own instructional programs. We hope this book will stimulate science teachers to keep abreast of cutting-edge approaches to science teaching that are now in research laboratories around the world and will soon appear on the educational horizon.

Acknowledgments

We are grateful to the people at Corwin Press: to Alice Foster for recommending and arranging our collaboration, and to Gracia Alkema and Faye Zucker for their patience during the completion of the manuscript. We are also indebted to Alfred Posamentier and Constanze Kaiser for their work on the book *Tips for the Mathematics Teacher: Research-Based Strategies to Help Students Learn* (for which Hope Hartman was a coauthor), which inspired and informed this book.

Hope Hartman appreciates Drs. Joseph Griswold and Daniel Lemons for the opportunities she had to work with and learn from them on their innovative and multidimensional efforts to restructure introductory biology, anatomy, and physiology courses. She also is grateful to the scores of biology, physics, and chemistry tutors who helped her to develop content-specific materials to help science learners. Hope also deeply appreciates her treasured friends, who gave her the emotional support to complete this manuscript during rather trying times: Dennis Haas, her "brother"; Susan Solomon, her "sister"; and Drs. Teres Scott, Michelle Rabin, and Sandy Bushberg. Hope's husband, Michael Holub, was a great source of support, as always.

Hope dedicates this book to the memory of two wonderful friends and colleagues, Drs. Jann Azumi and Nancy Duke S. Lay.

Neal Glasgow is grateful to Dr. Margaret Just, whose own educational experiences, scientific research, professional growth, and personal support highlighted and clearly defined the differences between science and science education. Her laboratory colleagues were always there to help define what science teachers and citizens should know about the way science is conducted, the information science research provides, and how students should experience science.

He is also grateful to Dr. David Bynum, whose critical view of teachers and teaching never failed to inspire him to bring more professionalism to the field. He is most indebted to his many students and teaching colleagues, who provided most of his learning and teaching questions and problems. Without their reality, there wouldn't be answers.

The joy of writing and general sanity was always enhanced with the helpful diversions of the cats, Roxy and Ringer. Lastly, without the work of the many caring educational researchers, this book would not be possible. We are deeply indebted to them and hope we have given them a louder voice.

About the Authors

Hope J. Hartman is Professor of Educational Psychology at the City University of New York Graduate School and University Center, and Professor of Education at the City College of the City University of New York, where she is Coordinator of Social and Psychological Foundations. Her area of specialization is improving cognition and affect through instructional techniques that emphasize active, meaningful, and self-regulated learning. Recently, she has begun to focus her attention on the use of technology in teaching and learning. She earned her doctorate in cognitive psychology at Rutgers University's Institute for Cognitive Studies and received the Northeastern Educational Research Association's Distinguished Paper Award for part of her dissertation research on comprehension monitoring and clarification. She has held positions as an educational researcher at Rockland Community College in New York and in the Newark Public Schools District Office in New Jersey. She served as Assistant Director of a K-12 thinking skills program (THISTLE) and as Assistant Professor of Educational Leadership at Montclair State College. Before joining the faculty at the City College of New York, she was Director of the Diamond Learning Program (City College Tutoring and Cooperative Learning Program). She also served as Chairperson of the Secondary Education Department at CCNY. Since 1988, she has received and worked on several grants for science curriculum development, including funding from the National Science Foundation. In addition to authoring many articles and book chapters, she is the editor of *Metacognition in Learning and Instruction: Theory, Research and Practice* (2001), coauthor (with Alfred S. Posamentier and Constanze Kaiser) of *Tips for the Mathematics Teacher: Research-Based Strategies to Help Students Learn* (1998), and author of *Intelligent Tutoring* (1992).

Neal A. Glasgow has been involved in education on many levels. His experience includes serving as a secondary school science and art teacher in both California and New York, as a university biotechnology teaching laboratory director and laboratory technician, as an educational consultant, and as a frequent educational speaker on many topics. He is the author of three books on educational topics: *New Curriculum for New Times: A Guide to Student-Centered, Problem-Based Learning* (1997), *Doing Science: Innovative Curriculum Beyond the Textbook for the Life Science Classroom* (1997), and *Taking the Classroom Into the Community: A Guide Book* (1996). He is currently teaching biology and art at San Dieguito Academy High School, a California public high school of choice, and continues to conduct research and write on educational topics as well as work on various personal art projects.

CHAPTER ONE

Instructional Strategies

THE TIP (1.1)

 Before beginning a lesson, show students an overview of the day's content.

What the Research Says

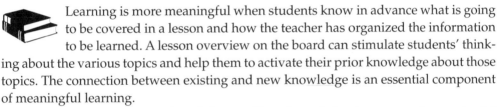 Learning is more meaningful when students know in advance what is going to be covered in a lesson and how the teacher has organized the information to be learned. A lesson overview on the board can stimulate students' thinking about the various topics and help them to activate their prior knowledge about those topics. The connection between existing and new knowledge is an essential component of meaningful learning.

According to Ausubel's (1960) theory of how knowledge is structured, meaningful learning depends upon lesson materials being organized in a way that makes them meaningful to the learner; that is, the learner needs to be able to connect the materials with ideas that already exist in the learner's cognitive structure. According to Ausubel, teachers can promote meaningful learning by using advance organizers: abstract, general, and inclusive introductory materials that provide a framework within which the material to be learned is preorganized. The framework provides a stable, general cognitive structure that students can use to subsume (or incorporate) specific information. Advance organizers help students to organize new material and to connect new material to their prior knowledge, thereby increasing the meaningfulness of the lesson and the likelihood students will learn and retain the information within it.

The teacher presents the advance organizer at the beginning of the lesson, before giving students information (e.g., lectures). Then the teacher provides the information, which the students take in or receive (reception learning). The organizer makes the information to be received more meaningful because it shows students in advance how the teacher has organized the material, and knowing concepts in advance helps students to activate relevant prior knowledge. This is Ausubel's recipe for "meaningful reception learning."

1

Classroom Applications

Do you remember being in a class, taking notes, and wondering whether the teacher was still talking about the same topic or had moved on to the next? Most students have had this experience more than once. Board or overhead projector outlines can serve a number of purposes. They can routinely inform students of due dates, upcoming events, and the like, and they can also be used to provide detailed outlines of current lessons. This technique often alleviates miscommunication problems and reduces the academic stress some students feel when faced with relatively ambiguous class structure.

For a lesson on digestion, you might create a grid or outline such as the one shown in Table 1.1 on the chalkboard, or you might design an appealing overlay for an overhead projector such as the overview of the lesson on "Our Solar System" shown in Figure 1.1, or you might create a computer presentation software slide (e.g., using PowerPoint).

Table 1.1   Structures and Functions of External Features of the Digestive System

Oral Cavity and Roles in Digestion

Structures	Physical Features	Locations & Boundaries	Functions
Tongue			
Teeth			
Salivary glands			
Nasal passages			
Glottis			
Epiglottis			
Esophagus			
Soft palate			
Hard palate			
Nasopharynx			

According to Novak (1998), there are two criteria for the design of an effective advance organizer:

1. The advance organizer must be based on the learners' specific existing relevant conceptual and propositional knowledge.

Figure 1.1.   Advance Organizer of a Lesson on the Solar System

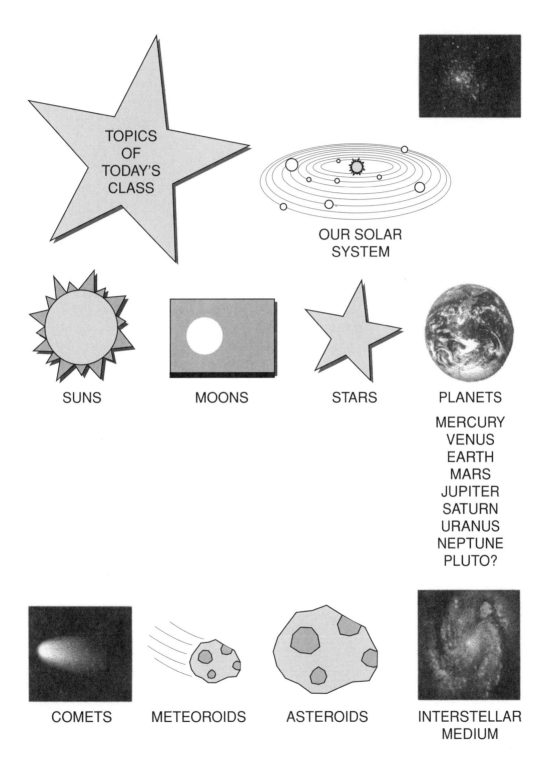

2. The advance organizer must organize and sequence the new information in relation to the learners' relevant prior conceptual and propositional knowledge.

The type of advance organizer displayed in the example in Table 1.1 is sometimes called a comparative organizer, because it encourages students to think about similarities and differences, in this case between structures of the oral cavity and their roles in digestion. The learners' relevant prior knowledge in this case includes structures of the oral cavity. This can also be considered an interactive advance organizer because, instead of having all of the details already filled in for each cell of the table, as is characteristic of reception learning, students are required to enter their own descriptions, a task characteristic of inquiry and/or discovery learning.

Precautions and Possible Pitfalls

When students set about turning advance organizers into notes, their focus turns to note taking, and you risk losing their attention. If time is an issue, you may consider handing out copies of your outlines or class notes to students and have them add to those, rather than having students use class time to copy information off the board or screen. Or, post them on a class Web site. Sometimes suspense or curiosity about the unknown is a useful motivation strategy. You can adapt the advance organizer for use in specific lessons where you want students to be unsure where you are headed. In addition, advance organizers that are too detailed can easily become meaningless chalkboard notes.

BIBLIOGRAPHY

Ausubel, D. (1960). The use of advance organizers in the learning and retention of meaningful verbal learning. *Journal of Educational Psychology, 51,* 267-272.

Novak, J. D. (1998). *Learning, creating and using knowledge: Concept maps as facilitative tools in schools and corporations.* Mahwah, NJ: Lawrence Erlbaum.

THE TIP (1.2)

 Use analogies to help students develop more valid conceptions.

What the Research Says

 When teachers use analogies to help explain concepts to students, students are able to construct more accurate conceptions of complex ideas. Joshua and Dupin (1987) conducted a study of 106 middle school students' (ages 12-14) ideas about electricity that included an examination of the students' conceptions of electrical circuits before their teacher covered the topic. The researchers examined the students' use (and lack of use) of their preconceptions to explain how a lightbulb works and how a battery works. They also looked at how these ideas changed after instruction. What they found was that the ideas became more internally consistent, but did not become more valid. When the teacher used an abstract, "thought experiment" analogy of a train on a closed-loop track to explain ideas about electrical circuits in a discussion, the students developed more accurate conceptions. The students were also able to use the analogy appropriately and to describe the limitations of the analogy. Table 1.2 shows the elements of the analogy between the train and the electrical circuit (Joshua & Dupin, 1987, p. 131). The teacher also drew a diagram showing the train analogy on the chalkboard and showed the connections with how an electrical circuit works.

Classroom Applications

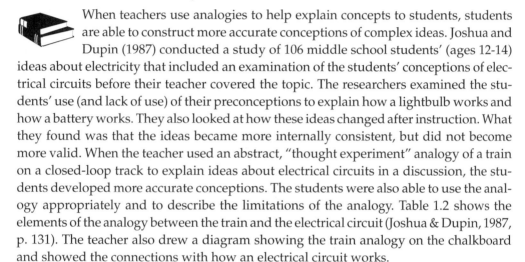

1. Do a concrete, hands-on classroom activity that involves the concept you are trying to teach, and follow the activity with a discussion.
2. Through the discussion, identify the students' preinstructional ideas about the concept.

3. Make sure that the students are aware of the different possible interpretations of individual concepts.

4. Have the students evaluate the competing interpretations.

5. Give the students a task that will enable them to test out and decide among these interpretations and will also help them to develop new interpretations and/or to refine old interpretations, as needed.

6. Have the students draw conclusions based on this task. Help them identify and try to reconcile major contradictions.

7. Give the students an analogy to the concept. Have them discuss the analogy, including its relevance and limitations.

In science, finding analogies that can help students to develop more accurate conceptions may be difficult, as relationships are sometimes abstract and skill oriented. For example, a city may serve as an analogy to a single cell in form and function. Both have boundaries, both have energy flow and waste problems, and the various structures in the two have differentiated functions. You might have students identify the structures and their functions within a cell and find analogies with those structures and functions in a city.

In earth science, you can help students to conceptualize ocean convection currents by analyzing the behavior of water in a large pot as it is being heated from the bottom. This analogy provides an example of the same idea on a different scale. Students can more easily picture the motions and effects of tides as well as undersea earthquakes and landslides if they think of the movement of the water in a child's plastic wading pool. When you hit the side of the pool, the water sloshes within its boundaries, much as an ocean does within its continental boundaries.

Often, you can help students to form concrete mental pictures of science concepts or processes by asking them to use their own life experiences to come up with their own analogies. Having students share these analogies can also provide you with valuable feedback, exposing misconceptions and errors in thinking.

Table 1.2   Analogy Between a Train and an Electrical Circuit

Train	Electrical Circuit
Cars	Electrons
Movement of cars	Movement of electrons
Rate at which cars pass a certain point along the track	Rate at which electrons pass a given point in the circuit (current intensity)
Mechanical friction (obstacle in the track)	Electrical resistance (atomic nuclei)
Men pushing train	Battery
Muscular fatigue of men	Wearing out of the battery
Vibration of the cars, noise and heat	Heat in the wires and battery, heat and light
Produced by collisions with obstacle on the track	In the bulb produced by the interactions of the electrons and atomic nuclei

Precautions and Possible Pitfalls

Students often have difficulty fitting new ideas into preexisting frameworks. Make sure that the framework you are using is very clear before you proceed to employ it as an analogy. Students must have a clear understanding of the

framework to be used in the analogy. For example, if students are not familiar with the underlying structures and functions of a city, they will be unable to make connections between those structures and functions and those of a cell; the analogy will only add to their confusion. In a rural environment, a better analogy for a cell might be a farm instead of a city. Adapt your application of this tip to your students' backgrounds and experiences. If your students have never boiled water or watched water boil, they have no starting point from which to compare or contrast the concepts involved. Good analogies are based on commonly shared experiences. They can also be biased socially, experientially, or culturally.

BIBLIOGRAPHY

Joshua, S., & Dupin, J. J. (1987). Taking into account student conceptions in instructional strategy: An example in physics. *Cognition and Instruction, 4*(2), 117-135.

THE TIP (1.3)

☑ Analyze your textbook and identify misconceptions about science that you don't want your students to learn.

What the Research Says

 Science textbooks sometimes contain misconceptions and alternative conceptions about science, so student use of such books can interfere with learning unless the teacher works to filter conceptual problems before students are exposed to them. Abimbola and Baba (1996) have developed a procedure for teachers to use in analyzing textbooks and identifying misconceptions. In their analysis of one textbook, *STAN Biology*, they found 117 misconceptions and 37 alternative conceptions distributed through 18 of the 22 chapters. One type of misconception involves the use of inaccurate or out-of-date terms to represent concepts; for example, *semipermeable membrane* has been replaced by *selectively permeable membrane* or *differentially permeable membrane*, to avoid any misunderstanding that the membrane is partially permeable or partially impermeable. Another type of misconception comes from statements that are wrong; for example, the statement "Oxygen is produced as a waste product" is erroneous because in the context of nutrition and photosynthesis, where it appears in the text, oxygen is really a useful end product of photosynthesis because it oxidizes food to release energy. As an example of an alternative conception, Abimbola and Baba note that the definition of dentition as concerning teeth does not mention that dentition also includes the arrangement of teeth. Abimbola and Baba recommend that teachers consider the number of misconceptions and alternative conceptions found in science textbooks and take care to choose books that contain the fewest of both.

Classroom Applications

 Read about and use or adapt the procedure that Abimbola and Baba developed for teachers to employ in analyzing textbooks and identifying misconceptions. In the sciences, words are often very context dependent. For example, the term *clone* can mean a variety of different things, depending on who is using it. Asexual bacteria routinely clone themselves and, in the process, duplicate their entire genome. The word *clone* has a very different meaning in that context from its meaning in the context of the science that produced Dolly the sheep. Even within the science community *clone* can mean a variety of things.

During a recent seminar, Dr. Bruce Alberts, president of the National Academy of Sciences, held up a secondary school science textbook and then read a few passages from it. The excerpts he read so oversimplified a complex biological topic and concept that the information given was almost no longer true. Textbooks often "dumb down" content to a point where the information suffers in validity.

The National Research Council's handbook *Science Teaching Reconsidered* (1997) provides guidelines for appropriate college science textbook selection that precollege teachers can adapt for their own textbook selection:

- To what extent is the text consistent with the course curriculum? To maximize students' benefit from the textbook, it should closely correspond with course objectives.

- To what extent is the textbook author's approach consistent with that of the course instructor? Lack of consistency between approaches of the text and teacher can easily confuse students.

Try awarding bonus points to students who find misconceptions in their textbooks and in reference books. Complain to publishing companies about errors and out-of-date information. Talk to colleagues at your school, in your district, and nationally and internationally about common scientific misconceptions, especially the ones most likely to affect your students' learning.

Precautions and Possible Pitfalls

Like any language, the language of the science changes, sometimes rapidly in definitions and contexts. Most science teachers are "teachers" more than they are scientists or "science people." There are no easy solutions for teachers interested in keeping up with the state of change within the language, processes, and progress of science. Textbooks always make sense if you know nothing else. Keeping current and enriching science textbook content requires science teachers to develop professional growth patterns out of the teaching paradigm. One way of doing this is by using the Internet, where many resources are available on misconceptions in science learning, including journal articles, conference proceedings, and information from project Web sites, such as C^3P (Comprehensive Conceptual Curriculum for Physics), which is based on findings from current research in students' preconceptions (see http://phys.udallas.edu/).

Keep in touch with your science discipline by attending science, not education, seminars, by attending in-service opportunities featuring scientists, and by forming relationships within the local science community. This will give you greater insight into how the content of your textbooks relates to the "real world" where science functions.

BIBLIOGRAPHY

Abimbola, I. O., & Baba, S. (1996). Misconceptions and alternative conceptions in science textbooks: The role of teachers as filters. *American Biology Teacher, 58,* 14-19.

National Research Council. (1997). *Science teaching reconsidered.* Washington, DC: National Academy Press.

THE TIP (1.4)

Be aware that students may come to your classroom with scientific misconceptions that may interfere with their acquisition of the information you want them to learn. To help students really understand science, you need an accurate view of your students' prior knowledge of a topic.

What the Research Says

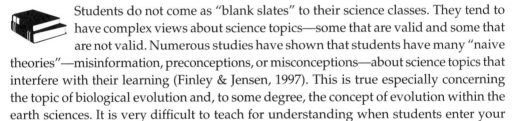

Students do not come as "blank slates" to their science classes. They tend to have complex views about science topics—some that are valid and some that are not valid. Numerous studies have shown that students have many "naive theories"—misinformation, preconceptions, or misconceptions—about science topics that interfere with their learning (Finley & Jensen, 1997). This is true especially concerning the topic of biological evolution and, to some degree, the concept of evolution within the earth sciences. It is very difficult to teach for understanding when students enter your classroom not believing in some basic concepts.

Misconceptions are faulty ideas that are based on false or incomplete information, limited experience, incorrect generalizations, or misinterpretations and are consistent with the student's basic understanding. Other causes of misconceptions include cultural myths, scientifically out-of-date information, and attempts to oversimplify content. In a study of college biology students, Anderson, Sheldon, and DuBay (1990) looked at the concepts of respiration and photosynthesis. Sample misconceptions include the simplistic definition that respiration is exhaling CO_2 and thinking that plants get their food from nutrients in the soil rather than manufacture their own food. Misconceptions can also arise from vague, ambiguous, or discrepant information. Some researchers view and refer to misconceptions as *alternative frameworks* or *preconceptions,* emphasizing the emergent nature of structures of knowledge. Some information students bring with them is an emerging foundation, parts of which can be built upon, parts of which must be revised, and parts of which must be discarded.

A critical component of teaching for conceptual change is the teacher's creation of situations that stimulate students to modify their prior knowledge into more scientifically valid forms. This is best begun with a survey activity designed to allow the teacher to assess students' initial ideas. The teacher needs an accurate idea of the students' prior knowledge as an instructional starting point.

Classroom Applications

One science concept for which teachers' preassessment of students' prior or current knowledge and understanding is strongly recommended is the biologically unifying concept of evolution. The concept of evolution within the earth sciences also calls for such preassessment. Most of the science community's larger professional organizations now call for the theme of evolution to be the central unifying concept in the teaching of biology. In a similar but slightly different fashion, physical evolution is a central thread in the earth sciences.

To assess students' prior knowledge of biological evolution and evolution within the earth sciences, you might give students several problems to solve or describe several situations for which they should provide explanations. The responses should provide you with important information. Consider these four examples:

In the Life Sciences

- In Mexico, certain species of blind cave fish (they have remnants of eyes, but these organs are not functional) exist in geographically close but isolated caves. How would biologists explain how these fish evolved from the same sighted ancestors as other fish, and why the fish in various caves look different from one another?

- Many antibiotics today are gradually becoming ineffectual against certain human bacterial diseases. Gradually, bacteria become resistant to antibiotics that have worked well in the past. How would microbiologists explain the existence of these antibiotic-resistant bacteria?

In the Earth Sciences

- Dinosaurs no longer exist, but many fossil and skeletal remains have been discovered in odd locations around the world. How would geologists explain the existence of dinosaur fossils in the Arctic regions, where the hostile environment could not support such large animals?

- Many species of sea turtles migrate long distances over hazardous routes to lay their eggs on specific beaches yet live the rest of their lives in totally different environments. How might geologists explain this phenomenon?

You will usually find that student views include a variety of ideas. Some Darwinian ideas and concepts may be mixed with other, non-Darwinian ideas. Plate tectonics and climatic change, central earth science concepts, help explain and answer the last two questions.

Some students may even mention divine intervention as an explanation of certain changes. Listening to your students' answers to such questions will give you a clear view of their perceptions of evolution.

You can structure such preinstructional assessments to reveal your students' views on and attitudes toward a variety of evolutionary concepts, including those concerning earth processes, origins, biological change, and other related concepts and human divergence. A typical instructional approach requires that you do the following:

- Challenge misconceptions, misinformation, and naive theories about science with scientific evidence and explanations.

- Present new science ideas and concepts.

- Ensure that students experience the success of seeing that the new ideas you present provide better explanations of the evidence.

It is clear that teaching and learning evolutionary concepts are difficult for both teachers and students. Research has shown that students exhibit an increase in their use of scientific or Darwinian explanations when teachers follow the steps laid out above.

Precautions and Possible Pitfalls

The problems you pose for your students must be at an appropriate level of complexity. In addition, the students must have some appropriate level of prior knowledge, so they can figure out what they need to learn to solve the problems. You also need to give them enough time and resources to address the problems, or you will not gain the information you desire. The topics within the questions must be appropriate for the ability level of the students and also must be challenging and motivating, not frustrating. Unless they are interested, students will not become totally engaged.

Occasionally, students' misconceptions may be based in misinformation they have learned from trusted friends or family members. Such misconceptions may be rooted in students' personal religious, cultural, or social beliefs, or in the beliefs of their parents. The topic or concept of evolution in the curriculum is an obvious example of an area in which students may hold misconceptions. You need to be very sensitive to the dangers to which you may expose yourself by aggressively attacking certain misconceptions. You may be able to avoid direct confrontation on sensitive issues by talking with students individually and privately when such issues arise. Structuring and providing avenues of respectful discourse within a class can also reduce the likelihood of undesirable confrontations.

The topic of evolution within the sciences, used here as an example, comes with many potential instructional pitfalls. To help you avoid them, we offer some specific recommendations for the teaching of evolution:

1. If the majority of your curriculum comes from textbooks, carefully select those that reflect the curricular content, arrangements, and balance you desire. Most textbooks have been reviewed as well as compared and contrasted with others. You can often find information on specific textbooks in research journals.

2. Balance evolutionary content within the total curriculum. The biological and earth science evolutionary theme, both scientific and cultural, has a past, present, and future. Give it a larger context within other science topics and concepts.

3. Address directly the likely cultural/religious concerns about evolution and the origins of the earth and human beings, and do so early on so as to break down any barriers that can keep students from hearing what you have to say. It is appropriate and fruitful to begin with a discussion of the nature of science and scientific inquiry.

4. Be careful about wandering into areas that are not science; do not contradict anything others have told students outside of the science context.

5. Encourage students to make a distinction between questions within the realm of science and questions of religion, and vice versa.

6. The integrity of the science curriculum and instruction cannot be based on personal beliefs; rather, it must be based on the best science research of the day. It is crucial that both students and teachers understand the progress of science and the progress of scientific advancement. An examination of the nature, rules, and philosophy of science may be a first step in addressing this issue.

BIBLIOGRAPHY

Anderson, C. W., Sheldon, T. H., & DuBay, J. (1990). The effects of instruction on college nonmajors' conceptions of respiration and photosynthesis. *Journal of Research in Science Teaching, 27*, 761-776.

Finley, F. N., & Jensen, M. S. (1997). Teaching evolution using a historically rich curriculum and a paired problem solving instructional strategy. *American Biology Teacher, 55*, 208-212.

THE TIP (1.5)

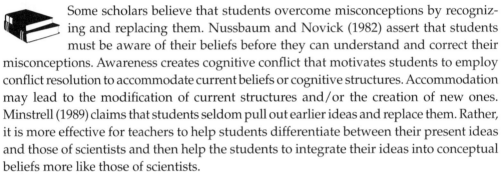

Use a conceptual change model to overcome students' misconceptions.

What the Research Says

Some scholars believe that students overcome misconceptions by recognizing and replacing them. Nussbaum and Novick (1982) assert that students must be aware of their beliefs before they can understand and correct their misconceptions. Awareness creates cognitive conflict that motivates students to employ conflict resolution to accommodate current beliefs or cognitive structures. Accommodation may lead to the modification of current structures and/or the creation of new ones. Minstrell (1989) claims that students seldom pull out earlier ideas and replace them. Rather, it is more effective for teachers to help students differentiate between their present ideas and those of scientists and then help the students to integrate their ideas into conceptual beliefs more like those of scientists.

Research on teaching for conceptual change suggests that students can be taught active processing strategies (e.g., predicting, explaining) that can help them notice and correct their misconceptions, thereby deepening their scientific understanding. Students can learn to distinguish similar concepts—such as force, impulse, and work—from each other and from properties of systems or objects (McDermott, 1984).

Direct, hands-on experience can help students to develop models of concepts based on their own observations, enabling them to make more accurate predictions and explanations (McDermott, 1991). Posner, Strike, Hewson, and Gertzog (1982) highlight three conditions for conceptual change: dissatisfaction with a current concept, perceived plausibility of a new concept, and perceived usefulness of a new concept. They also emphasize some aspects of the learner's "conceptual ecology," such as epistemological commitments about the nature of evidence, the importance of parsimony, and metaphysical beliefs (e.g., faith in nature's orderliness). Posner et al.'s conceptual change model emphasizes confronting existing concepts and facts, pointing out contradictions, seeking consistency, and making theory intelligible, plausible, and fruitful.

Classroom Applications

Apply or adapt one of the available conceptual change models. The following is an adaptation of Driver's conceptual change model (as cited by Skane & Graeber, 1993):

1. *Orientation:* Introduction to the topic and motivation.

2. *Awareness:* Recognition of misconceptions. This may occur in one of the following ways:

    a. *Independent recognition:* Without feedback from an external source, the student uses her or his own knowledge and reasoning, which interacts with the context to uncover a misunderstanding.

    b. *Disconfirmational feedback:* The student is exposed to information from an external source (e.g., lab experiment, instructor, tutor, book) that directly contradicts his or her conceptions; change occurs through cognitive conflict.

    c. *Relational recognition:* The student is exposed to information that is related to his or her conceptions, and this information helps the student to discover that those earlier conceptions are inadequate.

    d. *Induced recognition:* The student is told directly that his or her conceptions are invalid; the student is confronted with conflicting concepts and facts.

3. *Elicitation:* Explication of student ideas and misconceptions. The student disassembles concepts into their component parts, or deconstructs them (component knowledge and skills are broken into a learning hierarchy).

4. *Restructuring:* Integration of new and revised conceptions. The student is receptive to changing his or her conceptions. The student exchanges and clarifies ideas after exposure to conflicting meanings, recursively expanding and reworking information.

5. *Application:* Consolidation of new or restructured ideas. The student uses new or restructured conceptions to solve problems or answer questions.

6. *Review:* Reflection on concepts. The student considers what the concepts are; when, why, and how they are used; and what they are related to—how they fit into the big picture.

Precautions and Possible Pitfalls

As the scale at which science is conducted today continues to undergo reduction, there are more and more concepts that students simply cannot observe or experience directly. Molecular biology and atomic structures can usually be observed only indirectly. The equipment and expertise needed to bring such experiences, in a hands-on style, into K-12 classrooms are limited. For example, students can usually experience aspects of the work of the Human Genome Project or an atomic accelerator experiment only through paper lab simulations. Poor hands-on experiences that really don't demonstrate the concepts under study can increase confusion. Without effective alternative types of reinforcement strategies, teachers risk reducing their students' experiences to rote learning. The need for educators to survey and adopt sound instructional practices to confront and reduce scientific misconceptions has never been greater and will continue to be a challenge.

BIBLIOGRAPHY

McDermott, L. (1984). Research on conceptual understanding of mechanics. *Physics Today, 37,* 24-32.

McDermott, L. (1991). What we teach and what is learned: Closing the gap (Millikan Lecture 1990). *American Journal of Physics, 59,* 301-315.

Minstrell, J. (1989). Teaching science for understanding. In L. Resnick & L. Klopfer (Eds.), *Toward the thinking curriculum: Current cognitive research* (pp. 129-149). Alexandria, VA: Association for Supervision and Curriculum Development.

Nussbaum, J., & Novick, S. (1982). Alternative frameworks, conceptual conflicts and accommodation: Toward a principled teaching strategy. *Instructional Science, 11,* 183-200.

Posner, G., Strike, K., Hewson, P., & Gertzog, W. (1982). Accommodation of a scientific conception: Toward a theory of conceptual change. *Science Education, 66,* 211-228.

Skane, M. E., & Graeber, A. O. (1993, August). *A conceptual change model implemented with college students: Distributive law misconceptions.* Paper presented at the Third International Conference on Misconceptions and Educational Strategies in Science and Mathematics, Ithaca, NY.

THE TIP (1.6)

 Persist! True misconceptions tend to be deeply held and highly resistant to change.

What the Research Says

 Research shows that misconceptions are deeply entrenched and enduring, even after students learn new information that is inconsistent with their prior knowledge. Extensive and deep, meaningful learning must take place before new, correct knowledge can come to mind and be applied, instead of the old misconceptions (Pressley & McCormick, 1995). According to Duit (1991), prior knowledge affects students' observations, guiding them to information that is consistent with their own perspectives. Students selectively attend to information, seeking to confirm what they already "know." Sometimes students' prior knowledge is so strong that they won't even believe what they see. A videotape titled *A Private Universe* (Schneps & Sadler, 1992) shows that even students and professors at Harvard University are subject to deeply entrenched scientific misconceptions.

Classroom Applications

There is a point at which some aspects of science curriculum content may conflict with a student's entrenched misconceptions or alternative explanations for scientific phenomena. This situation can have detrimental effects on the overall learning and teaching environment for both the individual student and the class as a whole. Experienced teachers usually know where these trouble spots in the curriculum or pedagogy are and have plans to mitigate such situations. Talk to your colleagues about strategies they have found successful.

You may find it helpful to acknowledge to your students that other views or perspectives exist concerning particular concepts. It is important that you make sure you present the most current and accurate view science can provide, and perhaps the most prevalent alternative views, if you are comfortable. Students need to remember that you are coming from an informative, not a persuasive, perspective. If the class chemistry is right, this can open the door to respectful debate. If students comprehend and understand what you are presenting, you have done your job. They can then decide how they want to use the information.

Precautions and Possible Pitfalls

 Don't make the mistake of thinking that because you have given students the correct scientific information, they will automatically replace their old, faulty information with the new, accurate information. Usually a more substantive "conceptual change" approach is needed to eliminate misconceptions.

Also, be aware that what you say goes home to your students' parents. If you know that you are going into a controversial unit, communicate the nature of the unit with the parents ahead of time, and have alternative options available. Such planning will help parents to see you as a professional and as a person with empathy.

BIBLIOGRAPHY

Duit, R. (1991). Students' conceptual frameworks: Consequences for learning science. In S. M. Glynn, R. Yeany, & B. Britton (Eds.), *The psychology of learning science* (pp. 65-85). Hillsdale, NJ: Lawrence Erlbaum.

Pressley, M., & McCormick, C. B. (1995). *Advanced educational psychology for educators, researchers, and policymakers.* New York: HarperCollins.

Schneps, M. H., & Sadler, P. M. (Producers). (1992). *A private universe* [Videotape]. San Francisco: Astronomical Society of the Pacific.

THE TIP (1.7)

 Structure teaching and learning of science concepts and skills around problems to be solved, using a problem-centered or problem-based approach to teaching and learning.

What the Research Says

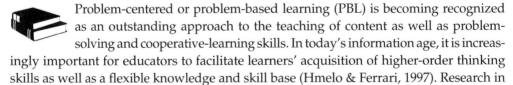 Problem-centered or problem-based learning (PBL) is becoming recognized as an outstanding approach to the teaching of content as well as problem-solving and cooperative-learning skills. In today's information age, it is increasingly important for educators to facilitate learners' acquisition of higher-order thinking skills as well as a flexible knowledge and skill base (Hmelo & Ferrari, 1997). Research in

cognitive science and education suggests that teachers can achieve these goals by arranging instruction and learning around carefully selected, designed, and constructed problems or problem-based learning scenarios. Problem-based learning stresses both content acquisition and the higher-order thinking skills students require to analyze problems, gather appropriate resources to address problems, and solve problems.

Often, more traditional teacher-centered teaching and learning require students to assimilate content based on the promise that they will need it beyond the test and the classroom. PBL is the learning that results from the process of a student's working toward the understanding or resolution of a problem. PBL calls for students to acquire knowledge in a more authentic context, within a more open-ended problem-solving scenario. Curricular models that incorporate PBL more clearly simulate the higher-order thinking skills and conditions within many advanced academic and career pathways. Within a problem-based classroom arrangement, students learn to learn and become more independent, confident thinkers as well as lifelong learners.

In examining a PBL curriculum, Dolmans (1994) found that students depended upon a combination of the following sources of information:

1. Initial problem discussion

2. Generation of learning issues

3. Reference literature

4. Course objectives

5. Test content

6. Other students

7. Tutors

Dolmans's work suggests that PBL has the metacognitive advantage of helping students identify and integrate information from a variety of relevant sources.

Classroom Applications

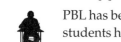 PBL has been in use in many science classrooms for a long time. Engineering students have been presented with the problem of creating packages for eggs that will allow the eggs to survive a drop from a given height without breaking. Physics teachers have used paper-airplane contests to help students learn and test the principles of flight. Many science research classes and contests stress problem solving or research as a vehicle for learning.

There is a difference between teaching static science knowledge from a textbook and teaching science as the dynamic inquiry and problem-solving practice it is. Engaging students in the process of doing science can make the textbook knowledge come alive as the principles it describes are applied to interesting problems. The best problems are those for which there is no one "right" recipe or pathway to the solution. To solve such problems, students must ask good questions, test experimental designs, analyze results, draw conclusions, and revise their designs as necessary. Following are a few examples.

In a biology class, a group of students wanted to find out what attracts birds to certain types of seeds placed in bird feeders. They thought the deciding factor was color, so to test this hypothesis, they used different colors of vegetable dye to color the same types of seeds. The students placed the different colored seeds in different feeders and gathered data for a week.

In a chemistry class, students conducted consumer science on various household cleaners. They looked at the ingredients and product claims and researched the chemical science behind the products, and then they conducted comparison tests to determine which one was the most successful at actual cleaning. Experimental design became a challenge as the students tried to quantify their results.

Students beginning a botany unit were presented with an envelope containing five seeds. The students were told they were free to conduct any type of research they wanted utilizing those seeds. They were also required to list 10 questions they thought they could answer with their seed experiments. The topics covered by their questions ranged from the effects of water and light to the effects of fertilizers and beyond. The seeds the students were given were for "quick grow" plants that matured in a 2-week time frame. This allowed the students to "multitask" as they continued to take part in other class activities. They acquired and used much of the traditional curriculum because they needed the information to make sense of their experiments and explain their results.

Students in a physics class who were exploring energy were asked to create plans for the most energy-efficient house possible. They collected information on alternative and traditional building materials and brought in samples of materials for testing. The students tested various energy sources, from gas to solar power, for efficiency and compared the costs. They found that they needed to apply the concepts and principles in their textbooks in order to quantify energy production, retention, and loss. Because of the large scope of this project, students worked in teams.

Precautions and Possible Pitfalls

 Students who are accustomed to a teacher-centered or more traditional instructional style often require a period of adjustment to PBL (Glasgow, 1996). PBL requires students to take more responsibility for their own learning. They need to be more active and less passive in identifying what they need to know to solve a problem, acquire resources, set the pace of learning, and demonstrate mastery. In many PBL scenarios, there are no limits on how far a student can explore a topic. This open-ended quality calls for a gentle introduction to the responsibilities that PBL entails. You may need to build in many intermediate steps and model the PBL process for your students to avoid their becoming frustrated. Early on, they may need reinforcement to help build their confidence. As students become familiar with PBL, they require less direct guidance and are able to work more independently.

BIBLIOGRAPHY

Dolmans, D. (1994). *How students learn in a problem-based curriculum.* Maastricht, the Netherlands: Universitaire Pers Maastricht.

Glasgow, N. (1996). *Doing science: Innovative curriculum for the life sciences.* Thousand Oaks, CA: Corwin.

Hmelo, C. E., & Ferrari, M. (1997). The problem-based learning tutorial: Cultivating higher-order thinking skills. *Journal for the Education of the Gifted, 20,* 401-418.

THE TIP (1.8)

 Use state and national standards to establish benchmarks for assessing your students' science literacy.

What the Research Says

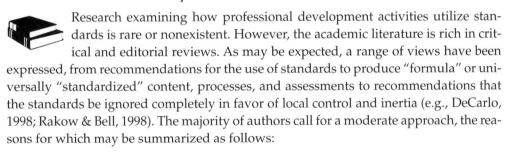 Research examining how professional development activities utilize standards is rare or nonexistent. However, the academic literature is rich in critical and editorial reviews. As may be expected, a range of views have been expressed, from recommendations for the use of standards to produce "formula" or universally "standardized" content, processes, and assessments to recommendations that the standards be ignored completely in favor of local control and inertia (e.g., DeCarlo, 1998; Rakow & Bell, 1998). The majority of authors call for a moderate approach, the reasons for which may be summarized as follows:

- The science standards are not a national science curriculum or a federal mandate.

- The standards do not contain specifications for a national exam.

- The standards do not constitute a set of rules, regulations, or approaches.

- The standards are designed to move stakeholders in the direction of (a) teaching science for conceptual change, (b) promoting integration of science and other content areas, (c) placing students in a position where they can see themselves as scientists and critical thinkers, and (d) providing a foundation upon which teachers can create experiences promoting inquiry, wonder, and understanding.

Overall, most of the literature calls for educators to use the various standards as a frame of reference for judging the quality of science education already provided. In addition, and most important, teachers should use the standards as tools that can serve and inspire them.

Classroom Applications

 When structuring a semester or yearlong science experience for your class, you will find that there are only so many resources that can contribute to the content and your instructional practices. Some teachers turn to textbooks and their colleagues for concrete help in structuring day-to-day activities. They trust textbooks to cover the mandated content and colleagues to help provide advice on timeline/pace, choice of specific content, and related activities. Most of these choices are based on the resources available at the school and the department's institutionalized instructional inertia. Try doing a little research—explore the various national frameworks, guidelines, and mandates.

Specific guidelines, mandates, standards, and frameworks, provided by national science organizations, filter through state and other bureaucratic agencies. Each state modifies and puts its own spin on the sources of guidance. Three valid and useful examples of national guidelines come from the National Academy of Sciences, the National Science Teachers' Association, and the American Association for the Advancement of Science (Project 2061). The overall usefulness of these documents has improved over the years. In the past, rarely would any of these guidelines filter down to the classroom teacher. Today, because of access to the Internet, they are available to everyone. So now, rather than turning first to textbooks or your colleagues, you can treat yourself to a more global perspective on how you and your students should experience science education.

In the recent past, the information in national science associations' guidelines was limited to what the organizations' leadership thought should be taught. Today, the thinking in these organizations has evolved and philosophies have expanded, and the guidelines include not only *what* should be taught but *how* science should be taught, learned, and experienced by students. Most of the guidelines now encompass suggested content, delivery, and assessment strategies and standards. However, most don't give direct, concrete examples or activities that are ready for the classroom. They only suggest how you might create and construct your own experiences for students that reflect their science education philosophies.

If you are designing your own instructional strategies and activities, these types of documents are the best and most current sources of information on science education you can find. They can be interesting and motivating, and you should visit and revisit them in support of your professional growth and inspiration.

Precautions and Possible Pitfalls

 Not all teachers keep current on the latest ideas in science teaching and learning. Department or school politics can be a problem. Curricular leadership can also come into play and cause conflict. The various standards, mandates, guidelines, and frameworks can be interpreted in different ways, and philosophical differences can be problematic. There is no way to predict how change will affect relationships within your school or department.

BIBLIOGRAPHY

DeCarlo, C. (1998). Standards that serve you. *Instructor, 108*(4).

Rakow, S. J., & Bell, M. J. (1998). Science and young children: The message from the National Science Education Standards. *Childhood Education, 74*(3), 164-167.

THE TIP (1.9)

 Use peer tutoring to help your students learn.

What the Research Says

 Peer tutoring can promote science learning at virtually all grade and school levels. Research shows that peers can scaffold one another's development of higher-level thinking and learning in science. In a study of seventh graders learning science, King, Staffieri, and Adelgais (1998) assigned students to three different tutoring conditions: explanation only, inquiry with explanation, and sequenced inquiry with explanation. Students were assigned to tutoring pairs and trained to tutor. Tutoring occurred over 5 weeks on content the teacher had already covered. The researchers measured cognitive, metacognitive, and affective variables, and found that students do not have to be tutored by other, "more competent" students to develop their thinking and knowledge in science. Students who were at the same age and ability levels helped each other learn in all three conditions.

A whole classroom of students helping other students has also been found to be an efficient and effective method of enhancing achievement. Fuchs, Fuchs, Mathes, and Simmons (1997) conducted a study in which 20 teachers participated in a study of classwide peer tutoring with 40 classrooms in elementary and middle schools. Half of the schools implemented classwide peer tutoring programs and half did not. Both urban and suburban schools participated, and the students came from diverse backgrounds, both culturally and linguistically. The researchers established three different categories of students: average achievers, low achievers without learning disabilities, and low achievers with learning disabilities. The peer tutoring programs were conducted 3 days a week, 35 minutes a day, for 15 weeks. Stronger students were paired with weaker students, and teachers reviewed each pair to ensure the individuals were socially compatible. In all pairs, students took turns serving in the roles of tutor and tutee. Student pairs worked together for 4 weeks, and then teachers arranged new pairings. The teachers received training on how to train their students to be tutors; this training included teaching students how to correct each other's errors. Achievement tests were administered before and after the peer tutoring program. Regardless of whether students were average achievers or low achievers, and regardless of the presence or absence of learning disabilities, students in the peer tutoring classrooms achieved at higher levels than did those in the classrooms without classwide peer tutoring.

Classroom Applications

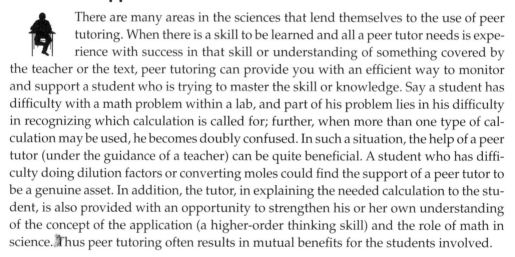

There are many areas in the sciences that lend themselves to the use of peer tutoring. When there is a skill to be learned and all a peer tutor needs is experience with success in that skill or understanding of something covered by the teacher or the text, peer tutoring can provide you with an efficient way to monitor and support a student who is trying to master the skill or knowledge. Say a student has difficulty with a math problem within a lab, and part of his problem lies in his difficulty in recognizing which calculation is called for; further, when more than one type of calculation may be used, he becomes doubly confused. In such a situation, the help of a peer tutor (under the guidance of a teacher) can be quite beneficial. A student who has difficulty doing dilution factors or converting moles could find the support of a peer tutor to be a genuine asset. In addition, the tutor, in explaining the needed calculation to the student, is also provided with an opportunity to strengthen his or her own understanding of the concept of the application (a higher-order thinking skill) and the role of math in science. Thus peer tutoring often results in mutual benefits for the students involved.

Precautions and Possible Pitfalls

Peer tutoring must be preceded by tutor training offered by the teacher. You will need to give tutors some instruction on how to conduct the sessions, what sorts of difficulties they should look for on the part of tutees, and what points they should stress in the sessions (based on your assessment of the class). You should mention any individual difficulties on the part of a tutee to the tutor prior to the sessions. Teach tutors also that their role is to guide student learning, not merely to solve problems for tutees. Students with severe learning disabilities may be too disruptive to benefit from classwide peer tutoring unless the tutors first receive individualized instruction from specialists in education for learning-disabled students.

BIBLIOGRAPHY

Fuchs, D., Fuchs, L., Mathes, P. G., & Simmons, D. (1997). Peer-assisted learning strategies: Making classrooms more responsive to diversity. *American Educational Research Journal, 34,* 174-206.

King, A., Staffieri, A., & Adelgais, A. (1998). Mutual peer tutoring: Effects of structuring tutorial interaction to scaffold peer learning. *Journal of Educational Psychology, 90,* 134-152.

THE TIP (1.10)

Use concept maps and Vee diagram graphic organizers to aid students' understanding of scientific concepts, systems, and procedures.

What the Research Says

Research has shown that concept maps and Vee diagrams help people learn how to learn. Concept maps also help students and teachers differentiate misconceptions from valid conceptions, decrease anxiety, improve self-confidence, and more. Novak, Gowin, and Johansen (1983) found that junior high school science students who were taught to use concept maps and Vee diagrams outperformed students who were not taught these strategies on tests of novel problem solving. Research conducted by Okebukola with Nigerian high school biology students showed that students who used concept maps had significantly better content mastery, better attitudes toward biology, and less anxiety than did those who did not use concept maps (cited in Novak, 1998). Regis and Albertazzi (1996) studied chemistry students ages 16-18 in a technical school who were taught concept mapping to aid their visualization of knowledge structures; the researchers also used the students' concept maps to document and explore changes in the students' knowledge structures as a result of learning. After 4 years of experience, Regis and Albertazzi note, "We have grown more and more impressed by the potential of this metacognitive tool to help chemistry teachers and learners to improve teaching and learning" (p. 1088). They found that concept mapping helps teachers to know what students know and to see how students relate concepts in their knowledge bases. This tool also shows teachers what misconceptions students have and lets teachers see how students reorganize their cognitive structures after specific learning activities. Concept maps benefit learners by making learning of new subject matter meaningful. Support has also been found for the use of concept mapping in the design of an artificial intelligence training program for the diagnosis of coronary problems (Ford et al., 1991).

The Vee diagram (or the knowledge Vee) was developed by Novak's retired colleague, Gowin, in 1977 to help students understand research. It is a V-shaped graphic organizer that helps learners systematically observe and measure all relevant variables by focusing on the specific principles and concepts that are involved in the event and the focus question. A Vee diagram consists of four basic sections: the focus question (top center); the event (bottom center); thinking, conceptual/theoretical elements (left side); and doing, methodological elements (right side). The elements on the left side of the diagram include the learner's worldview, philosophy/epistemology, theory, principles, constructs, and concepts. Those on the right side include value and knowledge claims, transformations, and records. All Vee diagram components interact to create new knowledge.

Concept maps, developed by Novak in 1972, are graphic representations of knowledge with the most general concept at the top, hierarchically leading to more specific concepts. Concepts appear in boxes or circles, with labeled connecting lines or arrows identifying relationships. The labels are words that link one concept to another, and labels are placed in the middle of linking lines. Figure 1.2 presents an example: The general concept *body fluid compartments* appears in a box, with lines drawn from it to linking words (e.g., *are, differ in*), which have lines drawn from them to more specific concepts (e.g., *intercellular fluid, chemical composition*), which are also in boxes. The linking lines from the more specific concepts (e.g., *intercellular fluid*) lead to still more specific concepts (e.g., *fluid within cells*), also in boxes. According to Novak, concept maps help to empower students, reduce the need for rote learning (memorization without understanding), and help teachers to negotiate meaning with students and to design better instruction. Students can use concept mapping successfully as individuals or in teams; the technique works equally well with concepts and events.

Classroom Applications

 Procedures for creating concept maps and Vee diagrams appear in the appendixes to Novak's book *Learning, Creating and Using Knowledge* (1998). You may need to model this learning tool as a classroom activity, using the board or an overhead projector. One way to help students acquire the skills they need to adopt these

Figure 1.2. Sample Concept Map on Body Fluid Compartments

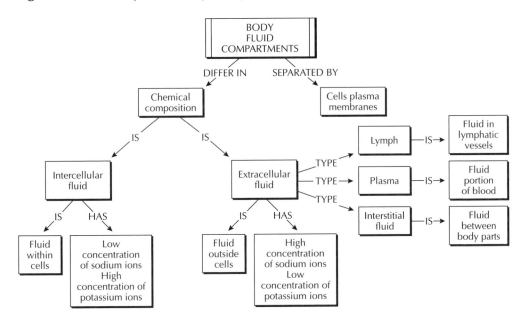

strategies is to allow them to use the concept maps and Vee diagrams they have created during their assessments or tests. This bestows immediate value and authenticity on the activity. Those students who authentically engage in the process of learning using these techniques will be immediately rewarded for their efforts, and those who find the techniques useful will adopt them. As a next step, you might reward students with grades for their finished Vee diagrams and content maps, but not allow them to use their diagrams and maps during assessment activities. In this way you can guide students through the learning of these techniques and encourage their adoption.

Cooperative learning arrangements can also be useful, as some students may be able to model the techniques for others. A good way to end a lecture or a period of note taking is to give students time to concept map their notes in class as you make yourself available for questions and provide guidance.

Precautions and Possible Pitfalls

Students are exposed to many types of study skills and strategies in their school careers. Some simply will not adopt new tools to replace their less effective techniques. Others already have study techniques that work for them. Guide your students through these concepts and give them the opportunity to learn them—some will buy into them and others won't.

BIBLIOGRAPHY

Ford, K. M., Canas, A., Jones, J., Stahl, H., Novak, J. D., & Adams-Weber, J. (1991). ICONKAT: An integrative constructivist knowledge acquisition tool. *Knowledge Acquisition, 3,* 215-236.

Novak, J. D. (1998). *Learning, creating and using knowledge: Concept maps as facilitative tools in schools and corporations.* Mahwah, NJ: Lawrence Erlbaum.

Novak, J. D., Gowin, D. B., & Johansen, G. T. (1983). The use of concept mapping and knowledge Vee diagramming with junior high school science students. *Science Education, 67,* 625-645.

Regis, A., & Albertazzi, P. (1996). Concept maps in chemistry education. *Journal of Chemical Education, 73,* 1084-1088.

THE TIP (1.11)

 Work directly with individual students as often as possible.

What the Research Says

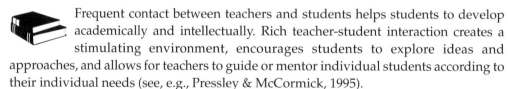 Frequent contact between teachers and students helps students to develop academically and intellectually. Rich teacher-student interaction creates a stimulating environment, encourages students to explore ideas and approaches, and allows for teachers to guide or mentor individual students according to their individual needs (see, e.g., Pressley & McCormick, 1995).

Classroom Applications

In a traditional classroom, it is not practical for a teacher to work with individual students for long periods of time. While your students are working individually on an exercise, you can visit with individual students and offer them some meaningful suggestions. Such suggestions might include hints that can move students who appear to be frustrated or bogged down on particular points toward solutions. You might also provide private advice to students on the form of their work. For example, some students are their own worst enemies when they are working with diagrams—they may create diagrams that are either so small they cannot do anything worthwhile with them or so inaccurately drawn that they prove to be relatively useless. Such small offers of support can move students along and give them that very important feeling of teacher interest.

In a case where a student is experiencing more severe problems, you might be wise to work with the individual after classroom hours. In this situation, you can have the student describe what he or she is doing as he or she works, justifying the procedure and explaining concepts. During such one-on-one tutoring sessions, you can gain valuable insight into a student's problems. Are they conceptual? Has the student missed understanding an algorithm? Does the student have perceptual difficulties? Spatial difficulties?

Precautions and Possible Pitfalls

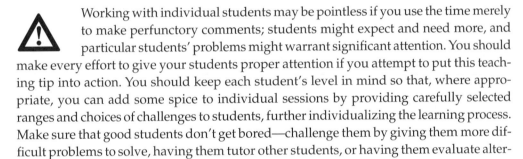

Working with individual students may be pointless if you use the time merely to make perfunctory comments; students might expect and need more, and particular students' problems might warrant significant attention. You should make every effort to give your students proper attention if you attempt to put this teaching tip into action. You should keep each student's level in mind so that, where appropriate, you can add some spice to individual sessions by providing carefully selected ranges and choices of challenges to students, further individualizing the learning process. Make sure that good students don't get bored—challenge them by giving them more difficult problems to solve, having them tutor other students, or having them evaluate alternative approaches to solving a problem.

Be aware that some students can become very needy. They may lack confidence or the ability to work comfortably in an independent manner, and this can compel them to begin to monopolize your time. When this occurs, give these students the same general attention that you give to others. If their demands begin to dominate the class, invite them to see you after school or at another time when you can give them undivided attention. To conserve time, consider creating a group of a few students with the same problems and address their needs together. Or have students who understand the material serve as tutors, mentors, or group leaders.

BIBLIOGRAPHY

Pressley, M., & McCormick, C. B. (1995). *Advanced educational psychology for educators, researchers, and policymakers*. New York: HarperCollins.

THE TIP (1.12)

 Use a learning cycle approach to science teaching to help students move from concrete to abstract understanding of scientific concepts.

What the Research Says

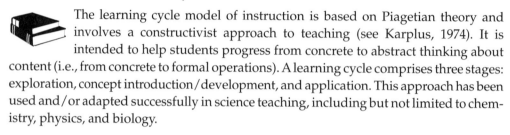 The learning cycle model of instruction is based on Piagetian theory and involves a constructivist approach to teaching (see Karplus, 1974). It is intended to help students progress from concrete to abstract thinking about content (i.e., from concrete to formal operations). A learning cycle comprises three stages: exploration, concept introduction/development, and application. This approach has been used and/or adapted successfully in science teaching, including but not limited to chemistry, physics, and biology.

- *Exploration:* Exploration involves students' getting hands-on experience working with the content that is to be the focus during the learning cycle. The teacher provides students with materials and guides their experience with them.

- *Concept introduction/development:* The teacher uses the students' experiences from their exploration to introduce the basic concepts to be learned.

- *Application:* The application phase of the learning cycle "challenges students to generalize the concepts of the lesson to other situations. They solve new problems by applying what they learned during steps one and two. Ideally, the teacher will assign tasks or problems that relate to students' everyday lives" (Barman, Benz, Haywood, & Houk, 1992, pp. 18-19).

By the end of a learning cycle unit, students are expected to have progressed from concrete thinking about scientific concepts to being able to deal with the concepts on a formal, abstract level.

Classroom Applications

This approach is inductive because it begins with specific, concrete experiences and gradually progresses to abstract generalizations about content. This approach is constructivist because it requires students to construct and reconstruct their own concepts. They use the knowledge they already have in combination with the information to be learned and apply this knowledge in different circumstances to build and refine concepts.

The Learning Cycle Model: Physics Example

Libby (1995) uses learning cycles to teach introductory chemistry. He describes the learning cycle as a three-phase process that provides students with opportunities to explore new material, to work with a teacher to recognize logical patterns in data, and to devise and test hypotheses. In Libby's approach, during exploration, the first phase, students evaluate data outside the classroom environment. Students attempt to identify significant trends and develop hypotheses that might explain fundamental scientific principles. During concept introduction, the second phase, the students and instructor work together in the classroom to evaluate student hypotheses and find concepts that work best in explaining the data. The third and final phase, application, involves an out-of-class application of the concept to new situations.

Griswold uses several techniques to help his students organize, understand, and remember what they have learned, one of which is the learning cycle. He designs lectures and laboratories to begin with the concrete and lead to the practice of formal operational functions, such as problem solving, using symbols and verbal reasoning. For example, initially small groups of students brainstorm together about how smoking can interfere with gas exchange in the lungs. Their sharing of ideas activates prior knowledge, reveals misconceptions, and identifies information gaps that need to be filled. This exploratory phase is followed by a dissection of the respiratory system and a study of its functions using demonstrations and videomicroscopy. Next, students analyze the issue of smoking using their new knowledge. Finally, they apply what they have learned to explain new situations, such as a change in function with physical exertion or pathology (see Griswold & Hartman, 1991). During application, students return to the original question on the impact of smoking with a new understanding of the mechanics of interference (Hartman, 2001).

Exploration. Do a brief demonstration or experiment and ask the students questions based on it, such as "What did you observe? How would you interpret or explain what you observed?" For example, show a lightbulb lighting from a setup with wire and a battery. Ask the students questions such as "Looking at the inside of the lightbulb, can you tell where the light originates? What is the difference between an open and a closed circuit?"

Concept introduction. Introduce the technical terms, formulas, rules, and so on that fit the analysis of what was observed during the exploration. Connect these concepts to the students' observations and interpretations. For example, describe a model of electrical current using and defining technical terms such as *current, flow, conductors, resistance, circuits,* and *volts.*

Application. Have the students use a critical concept to solve a new problem. This step helps the students generalize the concept beyond the initial concrete learning situation and the abstract concept introduction and helps them think about the concept more abstractly. For example, ask, "What is meant by 'short circuit'? What does the model predict the current will be under _____ circumstances?" (Fill in the blank in different ways to test students' understanding of the effects of different variables.)

The Comprehensive Conceptual Curriculum for Physics (C³P) is a learning cycle-based curriculum created by the Physics Department of the University of Dallas. It is designed to apply research on physics education to high school physics teaching. The department's Web site (at http://phys.udallas.edu/) provides numerous resources for teachers, including a sample learning cycle lesson on kinematics.

Another example of a classroom use of the learning cycle approach follows.

The Learning Cycle Model: Biology Example

Exploration

1. Pass around M&Ms for all students to eat.
2. Have students write brief descriptions of what they believe happens as their bodies digest the M&Ms.

To facilitate the inquiry process, ask questions such as the following:

- Where does digestion start?
- What parts of the body are involved in digestion?
- What is the function of each part?
- Where does digestion end?

Concept Introduction

1. Have students read about digestion in the material assigned.
2. Present a lecture on digestion.
3. Expose students to diagrams and simulations of the digestive system in books and videotapes as well as on the computer.
4. Have students write their answers to questions about digestion.
5. Discuss students' answers and provide feedback.

Application

1. Have students do a lab on digestion, applying what they have learned. Have them observe dissected animals in the lab, on video, or in a computer simulation. Have them diagram the structures and complete data matrices on their observations; have each student compare his or her results with those of a partner.

2. Have students solve problems about digestion.

3. Have students discuss how they might use their knowledge of digestion in their future professional activities—for example, those students who plan to become doctors, nurses, or physicians' assistants.

Lemons and Griswold determined that the original learning cycle model needed to be adapted to their students' goals and activities. Hence they modified the original learning cycle model, systematically integrating into it computer-based learning activities and simulations as well as formative and summative evaluations (see Hartman, 2001).

Figure 1.3.   Adaptation of the Learning Cycle in Biology

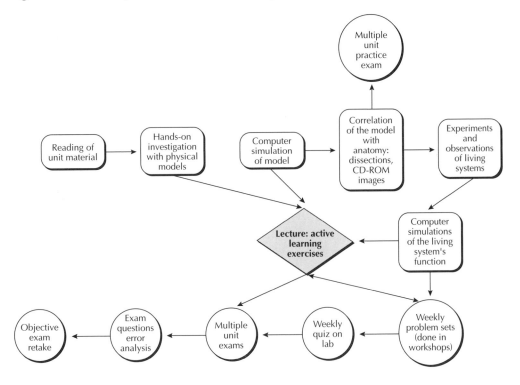

Precautions and Possible Pitfalls

The learning cycle might not always be the best approach for teachers to use. A study comparing the learning cycle approach to modeling in urban middle school science classes found that although both the modeling and learning cycle groups outperformed the control students in their use of integrated science process skills, students who were taught through modeling developed better integrated science process skills than did students who were taught using the learning cycle approach (Rubin and Norman, 1989). Rather than automatically using any commonly accepted approach, such as the learning cycle, you should carefully reflect on your own experiences in combination with the implications of what research has shown about the advantages and disadvantages of a variety of instructional methods for specific students and subject matters. Perhaps you will find that a combination of approaches is most effective in helping your students to develop even higher levels of integrated science process skills.

BIBLIOGRAPHY

Barman, C., Benz, R., Haywood, J., & Houk, G. (1992). Science and the learning cycle. *Perspectives in Education and Deafness, 11*(1), 18-21.

Griswold, J., & Hartman, H. J. (1991). *Restructuring introductory biology for success with minority students: A developmental approach.* Invited contribution to the colloquium "On Introductory Science Courses: New Approaches to Teaching and Learning," City University of New York.

Hartman, H. J. (2001). Metacognition in science teaching and learning. In H. J. Hartman (Ed.), *Metacognition in learning and instruction: Theory, research and practice* (pp. 173-201). Dordrecht, the Netherlands: Kluwer Academic.

Karplus, R. (1974). *The Science Curriculum Improvement Study (SCIS).* Berkeley: University of California, Lawrence Hall of Science.

Libby, R. D. (1995). Piaget and organic chemistry: Teaching introductory organic chemistry through learning cycles. *Journal of Chemical Education, 72,* 626-631.

Rubin, R. L., & Norman, J. T. (1989, April). *A comparison of the effect of a systematic modeling approach and the learning cycle approach on the achievement of integrated science process skills.* Paper presented at the annual meeting of the National Association for Research in Science Teaching, San Francisco. (ERIC Document Reproduction Service No. ED 305268)

THE TIP (1.13)

 Increase your awareness and your students' awareness of their personal learning styles. Try to improve the alignment between your teaching practices and your students' learning styles.

What the Research Says

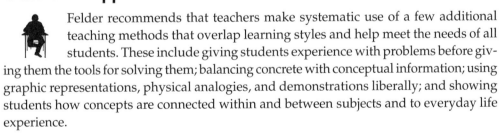 Tobias (1986) notes the negative features of many introductory college science courses, such as failure to motivate student interest, emphasis on passive learning, emphasis on competitive rather than cooperative learning, and reliance on algorithms rather than understanding. These features sometimes steer students away from careers in the sciences. Recent research suggests that the mismatch between teaching practices and students' learning styles may account for many of these problems. Felder's (1993) model of learning styles is especially appealing because it conceptualizes the dimensions of sensing/intuiting, visual/verbal, inductive/deductive, active/reflective, and global/sequential as continua rather than as dichotomous, "either/or" variables. Felder cites research to guide instruction for each of these styles.

Classroom Applications

Felder recommends that teachers make systematic use of a few additional teaching methods that overlap learning styles and help meet the needs of all students. These include giving students experience with problems before giving them the tools for solving them; balancing concrete with conceptual information; using graphic representations, physical analogies, and demonstrations liberally; and showing students how concepts are connected within and between subjects and to everyday life experience.

Precautions and Possible Pitfalls

Students and their parents often have entrenched views of how specific classes should be presented and experienced. If you venture too far from these "norms," student comfort levels can drop and student anxiety can rise. If you intend to present teaching or learning experiences (restructuring or reforming) that you feel might be new or unfamiliar to your students and their parents, consider clearly communicating with them about these new strategies early. You do not want to threaten students' potential success in your class or produce unneeded frustration.

Beware of the dangerous tendency to fall into the trap of labeling students, or allowing them to label themselves, as particular types of learners and then restricting your teaching and their learning to the dominant styles. By ignoring nondominant styles, you can limit students' intellectual growth and development. The goal of thinking about students' learning styles is to facilitate learning, not to constrain it.

Don't expect miracles of yourself. There can be an overwhelming number and variety of learning styles within a single class, and it is unrealistic for you to try to accommodate instruction to all of them on a regular basis. The key is to vary your instructional methods and present information in multiple modalities.

BIBLIOGRAPHY

Felder, R. M. (1993). Reaching the second tier: Learning and teaching styles in college science education. *Journal of College Science Teaching, 23*(5), 286-290.

Tobias, S. (1986, March-April). Peer perspectives on the teaching of science. *Change,* pp. 36-41.

THE TIP (1.14)

Highlight characteristics of your own mental models of content from your course, help students become aware of their own mental models, and help students identify and understand the differences between your models and theirs.

What the Research Says

In a review of the literature on the implications of cognitive science for the teaching of physics, Redish (1994) identifies four broad principles, each with corollaries, that physics teachers may find helpful as they think about their teaching. First is the *construction principle,* which states that people organize their knowledge and experiences into mental models and that individuals must build their own mental models. Second is the *assimilation principle,* which says that mental models control how individuals incorporate experiences and new information into their minds. Related prior knowledge and experiences form mental models into which individuals incorporate new knowledge and experience. Third is the *accommodation principle*, which emphasizes that sometimes existing mental models must be changed for learning to occur. Fourth is the *individuality principle*, which highlights the individual differences in people's mental models that result from their personal constructions. Different students have different mental models for learning and different mental models for physical phenomena.

Classroom Applications

Redish's four principles provide a framework that can help physics and other science teachers to plan, monitor, and evaluate their instruction, classroom activities, and learning assessments so as to maximize students' understanding of science. For example, Redish suggests that looking at the curriculum from the mental models perspective can help teachers to establish the goals of identifying the mental models they want students to develop, stimulate teachers to consider the character and implications of students' preexisting mental models, and help teachers realize the benefit of using touchstone problems to analyze and identify critical aspects of the curriculum. According to Redish, one implication of the individuality principle is that teachers need to think about how different students may arrive at the same answers but for very different reasons. To determine how their students reason, teachers should listen to students as they think aloud, without guiding them.

Use the "think-aloud approach" to highlight your mental models for your students. Talk through the steps you take while you are solving a problem so they can hear how you think about the problem and how you plan an approach to solving it based on the mental model or representation you have constructed.

Precautions and Possible Pitfalls

Don't always model error-free performance when demonstrating your mental models. This can lead to the false impression among students that successful scientists always "get it right"—selecting and using appropriate mental models—on their first attempts. It can be useful for you to make errors deliberately in front of students, so that they can observe how you use your mental models to self-monitor the implementation of your plan, assess the adequacy of your approach, and recover from errors to refine the mental models you have constructed so that they fit the problem situation.

Although mental models are often influenced by culture, don't make the mistake of assuming that students from similar cultural backgrounds will necessarily have similar mental models. The individuality principle is especially important in this context.

BIBLIOGRAPHY

Redish, E. F. (1994). The implications of cognitive science for teaching physics. *American Journal of Physics, 62*, 796-803.

THE TIP (1.15)

 Use the pair problem-solving method in class.

What the Research Says

Stress on Analytical Reasoning (SOAR), a program at Xavier University in New Orleans, has a record of success in teaching science to minority students interested in health sciences, physics, engineering, and mathematics (Fuller, 1998). One of the teaching strategies that educators in this program have found especially useful is pair problem solving. Whimbey and Lochhead (1982) describe this technique as a thinker and listener pair working on problems and rotating roles. Students take turns serving as thinkers (problem solvers), who externalize their thought processes by thinking aloud while analytic listeners track, guide, and question the problem-solving process as needed. This method makes problems more engaging and promotes self-monitoring and self-evaluation, giving students feedback on what is understood and what is still unclear. It encourages the development of skills in reflecting on beginning and later thoughts. It also teaches communication skills, fosters cooperation, and encourages the formation of study and support groups. Finally, pair problem solving exposes teachers and students to various solution approaches (Narode, Heiman, Lochhead, & Slomianko, 1987). By listening to their own thoughts, students gain awareness and control over problem solving. By externalizing their thoughts, students are able to see those thoughts from a fresh perspective. Together, pairs of students can discover errors, misconceptions, organizational problems, and other impediments to academic performance. The teacher needs to observe each pair, monitor progress, and provide feedback on the process. This approach has been demonstrated to be effective in helping students learn science and math (Whimbey & Lochhead, 1982).

Classroom Applications

 Set up thinker-listener pairs for cooperative problem solving. In each pair, the thinker verbalizes aloud *all* of the thoughts that arise as he or she goes through the process of completing an academic task. The listener actively attends to what the thinker says, examines the accuracy of the thinker's statements, points out errors, and keeps the thinker talking aloud. You will need to give students instructions about how to think aloud and how to serve as analytic listeners. In addition, as noted above, you should observe each pair, monitor progress, and provide feedback on the process.

Precautions and Possible Pitfalls

 Don't assume that students already know how to think out loud and how to be analytic listeners. Both skills require training, including demonstrations that you will need to provide. When teachers first start using this technique, they often discover how much they do automatically and intuitively. To think aloud for students effectively, teachers need to make what is implicit for themselves explicit for their students. Keep the following in mind:

1. People usually think faster than they speak, so sometimes thoughts trip over speech when students try to think aloud.

2. If students don't have adequate knowledge about a problem, they may not be able to think aloud effectively about how they are going about solving it.

3. Be aware that some students might be shy about thinking aloud because of their cultural/linguistic backgrounds, speech impediments, or simply peer pressure.

(For further details on how to develop skills in thinking aloud and analytic listening for pair problem solving, see Hartman, 1996.)

BIBLIOGRAPHY

Fuller R. G. (1998). ADAPT: A multidisciplinary Piagetian-based program for college freshmen. *Genetic Epistemologist, 26*(2) [On-line]. Available on Internet: http://www.piaget.org

Hartman, H. J. (1996). Cooperative learning approaches to mathematical problem solving. In A. Posamentier & W. Schulz (Eds.), *The art of problem solving* (pp. 401-430). Thousand Oaks, CA: Corwin.

Narode, R., Heiman, M., Lochhead, J., & Slomianko, J. (1987). *Teaching thinking skills: Science.* Washington, DC: National Education Association.

Whimbey, A., & Lochhead, J. (1982). *Problem solving and comprehension* (3rd ed.). Philadelphia: Franklin Institute Press.

THE TIP (1.16)

 Make realistic time estimates when planning your lessons.

What the Research Says

 Teachers need to have excellent time management skills if their students are to learn effectively. It has been said that "time + energy = learning." In planning their lessons, teachers sometimes confuse the amount of time allocated for instruction, such as a 50-minute class period, and the amount of time students are actually engaged in learning, which may be only 25 minutes out of the 50-minute period. The concept of engaged time is often referred to as *time-on-task*. Teachers often fail to take into account the *off-task* time they devote to managing student behavior, overseeing classroom activities, and dealing with announcements and interruptions (see Brophy, 1988).

Classroom Applications

Distinguish between time allocated for instruction and engaged learning time when you estimate how long it will take students to learn a particular set of materials. The time students actually spend learning is the key to how much they achieve.

Precautions and Possible Pitfalls

Be sure to include in your lesson plans time for your students to "digest" the material covered, time for you to monitor their comprehension of concepts and tasks, and time for you to engage in clarification as needed. If you look at a lesson only from the point of view of making sure particular material is "taught" or "covered," you are likely to underestimate the time students will need to understand, record, and remember what they have learned. Make sure that you allow sufficient time for students to take complete notes of the development you are doing in the lesson, so that they can effectively review for tests at home.

BIBLIOGRAPHY

Brophy, J. (1988). Research linking teacher behavior to student achievement: Potential implications for instruction of Chapter 1 students. *Educational Psychologist, 23,* 235-286.

THE TIP (1.17)

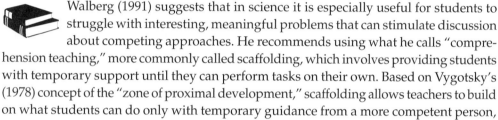

Provide students with temporary support (scaffolds) as they are learning complex skills or procedures. Gradually withdraw this support as students become more competent in performing the skills or procedures on their own, eventually phasing out your role entirely.

What the Research Says

Walberg (1991) suggests that in science it is especially useful for students to struggle with interesting, meaningful problems that can stimulate discussion about competing approaches. He recommends using what he calls "comprehension teaching," more commonly called scaffolding, which involves providing students with temporary support until they can perform tasks on their own. Based on Vygotsky's (1978) concept of the "zone of proximal development," scaffolding allows teachers to build on what students can do only with temporary guidance from a more competent person, gradually reducing and eventually removing this support as students become independent thinkers and learners who can perform particular tasks or use certain skills on their own. The zone of proximal development is the area within which the student can receive support from another person to perform successfully a task that the student cannot perform independently. Scaffolding has been found to be an excellent method of developing students' higher-level thinking skills (Rosenshine & Meister, 1992). Through scaffolding, teachers can gradually and systematically shift responsibility and control over learning and performance from themselves to their students.

Classroom Applications

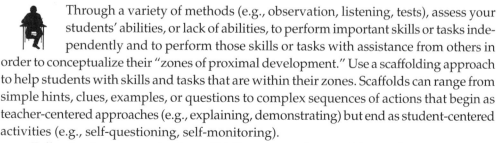

Through a variety of methods (e.g., observation, listening, tests), assess your students' abilities, or lack of abilities, to perform important skills or tasks independently and to perform those skills or tasks with assistance from others in order to conceptualize their "zones of proximal development." Use a scaffolding approach to help students with skills and tasks that are within their zones. Scaffolds can range from simple hints, clues, examples, or questions to complex sequences of actions that begin as teacher-centered approaches (e.g., explaining, demonstrating) but end as student-centered activities (e.g., self-questioning, self-monitoring).

Following is an example of a scaffolding approach to teaching students to construct graphic organizers of text they have read. This complex sequence of steps uses scaffolding to shift students from teacher direction and control over student creation of graphic organizers to student self-direction and self-control.

1. Show and explain to students a variety of traditional examples of graphic organizers, such as flowcharts, concept maps, and matrices, some made by professionals and some by students.

2. Inform students about what graphic organizers are and when, why, and how various types of them should be used. Jones, Pierce, and Hunter (1988-1989) provide information on why and how to create graphic organizers to comprehend text; their article includes illustrations of a spider map, a continuum/scale, a series of events chain, a compare/contrast matrix, a problem/solution outline, a network tree, a fishbone map, and a human interaction outline. Novak (1998) focuses on concept maps and Vee diagrams.

3. As a classroom or homework assignment, give students a partially completed graphic organizer to finish on their own. Give them feedback on their completions.

4. As a classroom or homework assignment, have students complete empty graphic organizer structures entirely on their own. Give them feedback on their work.

5. As a classroom or homework assignment, organize groups of students to create their own graphic organizers. Give students specific criteria for the construction and evaluation of graphic organizers, such as the following:

   a. The graphics are neat and easy to read.

   b. Ideas are expressed clearly.

   c. Ideas are expressed completely but succinctly.

   d. The content is organized clearly and logically.

   e. Labels or other strategies (colors, lines) are used to guide reader comprehension.

   f. Main ideas, not minor details, are emphasized.

   g. The graphic organizer is visually appealing.

   h. The reader doesn't have to turn the page to read all the words.

6. Once the groups complete their graphic organizers, have each group show theirs to the other groups. Have all groups critique the graphic organizers of all the other groups, giving the creators feedback based on the criteria used. Supplement the feedback as needed.

7. As a homework assignment, have students develop graphic organizers completely on their own, using the identified criteria. Have group members give one another feedback on the extent to which the graphic organizers created meet the established criteria.

8. Finally, have students create and critique their own graphic organizers, without support from others (students or teacher).

Precautions and Possible Pitfalls

To use scaffolding effectively, you must consider such issues as what types of support to provide to students, when and in what order to sequence different levels of support, and what criteria you will use in deciding when it is time to reduce or withdraw support. It is also very important that you make sure your scaffolding attempts are truly within your students' zone of proximal development. If they fall below this area, activities will be too easy because the students can really do them independently. If they are above this area, no amount of scaffolding will enable students to perform independently because the skills or tasks are too difficult given the students' prior knowledge and/or skills.

BIBLIOGRAPHY

Jones, B. F., Pierce, J., & Hunter, B. (1988-1989). Teaching students to construct graphic representations. *Educational Leadership, 46*(4), 20-25.

Novak, J. D. (1998). *Learning, creating and using knowledge: Concept maps as facilitative tools in schools and corporations.* Mahwah, NJ: Lawrence Erlbaum.

Rosenshine, B., & Meister, C. (1992). The use of scaffolds for teaching higher-level cognitive strategies. *Educational Leadership, 49*(7), 26-33.

Vygotsky, L. S. (1978). *Mind in society: The development of higher psychological processes* (M. Cole, V. John-Steiner, S. Scribner, & E. Souberman, Eds.). Cambridge, MA: Harvard University Press.

Walberg, H. J. (1991). Improving school science in advanced and developing countries. *Review of Educational Research, 61*, 25-69.

THE TIP (1.18)

 Use a variety of strategies to encourage students to ask questions about difficult assignments.

What the Research Says

 Several teaching approaches have been identified that can help students to overcome their reluctance to ask questions:

1. Avoid giving students the impression that any difficulties they are having are their own fault.

2. In cases where students have trouble with problems, do not indicate that the problems are simple.

3. Give external reasons for students' difficulties.

Research has shown that people can handle their neediness better if they can attribute the reasons for neediness to external causes. One study investigated asking questions as a kind of neediness (Fuhrer, 1994). Participants were 24 girls and 24 boys, with a mean age of 14 years. Students were confronted with the following situation: They were given an unformatted text that included typing mistakes and were asked to format the text according to a given pattern. The results were as follows:

1. The students showed the most willingness to ask questions when they could hold external circumstances responsible for their neediness.

2. Student willingness to ask questions decreased when students had the impression that the person they asked blamed them for the difficulty. In that case, asking a question hurt the student's self-esteem.

3. Students avoided asking questions if the person they asked indicated the task was simple.

Classroom Applications

Teachers should explicitly and implicitly encourage students to ask questions. Asking questions is not easy for students in many cases. Sometimes asking even simple questions requires both a minimum of knowledge/understanding and courage. You need to help students to feel that there are no such things as silly questions, although teachers sometimes give silly answers. Asking questions is one of the most valuable skills a person can develop. You may want to tell your students that "silly" questions are often the very best questions!

Take care to make positive comments on students' questions. For example:

- "Good question!"
- "Instead of getting grades for good answers, you should get grades for good questions!"
- "Your question shows that you've thought about this a lot."
- "Very interesting question!"

You can encourage students to ask questions by emphasizing the difficulties of the task or of the working conditions or by making understatements concerning your own abilities. Some examples are as follows:

- "Some aspects of this problem are hidden. Consequently, you might have some difficulties."
- "We never even talked about some of the steps needed to solve this problem."
- "Tomorrow we'll review how to solve that type of problem. A lot of students seem to be confused, so get your questions ready."
- "I didn't even see this problem."
- "Even today I have to struggle when asking questions in public."

If students begin to attribute their difficulties to their own lack of ability, try to direct their attention to external difficulties:

- "Make sure you pay careful attention to the difficult parts of this problem."
- "This is a new type of problem. We haven't discussed it yet, so you're not expected to know how to solve it now."
- "Do not expect your brain to work very quickly. It has been a long day."

Do not express doubt about students' capabilities or skills. For example, avoid statements such as the following:

- "I already answered that question three times."
- "Listen carefully to what I say!"

Instead, use statements such as these:

- "When students ask me a question a third time, that tells me something has gone wrong with my explanation."

- "Okay! We've covered a lot of facts—maybe too many."
- "Sometimes I explain things too quickly."

You can also have groups of students answer one another's questions, and then submit to you any questions they can't answer. Such group questions can save face for individual students.

Precautions and Possible Pitfalls

Beware of possible backfire! When you explain an assignment's difficulties as being based in external circumstances (e.g., very abstract, complex, or obscure; pressure for time; or the application of a very rarely used technique) you might encourage students, but you might also confirm their opinion that the assignment is too difficult. In that case, students would not be encouraged; rather, they may feel justified in stopping work on the problem, and their questioning will cease.

BIBLIOGRAPHY

Fuhrer, U. (1994). Fragehemmungen bei Schulerinnen und Schulern: Eine attributierungstheoretische Erklarung [Pupils' inhibition to ask questions: An attributional analysis]. *Zeitschrift für Padagogische Psychologie, 8,* 103-109.

THE TIP (1.19)

Make a lesson more stimulating and successful by varying the types and levels of questions you ask your students.

What the Research Says

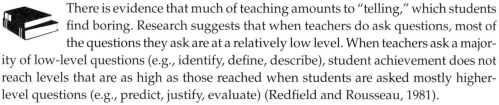

There is evidence that much of teaching amounts to "telling," which students find boring. Research suggests that when teachers do ask questions, most of the questions they ask are at a relatively low level. When teachers ask a majority of low-level questions (e.g., identify, define, describe), student achievement does not reach levels that are as high as those reached when students are asked mostly higher-level questions (e.g., predict, justify, evaluate) (Redfield and Rousseau, 1981).

Brown and Edmondson (1984) investigated the questions teachers ask and why they ask them. The participants in their study were 36 high school teachers from five schools, representing all subject areas. The researchers asked the teachers to give examples of the questions they asked, to explain how they used them, and to specify to whom the questions were addressed. Brown and Edmondson's findings, along with findings from previous research by Bloom, Engelhart, Furst, Hill, and Krathwohl (1956), Tisher (1971), and Smith and Meux (1970), led to a system of classifying the types of questions teachers ask in the classroom, which we describe below.

Classroom Applications

There are many types of questions you can use with students, as well as many you should avoid. Learning science requires understanding. When your class is considering a topic that requires thought and deduction, it is usually helpful to ask a lot of questions. Questions should be formulated with respect to long-term learning goals and should be succinctly structured to guide students' development so they can think like scientists. Questions can range from those that require low-level responses (e.g., recall of facts for definitions and descriptions) to those requiring intermediate-level responses (e.g., classifying and comparing/contrasting) to those requiring high-level responses (e.g., predicting, evaluating). Questions of the last type may have no definite answers; rather, they require students to make judgments. Questions may be classified into two main types: cognitive questions and speculative, affective, and management questions. Within each of these types, questions can be identified as low, intermediate, or high level.

Cognitive Questions

1. Students recall data, task procedures, values, or knowledge. This category includes naming, classifying, reading out loud, providing known definitions, and observing. These are low-level questions. For example: "How many stages are there in meiosis?"

2. Students make simple deductions, usually based on data that have been provided. This category includes comparing, giving simple descriptions and interpretations, and giving examples of principles. These are intermediate-level questions. For example: "How does meiosis compare with mitosis?"

3. Students give reasons, hypotheses, causes, or motives that were not taught in the lesson. These are high-level questions. For example: "What are possible explanations of global warming that are not in our book?"

4. Students solve problems using sequences of reasoning. These are high-level questions. For example: "What steps would you take to solve that problem? What order do they go in?"

5. Students evaluate their own work, a topic, or a set of values. These are high-level questions. For example: "Did I make any careless mistakes? How can I verify my answer?"

Speculative, Affective, and Management Questions

1. Students make speculations or intuitive guesses, originate creative ideas or approaches, and address open-ended questions (questions that have more than one right answer and permit a wide range of responses). For example: "Approximately how long will it take before the chemical reaction we're expecting takes place? How do you think we'll know if it worked? How else could we produce that reaction?"

2. Students express empathy and feelings. For example: "How do you think she felt when the incubator cooked all of the eggs she was trying to hatch for her science project?"

3. Students manage individuals, groups, or the entire class. This category includes checking that students understand a task, seeking compliance, controlling a situation, and directing students' attention. For example: "Which groups solved the problem? Which groups need help?"

There are many different questioning taxonomies available that you can consult to help you vary the types and levels of questions you ask. Sigel, McGuillicudy-DeLisi, and Johnson's (1980) taxonomy has three levels: low, intermediate, and high. You should spend most of your time questioning at intermediate and high levels.

- Intermediate-level questions require students to describe/infer similarities, sequence, and describe/infer differences. Students must analyze, apply their analysis, classify, estimate, and synthesize their findings.

- Higher-level questions require students to evaluate, verify, infer causal relations, and draw conclusions. Students must propose alternatives, predict outcomes, resolve conflicts, generalize from their findings, transform their findings, and plan based on their predicted outcomes.

Table 1.3 displays some examples of intermediate- and high-level questions that teachers of biology, chemistry, and physics might use.

Table 1.3   Examples of Intermediate-Level and High-Level Questions

Science Subject	*Intermediate Level*		*High Level*	
	Estimate	Synthesize	Verify	Infer Causality
Biology	If 2 animals heterozygous for a single pair of genes mate and have 276 offspring, about how many will have the dominant phenotype?	What does research on environmental cues show about biochemical and neural control of reproductive behavior?	Under what conditions might you infer that the mutations were caused by X rays?	How could you prove that those parents produce that probable composition of the F2 generation?
Chemistry	About how long do you expect it to take for the reaction to occur?	What did those theories suggest about the structure of an atom?	What causes diffraction patterns?	How could you check to make sure that you have written the correct electron configuration for an atom?
Physics	Approximately what is the mass of that drop now?	How could you summarize what you learned about electric fields from that experiment?	Why do you get a shock when you touch another person after walking on a synthetic rug?	How could you double-check the accuracy of your calculation of the electric field at the specified point in space?

Precautions and Possible Pitfalls

 Even good questions can lose their value if they are used too often. Avoid asking ambiguous questions and questions requiring only one-word answers, such as yes/no questions. Focusing on a particular questioning style without proper concern for the subject matter would be a misuse of this tip.

BIBLIOGRAPHY

Bloom, B. S., Engelhart, M. D., Furst, E. J., Hill, W. H., & Krathwohl, D. R. (1956). *Taxonomy of educational objectives: The classification of educational goals.* New York: David McKay.

Brown, G. A., & Edmondson, R. (1984). Asking questions. In E. C. Wragg (Ed.), *Classroom teaching skills* (pp. 97-120). New York: Nichols.

Redfield, D., & Rousseau, E. (1981). A meta-analysis of experimental research on teacher questioning behavior. *Review of Educational Research, 51,* 237-245.

Sigel, I. E., McGuillicudy-DeLisi, A. V., & Johnson, J. E. (1980). *Parental distancing beliefs and children's representational competence within the family context.* Princeton, NJ: Educational Testing Service.

Smith, B., & Meux, M. (1970). *A study of the logic of teaching.* Chicago: University of Illinois Press.

Tisher, R. P. (1971). Verbal interaction in science classes. *Journal of Research in Science Teaching, 8,* 1-8.

THE TIP (1.20)

Less = more. Streamline the content of your curriculum so that instead of teaching a broad survey course that covers many topics superficially, you focus on the most important content in enough depth that students can understand, remember, and apply what they have learned.

What the Research Says

Eylon and Linn (1988) report that, cognitively, students respond better to systematic in-depth treatment of a few topics than they do to conventional "in-breadth" treatment of many topics. Researchers are increasingly recommending that science teachers, as well as teachers of all subjects, streamline their curricula and focus more on limited sets of knowledge and skills. Students' misconceptions and lack of understanding of science basics reflect limitations of mental processing and memory. Ted Sizer, the well-known progressive educator, identifies "Less is more" as one of the major principles that should guide educational reform. (For more information, see Cushman, 1994.)

Classroom Applications

Examine the course(s) that students must take before taking yours to get the background for your course, and examine the courses that follow yours for which your course is expected to provide the background. Use this information to identify the key material your course must cover. Decide which chapters of your textbook you can forgo covering in your course to prevent overload and rote learning.

Precautions and Possible Pitfalls

Don't throw out diamonds in the rough or your favorite topics—there is a lot to be said for the effects of teacher enthusiasm on student motivation. Simply resign yourself to the fact that you might have less time to spend on some topics you particularly enjoy.

BIBLIOGRAPHY

Cushman, K. (1994). Less is more: The secret of being essential. *Horace, 11*(2) [Online]. Available on Internet: http://www.essentialschools.org

Eylon, B., & Linn, M. (1988). Learning and instruction: An examination of four research perspectives in science education. *Review of Educational Research, 58,* 251-301.

THE TIP (1.21)

 Take instructional planning and acclimatization time into account when you are shifting your students from simply receiving scientific knowledge to constructing and reflecting upon scientific knowledge.

What the Research Says

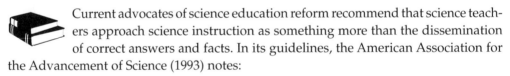 Current advocates of science education reform recommend that science teachers approach science instruction as something more than the dissemination of correct answers and facts. In its guidelines, the American Association for the Advancement of Science (1993) notes:

> Students should experience science as a process for extending understanding, not an unalterable truth. This means that teachers must take care not to convey the impression that they themselves or the textbooks are absolute authorities whose conclusions are always correct. (p. 187)

Yerrick (1998) conducted research that examined students' shared scientific discourse as a way to view standards for scientific thinking in both the scientific and formal classroom communities. This temporal view featured a "lower-track" group of science students and the instructor's attempt to challenge the students to adopt very different patterns of thinking, speaking, and acting as science students. The instructor's goal was to transform his lower-track classroom into an "ideal classroom community of authentic scientific inquiry." The goal was to change the pattern of communication typical of "school" discourse and replace it with discourse more typical of the science community. Yerrick analyzed videotapes of classroom discourse and found that students had been "shifted and sorted by discourse around teachers' factual answers" and that students resisted the shift to a more inquiry- or problem-based discourse.

The results of this investigation support a redefinition of expectations and a cautious approach toward a more authentic scientific discourse in the school science classroom. Discourse typical of and within the scientific community finds a very different context within the school classroom. Students do not have the same tools and mechanisms for coping with inquiry-based discourse as do participants within the scientific community. An attempt to shift the student role can create chaos, uncertainty, and dissent, and can strain group and class discussion. Sustaining more scientific discourse conflicts with many students' long-held beliefs that facts already exist and it is the student's job to arrive in class and learn them. Yerrick found many important differences between the views of science from a school perspective and from a scientific community perspective.

Classroom Applications

 Rethinking the role of the science teacher from that of giver of information to facilitator of learning takes planning. There is a cost to teaching students a new, powerful, and more scientifically authentic discourse. It changes the students' survival rules and devalues the students' existing discourse. When you intend to teach as the standards suggest, it is important that you balance the ideal vision with the reality of students' and parents' views of the traditional science classroom. Set realistic expectations.

Mediate and adjust the implementation of this type of alternative scientific thinking and discourse based on the following:

- *The demographics of your class:* Different groups present different problems. Balance the costs and benefits of the struggle to implement change. How much resistance can you endure? Total immersion may not be the best way to go. Science fair projects (or similar open-ended science experiences) are old but effective ways of immersing students in authentic science and discourse and can constitute a familiar, accepted, and relatively nonconfrontational strategy. Connect this approach with traditional instructional practices.

- *Your experience:* Novice teachers often have limited ways of viewing teaching from the perspective of instructional choices, student knowledge and experience, parent expectations and politics, and the nature of science. Put together a unit and share it with other department teachers who know the students, the institutional politics, and student demographics well.

- *Your department's philosophy:* It always helps to implement change on a departmentwide basis. Interact with colleagues (and administration) to present a unified strategy or at least to demonstrate acceptance and support.

- *Solid research:* Have the mandates, frameworks, research literature, and popular philosophies at hand when you interact with new curricula, pedagogy, and peers. Not only will this allow you to present support for change, but much of the literature offers practical, concrete examples and strategies that you can actually use.

- *Timing:* Trust is built over time. Many students, parents, and staff members will be more comfortable with a greater range of instructional ambiguity if you have their trust. Establish an environment of trust before you attempt to make changes to the way teacher-student business is conducted.

- *Communication:* Be proactive! Be clear on student assessment expectations in all graded activities before you begin an activity or unit. Try including the students in the construction of a rubric. If students do not find success in your new pedagogy or curriculum, you will need to defend your practices. Share any new strategies with parents beforehand, and clearly communicate your expectations and how work will be assessed.

Precautions and Possible Pitfalls

In Yerrick's study, the problems with implementation of the shift in the teacher's role included the following:

- Students criticized others for believing in unpopular, but correct, ideas.

- Groups excluded students for participating in unacceptable ways.

- Students found ways not to participate.

- The instructor's knowledge and authority were attacked and challenged because he did not emphasize answers. Some believed that if a teacher does not wield answers authoritatively over students, he or she possesses no authority over students.

- Students engage in classroom discourse for different reasons than do scientists. Opposing the discourse, new pedagogy, and teacher expectations brought students recognition and status.

Know the politics of the interactions at your school among students, teachers, departments, administrators, and parents. You will need the support of all these groups to make any changes to the expected science experience. Establish a base of trust with all those involved. Old norms of discourse can be replaced over time with careful redefinition of each stakeholder's role. Progress in implementing any reform is based upon agreement concerning what classroom science should be and why it should be rethought.

BIBLIOGRAPHY

American Association for the Advancement of Science. (1993). *Benchmarks for science literacy.* New York: Oxford University Press.

Yerrick, R. (1998). Reconstructing classroom facts: Transforming lower-track science classrooms. *Journal of Science Teacher Education, 9,* 241-270.

THE TIP (1.22)

Create a more authentic context, or "contextualize" science content, phenomena, and principles to serve a wider range of student interests and motivational levels.

What the Research Says

 The results of three separate studies (from chemistry, earth science, and technology perspectives) show that students in science classrooms who are not primarily interested in the sciences are poorly served. These studies found that the science curriculum is removed from authentic context and is thus unable to serve as a framework for knowing and instilling motivation for all but the most resilient students.

Schwartz (1999) describes a dominant chemistry class curriculum in which the presentation of chemistry is isolated from commonsense, everyday life and society, history, the philosophy of science, technology, school physics, and the chemical research context. Flannery and Hendrick (1999) describe an overemphasis on the learning of quickly forgotten facts that overshadows science history as a context for understanding how science functions. Tewksbury (1999) points out that in geoscience, or earth sciences, students learn principles in isolation from any cultural or social context. She suggests that, instead, students should probe the underlying influence of geology on human events, from prehistory and history to current economics and politics. All three of these studies point to a philosophy of teaching science in a rich, relevant, interdisciplinary style to engage a wider range of students, inspire students' interest, and meet students' needs. Data from all three studies indicate that a more interested and engaged student is more likely to learn, remember, and use information and experiences gained in the classroom. The recently formulated psychological theory of situated cognition (Brown, Collins, &

Duguid, 1989) emphasizes the importance of teachers' embedding learning and assessment experiences in authentic contexts. (We describe an instructional approach consistent with this theory, anchored instruction, in Tip 5.11.)

In his study of chemistry teaching and learning, Schwartz (1999) looked at how chemistry was present in a context of helping students to understand global warming, ozone depletion, alternative energy, nutrition, and genetic engineering. Student-centered learning featured activities to promote critical thinking and risk-benefit analysis as well as chemical principles. Looking at the context concept from the perspective of geoscience, Tewksbury (1999) found the subject could be approached from the perspective of its underlying influence on human events. This is a much deeper and subtler way to connect students, science, earth science, and nonscience topics with which many students are more familiar. Such instruction revolves around a series of geologic topics that have direct impact on and relevance to nonscience human issues and events. For example: "How have the unique geologic features of North Africa influenced human history in the area over the past 8,000 years?" "What are the geologic underpinnings of hydropolitics in North Africa?" "Mineral resources are unevenly distributed and exploited among regions in Africa—why is this the case? Predict the future for resource-rich nations of Africa."

Finally, Flannery and Hendrick (1999) suggest that the processes of technology and science and their relationship to society should be taught in a social history context. They provide the example of a discussion about Louis Pasteur and his adulation by the French public. Because Pasteur's popularity was based as much on nonscientific as on scientific factors, they use his career to illustrate concepts about science in its cultural context that they want their students to understand. This idea could include a multidisciplinary or interdisciplinary approach.

Overall, all three of the studies mentioned above suggest the need for an increase in scientific awareness and the societal and cultural roles individuals play as the results of science and technology activities filter through their lives. The researchers recommend that students develop a "working" literacy, not just an academic literacy. Science teachers, as curriculum designers, need to plan their units around motivating topics and locate the resources they need to provide their students with content that is relevant to them. Teachers need to align the science content of their units, both the type and the amount, with other interdisciplinary components within given topics.

Classroom Applications

It is often hard to view secondary education students as having academic "majors," but research indicates that many secondary courses are taught as if the students were majoring in those subjects. Often, the only thing that connects the various disciplines in the secondary school is the corridor between classrooms. Textbooks often support this notion, with overly detailed information packed into chapters based on the volume of what is known about specific disciplines. The science curriculum rarely includes science discipline content within the context of socially significant issues or the larger culture.

Scaffolding and constructivism are teaching and learning concepts that are accepted today as important tools in curricular construction. Consider the value of these models when you address the problems noted by researchers such as those cited above. In these models, content retention and overall interest in a subject are often based on students' ability to connect instruction to their lives, what they think is important, or some knowledge they already have on the subject. Concepts are added and misunderstandings are corrected, and, over time, concepts spiral around a cognitive framework facilitated by past experiences. Understanding grows as information is added and processes are experienced.

Do not be obsessed by "coverage" or rote learning. By encountering science in richer societal or cultural context, students experience a depth of coverage rather than a breadth of coverage.

Precautions and Possible Pitfalls

 Both parents and students have visions of what a science class is like, what science students do, and how science teachers teach. When you change the way science is traditionally taught, students need to see a clear path to success. Any doubt, insecurity, or threat to their success, their grades, or their visions of what they need to experience can cause concern for both students and parents. You will be asking students to move past the "chapter march" to engage in and experience science in a different way. Their comfort levels with this change will vary. Be very clear on your evaluation and assessment strategies. Include both parents and students in curriculum design, and orchestrate change slowly and carefully.

Also, if your science course is a foundation or prerequisite class for other courses, collaborate with your colleagues who teach those courses to make sure you can include content and instruction that will support the students who move into those teachers' classrooms.

BIBLIOGRAPHY

Brown, J. S., Collins, A., & Duguid, P. (1989). Situated cognition and the culture of learning. *Educational Researcher, 18*(1), 32-42.

Flannery, M. C., & Hendrick, R. (1999). Co-teaching and cognitive spaces: An interdisciplinary approach to teaching science to nonmajors. *Science and Education, 8,* 589-603.

Schwartz, T. A. (1999). Creating a context for chemistry. *Science and Education, 8,* 605-618.

Tewksbury, B. J. (1999). Beyond hazards and disasters: Teaching students geoscience by probing the underlying influence of geology on human events. *Science and Education, 8,* 645-663.

THE TIP (1.23)

 Put some of your specific content goals aside and present a more authentic view of the nature of scientific practice and how it is integrated into culture and society.

What the Research Says

 Bencze and Hodson (1999) found in a search of teacher education programs that many schools and school science curricula continue to promote a view of scientific practice that is locked in the philosophical mind-set of the 1960s and 1970s. This leaves many students with a deficient or distorted view of scientific inquiry.

The most common flaw in this mind-set is the creation of the illusion of certainty: Students are encouraged to regard the processes of knowledge building in the sciences as unproblematic, leading unambiguously and inevitably to "proven science." Scientists are regarded as experts whose views have authority conferred on them by the power of the scientific method and its universal application. The illusion is reinforced by heavy reliance on a didactic teaching style and by an approach to investigative work in which students spend the bulk of their time on cookbook-type exercises designed to reach particular, pre-determined outcomes. In this way, teachers and students conspire in perpetuating a false sense of security that manifests itself in reliance on "right" answers and a view of the expert as one who knows, rather than one who uses knowledge to refocus doubt.

Bencze and Hodson point out that despite the outpouring of scholarly writing and program guidelines such as those developed by the American Association for the Advancement of Science (Project 2061, first proposed in 1989) and the British National Curriculum (1994), change in science teacher preparation has been slow. The researchers also identify some other myths about scientific inquiry as perpetuated by science curricula:

- Science is a value-free activity.
- Scientific inquiry is a simple, algorithmic procedure.
- Experiments are decisive.
- Science proceeds via induction.
- Science comprises discrete, generic processes.
- Observation provides direct and reliable access to secure knowledge.

Classroom Applications

 Build integrated interdisciplinary components into your lessons. Include and emphasize the relationship between the nature of science content and scientific inquiry and each of the following:

- Society
- Technology
- Environment
- Societal decision making
- Historical context

Bencze and Hodson also suggest that teachers take a constructivist approach that features the fostering of intellectual independence through more self-directed learning and individual problem solving. In their version of a constructivist model approach to science teaching, students and teachers first explore their personal understanding of common phenomena and events, then formulate questions and hypotheses, identify problems, and seek possible solutions. Later, in a challenge phase, students are provided with alternative ideas to discuss and criticize. Finally, they are given the opportunity to explore these alternatives through hands-on inquiry and to reach consensus through discussion and debate. The focus of this inquiry is on cause-effect relationships.

Simple studies that Bencze and Hodson suggest include these:

- *Examination of the relationship between average litter size and life span in small mammals (biology):* How have humans affected the environments in which these mammals continue to live? This project depends on reference book data.

- *Examination of the relative attractive power of different colored lights on moths and other night-flying insects (physics, biology):* How do "bug lights" work? This project requires actual data gathering.

In each of these studies, the attempt to answer the questions within the investigation becomes the main focus. Science content is added, acquired, or taught as needed. The students' critical evaluation of the questions leads to a deeper understanding of causes and effects. Early tentative student knowledge is used as a vehicle to move students toward guided and self-directed desirable outcomes and to diminish or eliminate undesirable thinking.

It should be noted that interdisciplinary components don't always fit into every topic and lesson. You need to integrate appropriate concepts where they best fit, based on your background, your curricular objectives, the resources available, and where student inquiry takes you.

Precautions and Possible Pitfalls

 Do not abandon your already established teaching style entirely. Just as scientists and students develop expertise in doing science by engaging in scientific inquiry, so teachers develop expertise in supporting and encouraging more self-directed student learning. Students often go off in directions that are not supported by textbook knowledge. Orchestrating authentic research, no matter how simple, and creating interdisciplinary connections, require teachers to search for and gather new resources and learn new things on a regular basis, just to keep up with student projects. Depending on your comfort level, mix in more open-ended curriculum development and implementation with more easily controlled curricular activities. You can add to your open-ended units or revise them as your expertise in managing them grows.

BIBLIOGRAPHY

Bencze, L., & Hodson, D. (1999). Changing practice by changing practice: Toward a more authentic science and science curriculum development. *Journal of Research in Science Teaching, 36,* 521-539.

THE TIP (1.24)

 Have students role-play scientific concepts, systems, and phenomena.

What the Research Says

 Although extensive research has documented the importance of active learning in science (e.g., Walberg, 1991), there is relatively little literature available on the use of role playing or simulation as a teaching strategy in science. Nevertheless, many good science teachers at all school levels have been using role playing to provide concrete demonstrations of abstract concepts for years. Francis and Byrne

(1999) found that using role-playing exercises in the teaching of physics and astronomy "deepens student understanding and dramatically increases the level of classroom interaction" (p. 206). Research on learning and instruction suggests that students acquire, understand, retain, and use information more effectively when they learn it in realistic, meaningful contexts (Brown, Collins, & Duguid, 1989), and role playing can simulate such contexts. In addition, extensive research has shown the value of social interactions for enhancing students' learning, and constructivist approaches to science teaching emphasize the importance of students' working directly with and exploring knowledge through techniques such as role playing (Moussiaux & Norman, 1997).

Classroom Applications

 Role playing in the science classroom is structured so that students act out scientific principles as dramas or miniplays. For example, students might take on the roles of chromosomes in the different stages of meiosis or mitosis, or may enact the sequence of events in the process of digestion. McKeachie (1994) identifies several uses of role playing in the classroom:

- To illustrate course concepts
- To allow students to practice skills
- To stimulate interest
- To provide a concrete basis for discussion

Paul Francis has established a Web site where he provides free copies of role-playing lessons in astronomy and physics for teachers to use or adapt (http://msowww.anu.edu.au/~pfrancis/roleplay.html). Lesson titles include "Case Study: Star and Planet Formation" and "Runaway Greenhouse Effect." Although these lessons were developed for college students, they can be adapted for use with younger students.

Precautions and Possible Pitfalls

 Some people consider role playing and simulations so much fun that they don't think of these activities as learning, so they don't take the information seriously and retain it for future use. Try to prevent this by allowing your students to have all the fun without losing the emphasis on learning science. Teaching through the use of role playing has had plenty of success at the college level, so high school science teachers shouldn't worry that their students will see such activities as juvenile—your attitude is the crucial variable.

BIBLIOGRAPHY

Brown, J. S., Collins, A., & Duguid, P. (1989). Situated cognition and the culture of learning. *Educational Researcher, 18*(1), 32-42.

Francis, P. J., & Byrne, A. P. (1999). Using role-playing exercises in teaching undergraduate astronomy and physics. *Publications of the Astronomical Society of Australia, 16,* 206-211.

McKeachie, W. (1994). *Teaching tips* (9th ed.). Lexington, MA: D. C. Heath.

Moussiaux, S. J., & Norman, J. T. (1997). Constructivist teaching practices: Perceptions of teachers and students. In P. A. Rubba, P. F. Keig, & J. A. Rye (Eds.), *Proceedings of the 1997 Annual International Conference of the Association for the Education of Teachers in Science.* (ERIC Document Reproduction Service No. ED 405220)

Walberg, H. J. (1991). Improving school science in advanced and developing countries. *Review of Educational Research, 61,* 25-69.

CHAPTER TWO

Developing Students' Scientific Thinking and Learning Skills

THE TIP (2.1)

 Teach students how to read scientific textbooks by illustrating major concepts that underlie their organization.

What the Research Says

Even otherwise competent readers are not aware of the top-down structures underlying scientific texts. The findings of research conducted by Cook and Mayer (1988) suggest that students who don't understand the structure of scientific texts have problems representing the material, and thereby their comprehension and retention are impeded. Cook and Mayer found that students had difficulty sorting text into the categories of classification, comparison/contrast, enumeration, sequence, and generalization. They also found that a sample of junior college chemistry students outperformed controls on measures of comprehension after receiving 8 hours of training in analyzing, recognizing, and organizing relevant information in scientific texts. The text structure instruction included the modeling of reading strategies and explicit explanation of how to identify sequences (for example, how to put sequences into one's own words), how to identify the key words signaling sequences, and how to identify supporting evidence. Thus teachers can help to improve students' comprehension by developing students' thinking about how to read scientific texts, which can help them to focus on relevant information and use that information to create an internal representation. The research in this area addresses the important issue of domain-specific differences in cognitive processes such as reading. Whereas students reading science should concentrate on such text structures as classification, generalization, and comparison, students reading literature should concentrate on such structures as characters, plots, and settings.

Classroom Applications

 List the major conceptual categories that underlie the organization of your textbook (e.g., classification, comparison/contrast, sequence, generalization) on the chalkboard or create a handout showing the categories. Give your students definitions of the categories and show them how these are represented in the textbook. Ask students to give their own examples of where and how these concepts are represented in the text and give them feedback on the accuracy and quality of their examples. Help your students learn to use such reading strategies to integrate information provided at various points in the text and to integrate information found in the text with their prior knowledge.

You can further guide your students in acquiring textbook literacy by creating an open-book reading comprehension work sheet. The questions and answers can range from basic fill-ins to questions requiring application, analysis, and synthesis-type answers. You may also consider an open-book assessment activity. Just because students are allowed to use their books does not mean you can't create a rigorous test that will engage students in high-level thinking skills. By raising the stakes a little, you focus their attention and reward them for demonstrating their skills and new learning tools.

Precautions and Possible Pitfalls

 Students are always looking for an edge in assessing what is going to be on a test. Although it is always a good idea to teach reading across the disciplines, be careful not to send the message that your assessment is going to be based totally on your textbook if it is not. Some teachers use textbooks as reference only, whereas others use texts more directly in their instruction. Be clear from the beginning on what role the textbook will play in your class and especially in assessment.

BIBLIOGRAPHY

Cook, L. K., & Mayer, R. E. (1988). Teaching readers about the structure of scientific text. *Journal of Educational Psychology, 80,* 448-456.

THE TIP (2.2)

 Provide students with labeled illustrations of concepts in their textbooks to focus their attention on important explanatory information and to help them construct mental models.

What the Research Says

 According to Mayer (1989), labeled illustrations of information in scientific texts improve the meaningfulness to students of important material and help students think more systematically about this material. In Mayer's research, students who had backgrounds in automobile mechanics were given textual information on sequential operations of vehicle braking systems (e.g., "First, you step on the brake pedal. Second, the piston moves forward in master cylinder"; p. 241). One experiment compared students who were provided labeled illustrations with students who were provided no illustrations. In another experiment, students in the experimental group were given supplementary labeled illustrations, whereas students in one control group received unlabeled illustrations and students in another control group received labels but no graphics (illustrations). Students in both experiments were tested on their recall and transfer of explanatory and nonexplanatory ideas in the text. In both experiments, labeled illustrations improved students' ability to use explanatory information for creative problem solving (transfer) but did not improve their verbatim recall.

Classroom Applications

 When selecting a textbook for your course, examine each candidate book's illustrations to see how well they will support students' ability to focus on important information in the text and how well they will help students make connections among concepts so that they can construct accurate and meaningful mental models. If your chosen textbook does not provide sufficient illustrations, then select another text or supplement your primary text's illustrations with more meaningful, labeled illustrations.

Illustrations can also serve as sources of material that can be used in classroom activities and assessment. More and more standardized science tests require students to interpret illustrations. Evaluation and analysis of illustrations can reinforce concepts in ways that simple reading of a textbook cannot. For a somewhat new twist, have students create new illustrations based on the textbook content.

Precautions and Possible Pitfalls

Without support materials, you may be tempted to copy or make overhead transparencies from illustrations in published texts. However, you should be aware that most, if not all, textbooks are copyrighted, and their publishers forbid photocopying or other forms of reproduction of their contents without permission. If you want to make copies or transparencies from a particular textbook, consider calling or writing to the publisher to clarify your position and request permission to use the material. Textbook publishers are usually very understanding and cooperative; most will be happy to help you.

BIBLIOGRAPHY

Mayer, R. E. (1989). Systematic thinking fostered by illustrations in scientific text. *Journal of Educational Psychology, 81,* 240-246.

THE TIP (2.3)

 Help students read their science texts more effectively by teaching them to construct graphic organizers of the main concepts after they have finished a chapter.

What the Research Says

 Spiegel and Barufaldi (1994) focused on four of the same common science text structures as Cook and Mayer (1988)—classification, enumeration, sequence, and generalization—and a different one, cause and effect. Community college students in anatomy and physiology were taught to recognize these text structures and to construct graphic organizers of them after reading (postorganizers). Students who constructed postorganizers demonstrated superior memory on immediate and delayed posttests when compared with students who used rereading, highlighting, or underlining. Spiegel (1996) emphasizes the importance of providing students with explicit information on what graphic organizers are, when and why they are useful, and how to construct them after reading part of their science texts so that they use graphic organizers appropriately and effectively.

Classroom Applications

 Use an overhead projector to review a handout you have prepared for students that presents the main concepts in a textbook chapter and the relationships among those concepts in graphic organizer form. Choose one of the first chapters of their textbook for your model. The pre- and postreading organizers depicted here in Figures 2.1 and 2.2 are adaptations of two that were developed specifically for use with students for whom English is a second language (Carrell, Pharis, & Liberto, 1989).

Precautions and Possible Pitfalls

 Don't worry about the artistic quality of your students' pre- and postreading organizers. The important consideration is whether students can read their own organizers. Don't insist that your students produce one particular type of graphic organizer. Encourage them to experiment and see what works best for them individually.

Figure 2.1.   Prereading Map

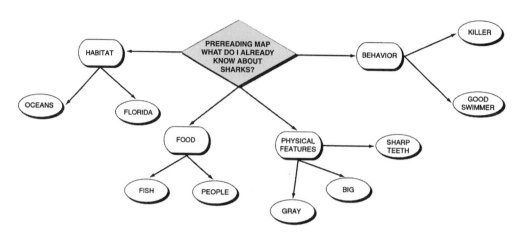

Figure 2.2.   Postreading Map

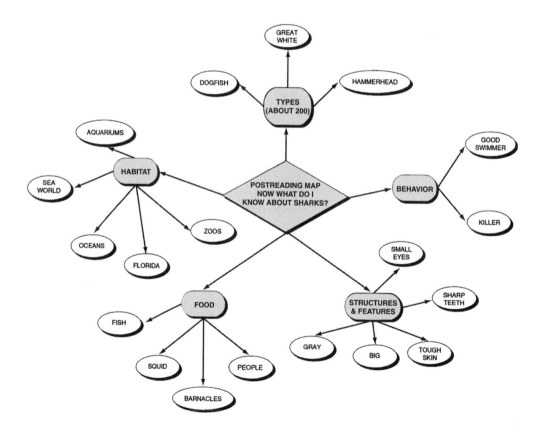

BIBLIOGRAPHY

Carrell, P. L., Pharis, B. G., & Liberto, J. C. (1989). Metacognitive strategy training for ESL reading. *TESOL Quarterly, 23,* 647-678.

Cook, L. K., & Mayer, R. E. (1988). Teaching readers about the structure of scientific text. *Journal of Educational Psychology, 80,* 448-456.

Spiegel, G. F., Jr. (1996). *Text structure awareness and graphic postorganizers of reading.* Workshop presented at the 10th Annual Conference of the Human Anatomy and Physiology Society, Portland, OR.

Spiegel, G. F., Jr., & Barufaldi, J. P. (1994). The effects of a combination of text structure awareness and graphic postorganizers on recall and retention of science knowledge. *Journal of Research in Science Teaching, 31,* 913-932.

THE TIP (2.4)

 Teach students to use self-questioning and think-aloud techniques so that they become more aware of and better able to control their reasoning and problem-solving skills.

What the Research Says

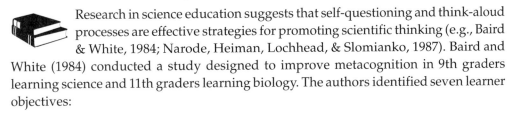 Research in science education suggests that self-questioning and think-aloud processes are effective strategies for promoting scientific thinking (e.g., Baird & White, 1984; Narode, Heiman, Lochhead, & Slomianko, 1987). Baird and White (1984) conducted a study designed to improve metacognition in 9th graders learning science and 11th graders learning biology. The authors identified seven learner objectives:

1. Increased knowledge of metacognition

2. Enhanced awareness of learning styles

3. Greater awareness of tasks' purposes and natures

4. More control over learning through better decision making

5. More positive attitudes toward learning

6. Higher standards for understanding and performance set by the students themselves, and more precise self-evaluation of their achievements

7. Greater effectiveness of students as independent learners, planning thoughtfully, diagnosing learning difficulties and overcoming them, and using time more productively

The instructional materials in Baird and White's study included a question-asking checklist, a notebook for evaluation of learning behaviors and outcomes, and a techniques workbook, where students tried out concept mapping. The authors' extensive research went through four phases and involved 15 methods of collecting data, including video- and audiotapes, classroom observations, questionnaires, and tests. Their results showed increased student control over learning and understanding of content.

Classroom Applications

How do scientists think, reason, and conduct their research? Some thinking and reasoning strategies are more conducive than others to making discoveries and bringing clarity of understanding. Below, we present a few basic suggestions concerning classroom activities that focus on strategies for improved reasoning and thinking.

Self-questioning and think-aloud techniques are routinely practiced within the context of research lab meetings. Science has gone from being a usually individual process to more of a group enterprise as reasoning and knowledge are distributed over many stakeholders within specific labs. The more diverse the group, the more beneficial shared reasoning and knowledge become.

- Use self-questioning and think-aloud techniques within students' laboratory groups to distribute reasoning and knowledge within these groups. This is especially important within the context of inquiry-based learning activities.

- Have students follow up on surprising results. Pay attention to unexpected findings in the control conditions, because these reflect either conceptual problems or experimental problems with the research.

- Have students engage in analogic reasoning in both formulating hypotheses and solving research or investigative problems. "Think aloud," using distant analogies as an explanatory device. Have students refer back to other experiences in which they used similar thinking frameworks. Make frequent use of analogies to explain things (scientists commonly converse in analogies).

- During self-questioning and think-aloud activities, make sure the students' current goal is not blocking them from considering alternative theories or ways of looking at experiments and other science activities.

Table 2.1 displays some examples of science-oriented self-questions. For ideas on how students can use self-questioning to guide their writing in science, see Tip 2.7.

Table 2.1   Examples of Science-Oriented Self-Questions

Planning	*Monitoring*	*Evaluating*
1. How can I design research to test this hypothesis?	1. Does the research design validly test this hypothesis?	1. How effective was my experimental design?
2. What are all of the critical variables that need to be considered?	2. Should I try a different approach?	2. To what degree were my conclusions justified by the results?
3. Which variables need to be controlled?	3. Am I recording all of the observations accurately?	3. What useful feedback did I get from others?
4. How should I record the data?	4. Am I observing and recording everything I'm supposed to?	4. How could I improve as an observer and recorder?

Precautions and Possible Pitfalls

 Given peer pressures, having your students critique one another's questions may pose a bit of a challenge for you. Avoid embarrassing individual students for asking ineffective questions by calling attention to particular questions in a whole-class setting.

Group work presents many potential pitfalls. Not all students will feel comfortable using these techniques or will buy into your strategies. You will have to decide how involved you want your students to become in this type of instructional strategy. If the work becomes too contrived, it loses its effectiveness. Monitor your groups closely. The more routine this type of discourse becomes and the more practiced the students, the more their comfort level will rise. To begin, consider having one group engage in these strategies while the others watch, as a way to keep control and guide and reinforce positive behaviors.

If you attempt to implement this tip, you should be aware that the use of self-questioning and think-aloud techniques is meant to be an enhancement to your instructional program and not a deterrent to student participation. If a technique doesn't seem to work with a particular class, you should replace it with a more effective approach.

BIBLIOGRAPHY

Baird, J. R., & White, R. T. (1984). *Improving learning through enhanced metacognition: A classroom study.* Paper presented at the annual meeting of the American Educational Research Association, New Orleans.

Brown, G. A., & Edmondson, R. (1984). Asking questions. In E. C. Wragg (Ed.), *Classroom teaching skills* (pp. 97-120). New York: Nichols.

Dunbar, K. (2000). How scientists think in the real world. *Journal of Applied Developmental Psychology, 21,* 49-58.

Narode, R., Heiman, M., Lochhead, J., & Slomianko, J. (1987). *Teaching thinking skills: Science.* Washington, DC: National Education Association.

THE TIP (2.5)

 Help students and yourself learn to ask better questions.

What the Research Says

Brown and Edmondson (1984) conducted research to investigate what questions teachers ask and why they ask them. Participants in their study were 36 high school teachers from five schools, representing all subject areas. In addition to asking their subjects to give examples of the questions they ask, explain how they use those questions, and identify to whom they address their questions, the researchers asked the teachers also to identify the types of errors students make when asking questions and to tell how they help students improve their questioning skills. The teachers identified seven types of mistakes that teachers make in asking questions:

1. *Delivery:* Questions are unclear; the teacher speaks too quickly, too slowly, too quietly, or too loudly. The teacher doesn't make eye contact with students while questioning.

2. *Structure:* The teacher makes unclear requests; he or she may use unclear vocabulary and or may ask questions that are too long or too complex.

3. *Target:* The teacher directs questions inappropriately, whether to an individual, a group, or the whole class.

4. *Background:* The teacher does not put questions into the proper context of the lesson, or there are problems with questioning sequences.

5. *Handling answers:* The teacher does not allow enough time for students to answer questions or accepts only answers that were expected.

6. *Discipline and management:* The teacher fails to avoid having students all calling out answers at the same time and fails to ensure that all students can hear both the questions and the answers.

7. *Level:* The teacher asks questions that are too hard or too easy for the specific students targeted.

Brown and Edmondson's subjects also made several suggestions for helping students ask better questions. They recommended that teachers provide students with models of good questions for students to observe, discuss effective questioning strategies, give students opportunities to practice questioning, and provide students with feedback on their questioning.

Classroom Applications

Making students aware of what constitutes a proper question may, in the long run, make them better learners and enhance their ability to pose better questions. You should demonstrate and discuss the characteristics of effective and ineffective questions. It may prove fruitful to have students critique one another's questions, either in pairs or in groups. Alternatively, as a homework assignment, you might give your students a list of student-generated questions to critique. There is a fair amount of information available about proper questioning techniques. Students need to know what features of classroom questions can make them effective as well as what can make them counterproductive.

Precautions and Possible Pitfalls

Teachers face a dilemma when it comes to student questioning, because students' questions sometimes give away the fact that they have not done their homework or the required reading. What should you do when a student has obviously not taken some basic responsibility for his or her own learning? Ideally, students' questions should reflect their misunderstandings concerning something they have read or experienced or their attempts to take the activity content further.

Your decisions about responding to student questions are personal ones. You might begin a questioning period by defining which types of questions you will consider for discussion. You might also look at any one student's questions as a sign that other students as well may have found the reading or activity difficult to understand. Carefully consider how you might respond to various kinds of questions before beginning a questioning activity.

BIBLIOGRAPHY

Brown, G. A., & Edmondson, R. (1984). Asking questions. In E. C. Wragg (Ed.), *Classroom teaching skills* (pp. 97-120). New York: Nichols.

THE TIP (2.6)

 Systematically and explicitly develop in your students the thinking skills that are important for understanding science.

What the Research Says

 A body of research on students' science thinking skills has shown there are developmental differences in students' abilities to interpret and evaluate evidence (see, e.g., Pressley & McCormick, 1995). Research has demonstrated that simply telling students what higher-level thinking strategies to use is unlikely to be successful. In order to use strategies effectively, students need not only descriptive information about what the strategies are but contextual information about when and why to use the strategies, as well as procedural information about how to use them (Schunk, 2000).

Classroom Applications

Provide students with strategic knowledge about the thinking skill you want them to develop. This should include knowledge about what the skill is, when and why to use it, and how to use it, as in the following example.

Strategic Knowledge About Justifying

What: Justifying is explaining one's reasoning: providing evidence underlying one's conclusions/reasoning, comparing obtained outcomes with achieved outcomes, and evaluating the degree of difference. For example:

The pancreas, a gland that synthesizes many biochemicals, produces digestive enzymes. While it produces enzymes involved in the digestion of starch, fats, and nucleic acids, it also produces the enzyme trypsin. Trypsin targets proteins for chemical digestion into peptides. Trypsin, along with the other enzymes, travels down the pancreatic duct then dumps directly into the small intestine.

When/why: One needs to employ justifying when one wants to evaluate evidence in order to assess whether it provides a sound basis of support for conclusions, decisions, and/or actions.

How: Understand the concept of evidence or support and its value for decision making about what one does, knows, or believes. Find evidence; weigh and compare evidence to a standard or set of criteria; evaluate the strengths, weaknesses, and degrees of difference of the evidence from the criteria; look at all possibilities. When there is strong support for one answer, interpretation, or approach and weak support for all the others, judge the one with stronger support to be the best answer, interpretation, or approach under the circumstances.

Precautions and Possible Pitfalls

Use of this strategy really has no potential pitfalls. Teaching content details, cause-effect relationships, and contextual connections separates these instructional strategies from rote-learning models. Most science content fits together logically once the connections are made, and the details relate very easily to centralized concepts.

However, we have one warning: Be consistent with this strategy. Compared with rote learning, learning this way requires that students have a more intimate understanding of the content and that they make a greater commitment. Students who are more comfortable with rote-learning models will need to adjust. You will need to be consistent with your expectations and help them to learn techniques for self-monitoring and evaluating their own effectiveness. You should also give students multiple opportunities to practice use of this strategy with feedback in a variety of situations and tasks, in order to promote long-term memory and students' ability to transfer the strategy to new situations.

BIBLIOGRAPHY

Pressley, M., & McCormick, C. B. (1995). *Advanced educational psychology for educators, researchers, and policymakers.* New York: HarperCollins.

Schunk, D. (2000). *Learning theories: An educational perspective* (3rd ed.). Upper Saddle River, NJ: Merrill.

THE TIP (2.7)

 Include teaching students how to write about science as part of traditional science content, because success in science, as in any field, requires mastery of discipline-specific systematic and reflective thinking about writing.

What the Research Says

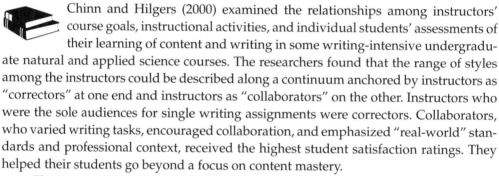 Chinn and Hilgers (2000) examined the relationships among instructors' course goals, instructional activities, and individual students' assessments of their learning of content and writing in some writing-intensive undergraduate natural and applied science courses. The researchers found that the range of styles among the instructors could be described along a continuum anchored by instructors as "correctors" at one end and instructors as "collaborators" on the other. Instructors who were the sole audiences for single writing assignments were correctors. Collaborators, who varied writing tasks, encouraged collaboration, and emphasized "real-world" standards and professional context, received the highest student satisfaction ratings. They helped their students go beyond a focus on content mastery.

The instructors in Chinn and Hilgers's study were very aware that their students would have to master discourse as well as knowledge in most fields to be accepted as professionals. Beyond content, their activities and writing assignments guided students through the intellectual, procedural, and social roles of scientists and engineers. Chinn and Hilgers's findings support the assumptions that underlie the National Academy of Science's teaching standards; the academy emphasizes the crucial role that instructors play in socializing students into authentic professional communicative expectations.

Research has demonstrated the importance of thinking systematically and reflectively—for example, planning, monitoring, evaluating, and revising in both problem solving and writing (Bereiter & Scardamalia, 1987; Schoenfeld, 1989). Research has also shown that self-questioning is an effective way of promoting reflective and systematic thinking. Student-generated self-questions have been found to be more effective than teacher-generated questions for promoting students' self-awareness and control over their own performance (Narode, Heiman, Lochhead, & Slomianko, 1987).

Classroom Applications

 More intensive attention to writing across content areas has been a goal of schools for many years. Chinn and Hilgers (2000) describe the most successful instructors in their study as having "created collaborative communities of apprentice scientists." Such teaching goes beyond grading student writing for grammar and style only. You need to make an effort to put students' science writing in its realistic context, so that they understand that writing plays a role in science much as mathematics does. Writing's role and character within your classroom's instructional practices might be characterized in one or more of the following ways:

- Writing activities involve realistic assignments that link classroom learning to professional utility, involve an audience other than the instructor, and require frequent interaction among students and between students and instructor.

- Writing is emphasized as a multipurpose tool for communicating and for learning content and literature relevant to the discipline.

- Assignments involve collaborative research and writing, and often take the form of major research projects culminating in oral presentations. Scientists collaborate, construct, and modify scientific knowledge.

- Critical peer review is routine, as it is within the science and engineering disciplines. Peer assessment and evaluation provide both writer and reviewer with opportunities to make sense of science content and process.

Keep in mind that mastery of discipline discourse is an incremental endeavor. One way in which you can assess and understand your students' learning experiences in science is by examining the composites of their experiences (as in final portfolios) at the end of the course, or at the end of their total science experience, if possible.

Remember, most of us can't simply decide one day to write and then expect to write well. Students need practice, help, and guidance in writing. Lab reports are common writing assignments in high school and college, and elementary and junior high school teachers should start the preparation early, so that students have adequate time to develop the requisite skills.

The following questions are samples of some types that students might use to guide their own thinking and writing for a lab report:

Experimental Approach

- What is the problem and how can it be defined?
- What is my hypothesis and its rationale?
- How did I test the hypothesis? What were my experimental procedures?
- What criteria did I establish for accepting or rejecting the hypothesis?

Gathering Scientific Information

- What phenomena did I observe?
- What equipment, materials, and measurement instruments did I use, and how did I use them?
- What observational/experimental data do I have?
- How have I recorded my data?

Results

- How should I organize the data?
- How should I present the data in the report? What kinds of tables might I use?
- What relationships do I see in the data?
- What techniques should I use to analyze the results?

Conclusions

- Should I accept or reject the hypothesis based on the results?
- Are there any generalizations I can make based on the data?
- What are the implications of my results?
- What are the limitations of my study?

Self-Assessment of Writing

- Do I have all of the information in the proper sections?
- How good are the organization, grammar, and spelling?
- How good is my sentence structure? Are there any fragments or run-on sentences?
- How clear and convincing is the support for my main argument?

Precautions and Possible Pitfalls

In Chinn and Hilgers's study, many of their undergraduate subjects complained about having to divide their focus and effort between science content and learning expository writing. Students with instructors who limited writing to one big assignment saw writing in a less positive light. Writing should be an ongoing class expectation and habit. Chinn and Hilgers found that instructors' messages about the reasons they required their students to write were sometimes partially developed or unclear. The commitment must be there—your students need to be convinced that you care as much about good writing as about good content. Feedback from you on a single writing assignment can help to teach your students much about the collaborative nature of science and the overall need to communicate effectively.

In regard to peer editing, Chinn and Hilgers found a gender gap: Female students were more likely than males to take the position of devil's advocate and to be critical reviewers. The students' main concerns with their peer editors' feedback on their writing were the lack of positive comments and the lack of helpful hints. The comments the peers made were discouraging and not motivating. These are good points—you need to teach your students how to be critical reviewers if you decide to use this strategy.

Communication technique is a big part of science. Its inclusion as curricular content does not need to be justified. The limited time you have to assess and evaluate writing can be a big deterrent to expanding the role of writing in your class. With collaborative work, peer reviewing, and other rewriting strategies, the final products can come across your desk much more polished and requiring less evaluation.

Resist the temptation to provide students with possible questions such as those listed above, because students are likely simply to use those questions without making them their own. If students are really to become more systematic and reflective about their science writing, they must have personal connections to and ownership of their questions. In addition, their questions cannot be generic; they must be tailored to the specific writing task.

BIBLIOGRAPHY

Bereiter, C., & Scardamalia, M. (1987). *The psychology of written communication.* Hillsdale, NJ: Lawrence Erlbaum.

Chinn, W. U., & Hilgers, T. L. (2000). From corrector to collaborator: The range of instructor roles in writing-based natural and applied science classes. *Journal of Research in Science Teaching, 37,* 3-25.

Narode, R., Heiman, M., Lochhead, J., & Slomianko, J. (1987). *Teaching thinking skills: Science.* Washington, DC: National Education Association.

Schoenfeld, A. H. (1989). Teaching mathematics thinking and problem solving. In L. B. Resnick & L. E. Klopfer (Eds.), *Toward the thinking curriculum: Current cognitive research.* Alexandria, VA: Association for Supervision and Curriculum Development.

THE TIP (2.8)

 Require students to use a learning log or an evaluation note-book to help them become better learners.

What the Research Says

Numerous studies have demonstrated that students often do not know what they don't know. Research has also shown that students can become aware of their strengths and weaknesses as learners and can learn to take greater control over their own academic performance. Baird and White (1984) conducted one such study with 64 students from two 9th-grade science classes and one 11th-grade biology class. There were four phases to this study:

1. *Exploration:* This phase lasted 4 weeks and involved the researchers' getting to know the students and seeking their consent for cooperation and participation in the rest of the study.

2. *Awareness:* This phase lasted 5 weeks for Grade 9 and 3 weeks for Grade 11. During this phase, the students began thinking about themselves as learners. They reflected on their attitudes, on their learning difficulties, and on strategies for overcoming these difficulties.

3. *Participation:* This phase lasted 7 weeks for Grade 9 and 6 weeks for Grade 11. The students began using question-asking checklists and evaluation notebooks. The teachers gave the students a considerable amount of help in using these materials during this phase.

4. *Responsibility-control:* This phase lasted 7 weeks for Grade 9 and 3 weeks for Grade 11. During this phase, the teachers' role virtually ceased and the students used the materials on their own. The teachers monitored student behavior and attitudes and intervened only as needed.

The question-asking checklist used in this study included 10 different categories, each of which had its own icon and set of questions. The 10 categories were topic, detail, task, approach, change in knowledge, increased understanding, progress, completion, satisfaction, and future use of knowledge. Questions for the approach category were as follows:

- How will I approach the task?
- How hard will it be?

- How long will it take?
- Is there another way of doing it?
- Why am I doing the task?
- What will I get from it?
- What will I make of the result?

During Phases 3 and 4 of the study, the students recorded in their evaluation notebooks their own evaluations of their use of the questions from the question-asking checklist for most of their science lessons.

Baird and White collected data from 15 different sources, including the evaluation notebooks, classroom observations, audio and video recordings of lessons, interviews, questionnaires, and teacher-made tests. The results showed that at the beginning of the study neither the 9th graders nor the 11th graders were clear about their learning difficulties, and neither had any strategies for overcoming those difficulties. During Phase 3 the students became more aware about themselves as learners, and during Phase 4 they improved in their ability to control their own learning.

Classroom Applications

 Develop and maintain a habit of having your students keep "learning logs." Such logs represent an individual, flexible method for student reflection and teacher feedback. At the end of each week or at the end of a unit, have your students take a moment of class time to reflect on the activities they have experienced, what they have learned, what they are confused about or have not understood, and where they need help.

To begin, create a simple form with triggers and clues about self-reflection and self-questioning for students to insert in their learning logs to act as a model and guide. Then ask your students to reflect on their attitudes, their learning difficulties, and possible strategies for overcoming these difficulties. Not only will the act of keeping learning logs facilitate your students' reflection, self-questioning, and self-discovery, the logs themselves can be a valuable source of feedback for you if you choose to collect them. Students will often write down things they will not verbalize. In contrast to the postactivity learning log, a "prelearning log" can help begin the development of mental constructs and a concrete context for the learning experiences to come.

It is important to note that, like student "portfolios," learning logs are very much based in the vision and needs of the individual instructor. There is no one correct way to use learning logs. It is clear that students who learn to use this technique will eventually need to be weaned off of the teacher development tool so that they can begin to make the technique their own.

Precautions and Possible Pitfalls

 Be careful not to impose your own checklist continually on your students. Students must formulate their own lists, so that the items are meaningful and useful to them. Students should have a feeling of ownership of their lists, and their questions should be adapted to specific problems.

BIBLIOGRAPHY

Baird, J. R., & White, R. T. (1984, April). *Improving learning through enhanced metacognition: A classroom study.* Paper presented at the annual meeting of the American Educational Research Association, New Orleans.

THE TIP (2.9)

 Teach students to read for understanding, not just to encode the information to be learned.

What the Research Says

 When reading scientific texts, students often try to learn big words, facts, and details by rote instead of trying to understand ideas. Many such students learn so that they can "report back" information, but not so that they can apply it. However, some students try to understand and accommodate their beliefs to the information in their texts; Roth (1991) describes these students as "conceptual change readers." They activate their prior knowledge and recognize when that knowledge is somewhat inconsistent with the meanings described in their texts. Conceptual change readers think about these meanings and work to resolve the discrepancies to refine their own thinking. Roth labels this clarification aimed at addressing misconceptions a "conceptual change strategy." Students employing this strategy exhibit the self-awareness and self-regulation that are the essence of independent learning. In a recent study, Hartman (2001) found that students who accurately self-evaluated their correct answers on a biology reading comprehension test had higher biology course grades than did students who did not accurately self-evaluate their correct answers.

Classroom Applications

 Provide students with an expert model of reading for understanding by reading to them and thinking aloud, demonstrating how you recognize and reconcile discrepancies between your prior knowledge and information in the text. You might pose questions aloud for yourself, such as "Is there anything that seems unclear to me?" and "What should I do to clarify my understanding?"

One especially useful technique is to model being confused about what you have read, letting students hear you think out loud as you refine your thinking. For example, you might say:

> I'm confused. Now how is an independent variable different from a dependent variable? They're both important if you're looking at cause-and-effect relationships. One of them represents the cause and one represents the effect, but which is which? The book says, "If the relationship being plotted is one of cause and effect, the variable that changes as a result of changes in the independent variable is the dependent variable." That must mean that the independent variable is the "cause" and the dependent variable is the "effect."

In class, ask students questions such as "Do you ever question yourself about how well you understand something you are reading?" and "What do you do when you discover that the book contradicts your existing understanding of something?" Discuss the strategies they use to clarify their thinking while reading, and suggest additional techniques as appropriate. Have students do homework assignments that require them to identify sources of confusion in their textbooks and to explain how they achieved understanding.

Try reading to your students interesting science newspaper articles that present new science information; discuss how the information relates to and adds to the knowledge the students have gained in class and from their textbooks. The *New York Times* Web site has a great science section that features very informative and unbiased articles (http://nytimes.com/pages/science/index.html). For high school and younger students, such articles are more appropriate reading than the academic science literature. Good science journalists generally filter through hard-core research content and present the essence of scientific findings in language that is appropriate for the secondary classroom.

Precautions and Possible Pitfalls

 When choosing science articles to read to your class, consider carefully. Students are not easily impressed with science writing. You may want to concentrate on subjects and writing styles that connect and relate to the students' own lives. Controversy is always a good selling point. Choose articles on topics your students might have strong opinions about. Students may initially resist your efforts to teach them to think about their thinking because it requires work. Assure them that the effort will pay off in the long run, and that with time and practice they can internalize this type of thinking and use it automatically as needed. Developing good and informed consumers of science and technology is one of the main goals of science education. This technique provides great practice.

BIBLIOGRAPHY

Hartman, H. J. (2001). Metacognition in science teaching and learning. In H. J. Hartman (Ed.), *Metacognition in learning and instruction: Theory, research and practice.* Dordrecht, the Netherlands: Kluwer Academic.

Roth, K. (1991). Reading science for conceptual change. In C. M. Santa & D. E. Alvermann (Eds.), *Science learning: Processes and applications* (pp. 48-63). Newark, DE: International Reading Association.

THE TIP (2.10)

 Some students do not think they have control over their academic successes and failures; help these students learn to monitor and control their own explanations of their successes and failures.

What the Research Says

Students often get into ruts in science, falsely thinking that because they haven't done well in science in the past, they won't now or in the future. However, extensive research has shown that students can learn to control their own academic destinies. One body of research focuses on students' attributions for their success and failure. This research shows that people tend to give one of four common reasons for their successes and failures: ability, effort, task difficulty, or luck. Attributions can be divided into two dimensions: stable/unstable and internal/external. *Stable/unstable* refers to how consistent the attributions are over time. That is, to what extent does the person use the same types of reasons to explain her or his success or failure over and over again (stable)? Does the person give one kind of reason on one occasion and another type of reason another time (unstable)? For example, Lillian says that solving mass problems in physics is always too difficult for her (stable), but she also says that in chemistry some balancing equation problems are easy for her and some are too difficult (unstable).

Internal/external refers to where the person assigns responsibility for her or his successes and failures: inside the self or outside the self. For example, Lillian says she didn't do well on her test about the Holocaust because she didn't study enough (internal), and she says she didn't do well on her first science test because her family interfered with her study time (external). She says she got a good grade on her second science test because she was lucky (external).

Students' explanations of their successes and failures have important consequences for their future performance on academic tasks. As noted above, researchers have found that students attribute their successes and failures to one of four common causes: ability ("I'm just not a good writer"), effort ("I could do it if I really tried"), task difficulty ("The test was too hard"), or luck ("I guessed right") (Alderman, 1990, p. 27). These attributions are related to (a) the individual's expectations about likelihood of success; (b) the individual's judgments about his or her ability; (c) the individual's emotional reactions of pride, hopelessness, and helplessness; and (d) the individual's willingness to work hard and self-regulate his or her efforts.

Classroom Applications

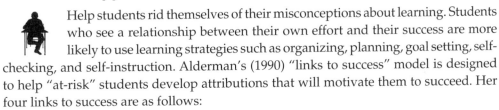 Help students rid themselves of their misconceptions about learning. Students who see a relationship between their own effort and their success are more likely to use learning strategies such as organizing, planning, goal setting, self-checking, and self-instruction. Alderman's (1990) "links to success" model is designed to help "at-risk" students develop attributions that will motivate them to succeed. Her four links to success are as follows:

1. *Proximal goals:* These are short-term rather than long-term goals, specific rather than general, and hard (but reachable) rather than easy. For example: "This week I'll manage my time so that I have 3 extra hours to study." Teach students to anticipate and overcome obstacles, monitor their progress while they pursue their goals, and evaluate whether or not they have achieved their goals at the end of the specified time ("I'll know whether or not I have accomplished this goal by writing down how much time I study and comparing that to how much I studied last week. Possible obstacles to achieving this goal are . . . I will overcome these obstacles by . . . ."). When students don't achieve their goals, teach them to determine why and what they could do differently next time.

2. *Learning strategies:* Students need to apply effective techniques, such as summarizing and clarifying, that emphasize meaningful learning and can be used across subjects and situations, instead of ineffective approaches, such as repeating, which tends to emphasize rote memorization.

3. *Success experiences:* Students evaluate their success in achieving their proximal goals. Learning ("How much progress did I make?") rather than performance ("What grade did I get?") is the goal.

4. *Attributions for success:* Students are encouraged to explain their successes in terms of their personal efforts or abilities. The teacher's role is to give students feedback on why they succeeded or failed and help students give appropriate explanations. Was an answer incorrect or incomplete? Did the student make a careless mistake? Make sure students understand why their incorrect answers are incorrect. Ask questions such as "What did you do when you tried to answer that question/solve that problem?"

Precautions and Possible Pitfalls

Feelings of helplessness are created over a period of time when an individual believes that his or her failures are due to lack of ability, so it is important for students to learn that they can improve their abilities if they use proper strategies and make appropriate efforts.

BIBLIOGRAPHY

Alderman, M. K. (1990). Motivation for at-risk students. *Educational Leadership, 48*(1), 27-30.

THE TIP (2.11)

 Teach your students the study skills, approaches, and orientations that are most appropriate to the learning environment that you create.

What the Research Says

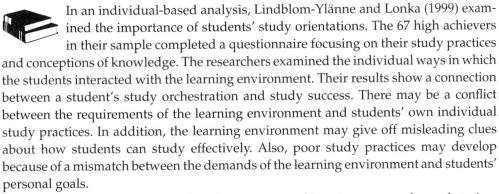 In an individual-based analysis, Lindblom-Ylänne and Lonka (1999) examined the importance of students' study orientations. The 67 high achievers in their sample completed a questionnaire focusing on their study practices and conceptions of knowledge. The researchers examined the individual ways in which the students interacted with the learning environment. Their results show a connection between a student's study orchestration and study success. There may be a conflict between the requirements of the learning environment and students' own individual study practices. In addition, the learning environment may give off misleading clues about how students can study effectively. Also, poor study practices may develop because of a mismatch between the demands of the learning environment and students' personal goals.

Research suggests that students' conceptions of learning, approaches to learning, and levels of processing learning activities can be divided into two categories: surface-level reproduction (or memorizing) and deep-level transformation (or construction) of knowledge. The latter is associated with more meaningful learning.

Lindblom-Ylänne and Lonka also considered how the students in their sample self-regulated their learning environments. Students may differ in their abilities to self-regulate and in how much they depend on external regulation; some may lack self-regulatory skills altogether. Self-regulation is most often related to deep-level learning, whereas external regulation is more likely to be associated with surface-level knowledge reproduction.

Successful students in Lindblom-Ylänne and Lonka's study were able to use flexible strategies according to the course demands, and also used the strategies that were the most appropriate to specific learning environments. Thus the development of students' metacognitive skills is a very important component in the development of good study practices as well as in the replacement of less effective learning habits with more effective ones.

Classroom Applications

Many students have difficulty "studying" science topics yet do very well in other disciplines. The skills that work for a student in one discipline don't always transfer to others, and this can be especially true for science classes. Students often gauge their overall success, failure, reward, and frustration according to how much "effort" they feel they have brought to a learning activity. When you hear an "effort" argument from a student, it often means that the student's effort has been misguided or ineffective. This can lead the student to "opt out" of the learning environment. Effort arguments often result from conflicts between the class environment and students' study skills and habits. The same amount of effort that students exert in one class may not yield the same level of success in others. How can you help these students?

Lindblom-Ylänne and Lonka's research points to a need for quantitative analysis of students' approaches to studying and learning orientations. Just asking your students to describe their own subjective definitions of learning can give you great insight and can lead students into self-reflection about their own studying and learning styles. You can pose your questions in the form of a student self-assessment inventory; this activity will also provide your students with an opportunity to talk with you about their results. Once you have the information you need about your students' learning orientations, you can reorganize the learning environment as necessary.

Where do you find the resources to create a student self-assessment inventory? One way is by using an Internet search engine; insert the phrase *learning styles* and you will find many Web sites that contain information on how to assess learning styles and how to design effective personal study strategies. Also, many books and papers are available that provide tools for gathering student self-assessment information.

The lack of effective study strategies interferes with your students' ability to be successful in your class. Students with disintegrated perceptions of their learning environment often lack commitment to the academic environment and to the purposes of studying. You may serve your students' needs in a richer and more meaningful way if you take time out from class work on more specific content goals and objectives to address these issues.

Numerous print and on-line resources on programs and materials are available to help students develop study skills specifically oriented toward science. An early program with a history of success with high school students in science is Stress on Analytical Reasoning (SOAR), and an early successful program for helping students make the transition from high school to college by developing their ability to think abstractly instead of concretely is Development of Reasoning in Science (DORIS). Both of these programs use the learning cycle approach described in Tip 1.12 (see also Nickerson, Perkins, & Smith, 1985). One especially useful print resource is Narode, Heiman, Lochhead, and Slomianko's book *Teaching Thinking Skills: Science* (1987).

Precautions and Possible Pitfalls

 Teachers need to cultivate the ability to determine what really motivates and rewards their specific students to replace or reorganize their study efforts. The teaching of effective study skills needs to become an ongoing part of a "hidden" curriculum. Don't be too disappointed if your efforts to teach study skills do not produce the desired or expected results. Different students require different levels of "guided practice," attention, and external versus internal reward structure.

BIBLIOGRAPHY

Lindblom-Ylänne, S., & Lonka, K. (1999). Individual ways of interacting with the learning environment: Are they related to study success? *Learning and Instruction, 9,* 1-18.

Narode, R., Heiman, M., Lochhead, J., & Slomianko, J. (1987). *Teaching thinking skills: Science.* Washington, DC: National Education Association.

Nickerson, R. S., Perkins, D. N., & Smith, E. E. (1985). *The teaching of thinking.* Hillsdale, NJ: Lawrence Erlbaum.

THE TIP (2.12)

 Have your students reflect on and evaluate their use of strategies when reading science and compare the strategies they use with those of other students. Provide them with suggestions on how to experiment with additional strategies and encourage them to try out new strategies, if needed.

What the Research Says

Recent studies show that, in general, good readers who are good students appear to have more awareness and control over their own cognitive activities while reading than do poor readers. In her characterization of "expert readers," Baker (1989) notes that research on metacognitive strategies indicates that such readers interact with their own domain-specific knowledge while reading. For example, experts and novices in science differ in how they budget and regulate their reading time.

Individuals' abilities to learn science from texts sometimes depend upon the relative effectiveness of various reading strategies. Research comparing good and poor readers has identified a variety of metacognitive skills that enhance reading comprehension. According to Brown (1980) and others, good readers regularly plan, attend to task demands, predict, use strategies to increase their comprehension and meet task requirements, check, monitor, reality test, control, and coordinate their learning. Four effective reading comprehension strategies that Jones, Amiran, and Katims (1985) have noted are organizational thinking, contextual thinking, reflective thinking, and imagery strategies. Long and Long (1987) found that good comprehenders in college are more mentally active while reading than are poor comprehenders. Good comprehenders engage in mental interactions with the text through visualizing, self-questioning, and inferring. Although poor comprehenders engage in some metacognitive activities, such as skimming, rereading, and pointing to key words, they perform behaviors similar to those of good comprehenders, but without mentally activating operations needed for understanding.

In a recent study involving 27 seventh-grade students and their classroom teacher, Spence (1995) examined the relationships between metacognition and science reading comprehension. He also explored the differential effects of science reading instruction on science reading metacognitive awareness, science reading metacognitive self- management, and science reading comprehension. Spence found significant correlations between metacognitive awareness and science comprehension task success and a positive association between metacognitive self-management and science reading comprehension. He also found an interaction between the treatment effect (type of reading instruction) and gender and ability: Lower-ability readers and males gained more from the instructional treatment than did higher-ability readers and females. These findings suggest that explicit instruction in reading strategies can have a significant impact on students' ability to understand what they read in science. They also suggest that the success of reading strategies may be affected by gender.

Classroom Applications

Get your students to think and talk about the strategies they use to read material in science. An interesting way of doing this is to perform an inquiry into classwide reading strategies. First, ask your students how they read. Then ask them about their familiarity with specific high-level reading strategies, such as skimming, self-questioning their understanding of the material, forming mental images, reviewing, summarizing, self-testing their memories, predicting, and retrieving their prior knowledge about the topic of their reading. Once you are sure your students understand what the strategies are, why they are beneficial, and how they are used, have all students read the same science material and reflect on which strategies they actually use. Compile the results classwide, and then discuss the implications of the results for improving the students' understanding of and ability to use what they learn from reading science. Be sure to discuss how reading science is different from reading literature and other subjects, and how reading to discuss something in class is different from reading to prepare for a test or for other purposes.

Precautions and Possible Pitfalls

Make sure your students understand that there are many individual differences in how students read science, and that there is no one correct strategy for undertaking such reading. Perhaps the only really wrong strategy is to read for rote memorization of facts in isolation, with no concern for understanding of ideas and their relationships. The use of metacognitive and other reading strategies is very personal. What works for you may not work for your students, and what works for one student may not work for another. Also, make sure that your students understand that the reading strategies they choose should depend upon the context. It is not necessarily appropriate to use the same strategies all the time.

BIBLIOGRAPHY

Baker, L. (1989). Metacognition, comprehension monitoring, and the adult reader. *Educational Psychology Review, 1*(1), 3-38.

Brown, A. L. (1980). Metacognitive development and reading. In R. J. Spiro, B. C. Bruce, & F. Brewer (Eds.), *Theoretical issues in reading comprehension* (pp. 453-481). Hillsdale, NJ: Lawrence Erlbaum.

Jones, B. F., Amiran, M. R., & Katims, M. (1985). Teaching cognitive strategies and text structures within language arts programs. In J. W. Segal, S. F. Chipman, & R. Glaser (Eds.), *Thinking and learning skills: Vol. 1. Relating instruction to research*. Hillsdale, NJ: Lawrence Erlbaum.

Long, J. D., & Long, E. W. (1987). Enhancing student achievement through metacomprehension training. *Journal of Developmental Education, 11*(1), 2-5.

Spence, D. J. (1995, April). *Explicit science reading instruction in grade 7: Metacognitive awareness, metacognitive self-management and science reading comprehension*. Paper presented at the annual meeting of the National Association for Research in Science Teaching, San Francisco. (ERIC Document Reproduction Service No. ED 388500)

THE TIP (2.13)

 Help your students to acquire and use the processes involved in self-regulating their learning.

What the Research Says

 Recent research suggests that self-regulated learners differ from other-regulated learners in numerous ways, but that self-regulatory abilities can be taught. Zimmerman (1998) defines *self-regulation* as self-generated thoughts, feelings (motivation, self-beliefs), and actions (strategies) for achieving goals, both academic and nonacademic. Self-regulation is multidimensional and context specific, and involves the selective use of self-regulatory processes, depending upon the situation and the perceived outcomes. Self-regulatory processes include goal setting (specifying intended outcomes or actions, specific and short-term) and self-efficacy, task strategies (analyzing tasks and identifying specific effective strategies), imagery (recalling or creating), self-instruction (engaging in overt or covert self-talk, e.g., self-questioning, to guide performance), time management (estimating, budgeting, planning practice, scheduling), self-monitoring (observing and tracking one's own performance and outcomes), evaluating and conse-quenting (making rewards contingent upon successful completion of important daily activ-ities), environmental structuring (selecting/creating effective learning setting), and selective help seeking (choosing specific models and the like to aid learning). Based on extensive research, Zimmerman has developed a cyclic model of academic self-regulation that teachers can use to help their students become self-regulating learners.

Classroom Applications

Zimmerman's cyclic model of self-regulated academic studying consists of the following elements:

1. *Self-evaluation and self-monitoring:* Students systematically observe and record their use of study strategies to assess the effectiveness of their current approaches. Students are often unaware of both the specific strategies they use to study sci-ence and how effective they are. For example, what strategies do students use when they are confused about something they are reading in a science book? How effective are their clarification strategies? Teachers can develop and distribute strategy self-observation rating forms for students to use and give assignments and/or quizzes to help students assess the effectiveness of their strategies. If stu-dents trade and grade homework papers of their peers, they can learn about the

strategies other students use and assess their effectiveness. Students use their experiences to identify their own specific strengths and weaknesses in the use of a variety of strategies.

2. *Goal setting and strategic planning:* Students examine their learning outcomes in relation to the specific strategies they use, and they understand the connection between their use of specific strategies and the specific results associated with them. For example, students often complain that they don't understand or remember much of what they read in their science texts. What strategies do students use and how well do they work? What other strategies might they use? A goal for a particular week might be to assess which is more effective for them when learning science from text, writing outlines of chapters or constructing graphic organizers of them? How useful is each strategy in helping students to acquire the basic concepts, understand them and how they relate to other concepts, and remember the information during a test? Rather than simply relying on the strategies students bring with them to your class (e.g., outlining), introduce your students to new strategies (e.g., graphic organizers) so that they can expand their options. Learning goals should be specific and short-term.

3. *Strategy implementation and monitoring:* Teachers provide repeated opportunities for students to practice a new strategy and receive feedback on their performance. Students rate the extent to which and how effectively they implemented the targeted study strategy. For example, if they created a graphic organizer, did they complete it? How easy was it to use? Was it too messy? Was it an effective structure? How good were the labels and connections?

4. *Strategic outcomes monitoring:* Students use feedback to determine the outcomes of their strategy use and to judge its effectiveness. Whenever possible, students should try to compare their performance using a new strategy with their performance when using another strategy. They should also judge whether their current strategy repertoire is adequate or they should try another approach. Teachers continue to provide opportunities for students to implement and judge the effectiveness of their learning strategies and monitor students' needs to learn additional strategies.

Precautions and Possible Pitfalls

One common misconception among students about their studying is that they just have to do more of it. However, studying more while using ineffective study strategies is unlikely to produce better learning. Students need to learn that the key to more effective learning might be to change some of the study methods they use. This awareness might trouble students, because changing one's study strategies takes time and effort. However, they are likely to save time in the long run if they take the time now to develop effective strategies. Students will gradually internalize the effective strategies that they use repeatedly and will eventually be able to use them selectively, automatically, and efficiently.

BIBLIOGRAPHY

Zimmerman, B. J. (1998). Academic studying and the development of personal skill: A self-regulatory perspective. *Educational Psychologist. 33*, 73-86.

CHAPTER THREE

Emotional Aspects of Science Learning

THE TIP (3.1)

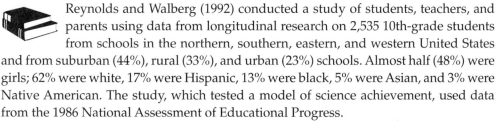

High school students' attitudes toward science are affected by several variables, some of which teachers and family members can influence.

What the Research Says

Reynolds and Walberg (1992) conducted a study of students, teachers, and parents using data from longitudinal research on 2,535 10th-grade students from schools in the northern, southern, eastern, and western United States and from suburban (44%), rural (33%), and urban (23%) schools. Almost half (48%) were girls; 62% were white, 17% were Hispanic, 13% were black, 5% were Asian, and 3% were Native American. The study, which tested a model of science achievement, used data from the 1986 National Assessment of Educational Progress.

Reynolds and Walberg found that science attitude, one of the components of their model, was most strongly affected by student's past attitude, home environment, motivation, and past achievement in science. Science attitude was defined by two major characteristics: interest and usefulness. Interest was assessed using the sum of three items focusing on enjoyment, ability, and understanding of science; usefulness was assessed using the sum of items on the value of science for solving everyday life problems, logical thinking, adult usefulness, and career relevance.

Classroom Applications

You can do action research on the variables affecting science attitudes among your students and design instructional interventions that meet the needs of individual students.

1. Find out about each student's prior attitude toward science and how it developed. At the beginning of the year, ask students to write biographies about themselves as science students, and identify the critical variables that you want them to address in these essays.

2. Ask your students to include in their science biographies information on their home environments, motivations, and past achievement in science.

To further your action research, consider providing your students' parents with course outlines. Allow them the opportunity to express their own attitudes and concerns about potentially sensitive science content. This can be especially useful for teachers of biology. Some students come with very entrenched attitudes toward particular content or activities typical of specific science classes. Be willing and prepared to provide alternative instruction on sensitive topics, such as those involving dissection and those concerning certain health or reproduction issues.

Precautions and Possible Pitfalls

 Any study based on self-reports is limited in its potential validity, so beware of making assumptions about students based on their self-reported data. Your observation of students' behavior, including verbal and nonverbal communications, is an important tool for assessing students' science attitudes, including how your students feel about your working in partnership with their home environments.

Although research suggests that both elementary and secondary students generally value parental involvement in education (e.g., Hartman-Haas, 1983), some high school students are struggling with independence issues and don't want their families involved. It may be wise for you to provide your students with the choice of opting out of writing this part of the biography.

BIBLIOGRAPHY

Hartman-Haas, H. J. (1983, April). *Family educational interaction: Focus on the child.* Paper presented at the annual meeting of the American Educational Research Association, Montreal.

Reynolds, A. J., & Walberg, H. J. (1992). A structural model of science achievement and attitude: An extension to high school. *Journal of Educational Psychology, 84,* 371-382.

THE TIP (3.2)

 If you have students who are not highly motivated to learn science, incorporate motivational skills training into your science instruction.

What the Research Says

 Training unmotivated students in motivational skills can improve both their motivation and their achievement. McCombs (1984) describes one study that involved giving students seven skill-training modules, the titles of which were "Introduction," "Self-Knowledge," "Career Development," "Goal Setting," "Stress Management," "Effective Communications," and "Problem Solving." The study utilized three different instructional formats: teacher-led instruction, small group work, and individual, self-paced instruction. The students were U.S. Air Force trainees who were required to learn technical material. One group of students received motivational training before learning the technical content; a control group learned the content without participating in motivational training. Students in the motivational training group showed higher levels of motivation and achievement than did students who had not received this training. McCombs concludes that it is possible to develop students' motivational skills through training, and that the combination of the three instructional formats is an important component of the success of such training.

Classroom Applications

 You may employ a variety of techniques in motivational skills training. We describe a few below, with reference to the seven modules used in McCombs's research, as noted above:

1. *Introduction:* Explain the purpose of motivational skills training. Introduce students to the concepts of personal responsibility and positive self-control, and how these attitudes engender feelings of competence. Introduce students to strategies for controlling negative attitudes, such as monitoring self-messages and focusing on positive self-talk.

2. *Self-knowledge:* Help students examine conflicts in their own values and beliefs and give them strategies for resolving such conflicts. Explain the role of values and beliefs in helping them define themselves and establish priorities based on what is most important to them.

3. *Career development:* Use students' self-knowledge to help them examine career options, develop decision-making skills, and make career goals and plans.

4. *Goal setting:* Describe for students the purpose of goals as motivating and directing behavior, explain the difference between short- and long-term goals, teach students how to think systematically about and set personal goals, and give them exercises that require them to set specific short- and long-term goals.

5. *Stress management:* Explain and demonstrate a variety of stress reduction techniques, such as deep breathing, creative visualization, positive self-talk, and progressive muscle relaxation. Explain how negative self-talk, misconceptions about learning, and erroneous perceptions can produce stress. Explain the importance of reducing anxiety before it gets out of control and interferes with learning and/or test performance.

6. *Effective communications:* Explain to students the importance of speaking, listening, and giving feedback effectively so that others can understand their wants, needs, feelings, and concerns. Teach students such listening strategies as paraphrasing, "reflecting the feeling," and showing empathy. Teach them to think about how they are speaking (e.g., tone, pace, volume) in addition to what they are speaking about. Teach them to be aware of their own and others' nonverbal communications. Finally, teach them to be sensitive to cultural differences in communication.

7. *Problem solving:* Show students how they have been using problem-solving approaches throughout their motivational skills training and in other areas of their lives. Explain and demonstrate a model for effective problem solving, and give students practice applying the model to a variety of problems.

Precautions and Possible Pitfalls

 Use a combination of these three formats for motivational skills training: (a) Some material is presented by a teacher; (b) Some work is done in small groups; and (c) Some work involves students working alone, self-pacing their instruction. You can make motivational material more personally relevant and meaningful to your students by describing some of your own experiences, showing genuine personal interest in the students, being a positive role model, and conveying how motivational skills will help students in their future endeavors.

BIBLIOGRAPHY

McCombs, B. (1984). Processes and skills underlying continuing intrinsic motivation to learn: Toward a definition of motivational skills training interventions. *Educational Psychologist, 19,* 199-218.

THE TIP (3.3)

 Be aware of students' different levels of test anxiety as this anxiety relates to different subject areas, and use a variety of techniques to help students to overcome their anxiety.

What the Research Says

 Students have differing degrees of test anxiety for different subject areas. Everson, Tobias, Hartman, and Gourgey (1993) compared 196 first-year college students' self-reports of test anxiety in mathematics, physical sciences, English, and social studies. The researchers administered the Worry-Emotionality Scale, on which the students rated their anxiety about tests in one of these four subjects. The students were asked to imagine that they were taking a test in mathematics, for example, and to rate each item on a 5-point scale on which responses ranged from 1: "I would not feel that way at all" to 5: "I would feel that way very strongly." Items included "I would feel my heart beating fast" and "I would feel that I should have studied more for that test." In rank order, from most test anxiety to least test anxiety, the subjects were physical sciences, mathematics, English, and social studies.

Among elementary and secondary school students, test anxiety often develops from a combination of factors, including parents' early reactions to their children's poor test performance, students' comparison of their performance with that of other students as well as their own prior test performance, and increasingly strict evaluation practices as students progress through school. For low-achieving students, failure experiences tend to increase test anxiety. For high-achieving students, unrealistically high self-expectations, parental expectations, and peer expectations tend to increase test anxiety. Some classroom practices also affect test anxiety. When teachers present material in an organized way and make sure that it is not too difficult, the performance of test-anxious students tends to improve.

Classroom Applications

 Test anxiety interferes with test performance. When students are anxious, they waste mental energy that they could be using to answer the test questions. There are many strategies that you can suggest and demonstrate to your students to help them relax. First, find out what strategies they already use. Then you might share with them some of the techniques you use to relax.

Try to reduce the pressure many students feel from being evaluated based on tests. Using other assessment strategies, in addition to tests, can help reduce this pressure and your students' corresponding test anxiety. Help your students to improve their study strategies and test-taking skills.

Help your students learn to differentiate between constructive and destructive kinds of anxiety. For example, constructive or facilitative anxiety can lead students to see tests as challenging experiences. Destructive or debilitative anxiety, in contrast, leads students to see tests as negative self-evaluation experiences.

Teach your students to become aware of their anxiety and how they can control it before, during, and after testing. For example, you might ask them, "What thoughts go through your mind before you take a test?" or "What kinds of thoughts do you have while you are taking a test?" Demonstrate and encourage their use of assorted relaxation techniques, such as those described below.

Deep Breathing

Sitting erect, breathe in deeply through your nose and hold your breath for a count of 8 to 10. Then slowly exhale through your mouth, for a count of 8 to 10. Repeat this procedure several times until you feel relaxed.

Muscle Relaxation

Tension relaxation. Tighten and then relax a muscle or set of muscles, such as your shoulders, that normally store considerable tension. Hold the muscles in a tensed state for a few seconds and then let go. Repeat this sequence with the same muscles a few times and then move on to other muscles.

Self-hypnosis. Sit up straight in a chair with your arms and legs uncrossed, feet flat on the floor, and palms on top of your thighs. Progressively relax your body, from toes to head, systematically focusing on one part at a time. Concentrate on tuning in to your bodily sensations, allowing your muscles to relax, becoming more aware of what it feels like when your muscles are relaxed. Talk to yourself (aloud or silently), telling yourself to loosen up and lessen any tightness. When the body is relaxed it is more receptive to positive self-talk, so build up your self-confidence at this point. For example, you might say to yourself, "I know I can do well on this test!"

Creative Visualization

Minutes, days, and weeks before testing, use suggestions such as the following to guide your students in engaging in success imagery.

Olympic success. Try what the Olympic athletes do to develop confidence in their performance. Picture yourself in a tense situation, such as taking a test, and visualize yourself looking over the test, seeing the questions and feeling secure about the answers. Imagine yourself answering the questions without too much difficulty. Complete the picture by imagining yourself turning in the completed test and leaving the room assured that you have done your best.

Relaxing place. Where do you feel most at peace? Identify a spot where you feel relaxed, and use all of your senses to imagine yourself there and to experience how you feel when you are there. If your spot is the beach, for instance, "watch" the waves with their white-caps rolling up the shoreline and onto the beach. "Listen" to the waves and the seagulls. "Smell" the salty air and "feel" your fingers and toes in the warm, soft sand.

Precautions and Possible Pitfalls

 Whatever you decide to do to help your students reduce their test anxiety, you must do it with a modicum of reserve, assessing your students and their likely reactions to the techniques outlined above. Not all suggestions work with all students. Be sure to encourage students not to give up if the first relaxation technique they try doesn't work. Often individuals need to practice such techniques for a while to be successful, and students often need to experiment with a variety of techniques to determine which ones work best for them. Ask your students specific questions to see whether gender and/or cultural differences might affect the use of the above suggestions and to elicit ideas you had not previously considered.

BIBLIOGRAPHY

Everson, H. T., Tobias, S., Hartman, H. J., & Gourgey, A. (1993). Test anxiety and the curriculum: The subject matters. *Anxiety, Stress and Coping, 6*, 1-8.

Hartman, H. J. (1997). *Human learning and instruction.* New York: City College of City University of New York.

THE TIP (3.4)

 Make sure that you include emotional (affective) objectives in your science lesson plans. Students *can* develop more positive attitudes toward science.

What the Research Says

 Research indicates that teachers seldom incorporate affective objectives into their lesson plans, despite the availability of guidelines for teachers to use in doing so.

Classroom Applications

 One lesson plan model, the "rich instruction" model (Hartman & Sternberg, 1993), systematically incorporates affective objectives into lesson design, along with thinking skill objectives and, of course, content objectives for science. The general lesson plan model includes three sections:

1. Objectives (content, thinking, and affective)

2. Lesson plan core (immediate purpose and long-term benefit, students' prior knowledge and its activation, and instructional methods)

3. Transfer (within subject, across task; across subject; to everyday life; practice for automaticity)

Following is an example of the objectives section as operationalized by David McNamara, a high school science teacher:

1. *Explicit objectives:* Teachers determine how they will achieve the targeted objectives, using a variety of instructional techniques and modalities.

   a. *Content.* Subject matter of lesson (e.g., Students will understand that science is not value-free). Topic: genetic engineering.

   b. *Thinking skills.* Specifically targeted for improvement in this lesson: both cognitive and metacognitive dimensions explicitly addressed (e.g., encoding, evaluating).

   c. *Attitudes.* Specifically targeted for improvement in this lesson (e.g., predispositions and open-mindedness).

Predispositions

Students enter classes with their own personal and cultural attitudes toward authority figures, their role as students, the importance of learning, and the value and usefulness of knowledge and skills. All of these factors affect students' willingness to participate in class, to persevere with academic tasks, and to take intellectual risks. Students' predispositions affect their perceptions of the relationship between schooling and future needs/goals as well as their willingness to pursue further education (Bloom, 1977; Bruner, 1966; Carroll, 1963; Nickerson, 1981). A student entering a classroom who is predisposed to learn from and use what the teacher presents is likely to have a learning experience that is different from that of a student who views school as a rite of passage or merely a social meeting place.

Following are some suggestions for improving on students' predispositions:

- Discuss the short- and long-term benefits intended for each topic/task.
- Cultivate student self-control over learning and performance (e.g., time management).
- Encourage students to challenge and question authority.
- Systematically relate schoolwork to students' everyday lives and future goals.
- Model, encourage, and reward all of the following: persistence, intellectual risk taking, tolerance for ambiguity, intrinsic motivation, and delayed gratification.
- Use the following positive self-talk, or "self-coaching," suggestions (based on the work of Collins-Eiland, 1985) to help students control their own predispositions:

    Fire up: Before working on an academic task, say something positive to yourself to increase your motivation, interest, involvement, meaning, or appreciation for the task at hand (e.g., "Okay, I'm going to learn to write a good report because someday I hope to publish my work!").

    Coax: Force yourself to do something you're not looking forward to by saying, "I will feel better when I finish this."

    Encourage: While working on a task, keep your mood positive and help yourself keep going until you're finished by saying, "This isn't as bad as I thought it would be" or "I'm getting there, slowly but surely!"

    Reward: After a task is finished, say something nice to yourself to reward a good performance. If your overall performance was poor, try to find some small success in it (e.g., "I did well on that part" or "Well, at least I got part of it right.").

Open-Mindedness

The extent to which students' mental attitudes are open or closed affects how they process information. Being open-minded is often associated with being free of any bias or prejudice that may inhibit consideration of new ideas. Ennis (1987) and others identify open-mindedness as one of the key attitudes underlying critical thinking. It allows an individual to determine objectively whether or not to accept or reject particular information. Perry (1970) has suggested that open-mindedness is one of the characteristics of intellectually mature college students. Rokeach's (1960) formulation of the concept suggests that students who are open-minded are more likely than those who are closed-minded to see connections between beliefs, whereas students who are closed-minded tend to treat beliefs as isolated things. Consequently, open-minded students might be more likely than closed-minded students to see relationships between concepts across subject areas as well as connections between knowledge and skills learned in school and nonschool applications. Following are some suggestions for enhancing students' open-mindedness:

- Help students view the world relativistically (in terms of degrees and alternatives) rather than absolutely (that is, in terms of all or none, or one right answer or way).

- Model withholding judgment and encourage students to do so until they have gathered sufficient evidence and reasons.

- Model respecting the rights of others to have beliefs and values different from one's own, and encourage students to do so also.

- Have students argue from positions different from their own and show them how to use opposing viewpoints as tools for critically evaluating lines of reasoning.

- Help students avoid overgeneralizing the implications of ideas and events.

- Accept students' valid answers and methods even if they are not the ones you or your textbook had in mind.

- Identify relationships between ideas instead of treating ideas in isolation.

- Cultivate the habit of differentiating between fact and opinion.

Precautions and Possible Pitfalls

This is a complex lesson plan model, and teachers are not expected to implement it all at once. Pick a part of the model you want to work with, in this case the affective component, and develop it along with your science content objectives. The three sets of objectives should be viewed as a goal for a unit of instruction, with each lesson in the unit structured to achieve specific objectives toward this goal, so that each unit systematically incorporates all three types of objectives.

BIBLIOGRAPHY

Bloom, B. S. (1977, November). Affective outcomes of schooling. *Phi Delta Kappan*, pp. 193-196.

Bruner, J. (1966). *Toward a theory of instruction*. New York: W. W. Norton.

Carroll, J. (1963). A model of school learning. *Teachers College Record, 64*, 723-733.

Collins-Eiland, K. (1985). *How to coach or cajole yourself into almost anything: Self-coaching for affect control*. Galveston: University of Texas, Medical Branch.

Ennis, R. (1987). A taxonomy of critical thinking dispositions and abilities. In J. Baron & R. F. Sternberg (Eds.), *Teaching thinking skills: Theory and practice* (pp. 9-26). New York: W. H. Freeman.

Hartman, H. J., & Barell, J. (1989). The flip side of cognition: Attitudes which foster thinking. *Intellectual Skills Development Association Journal, 4*(1), 3-12.

Hartman, H. J., & Sternberg, R. J. (1993). A broad BACEIS for improving thinking. *Instructional Science, 21*, 401-425.

Kobella, T. R., Jr. (1989, April 1). Changing and measuring attitudes in the science classroom. *Research Matters—to the Science Teacher* (no. 8901) [On-line]. Available Internet: http://www.narst.org/research/attitude.htm

Nickerson, R. S. (1981). Thoughts on teaching thinking. *Educational Leadership, 39*(2), 21-24.

Perry, W. (1970). *Forms of intellectual and ethical development in the college years: A scheme*. New York: Holt, Rinehart & Winston.

Rokeach, M. (1960). *The open and closed mind*. New York: Basic Books.

THE TIP (3.5)

When you are trying to determine how to motivate students' interest in science, differentiate between personal and situational interest and use both forms to increase your students' motivation to learn. Remember that you need to stimulate as well as maintain student interest.

What the Research Says

Teachers can draw on different types of interest that students have in science. Personal interest is what students bring with them to the classroom or other environment; situational interest is something that students acquire by participating in activities in the classroom or other situations. Whereas personal interest emphasizes the importance of working with individual differences in motivation, situational interest emphasizes the importance of the teacher's creating an appropriate setting to develop students' interest in science. Teachers should also differentiate between factors that stimulate student interest and those that maintain student interest. Situational factors, such as interactive exhibits at museums, tend to stimulate interest in science (Paris, Yambor, & Packard, 1998), whereas personal factors, such as setting task-mastery goals, tend to maintain student interest and produce more active cognitive engagement in science activities. The strength of students' goals has been found to be related to students' personal motivation and attitudes toward science (Meece, Blumenfeld, & Hoyle, 1988).

Classroom Applications

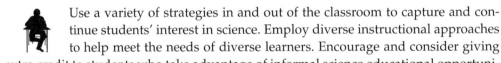

Use a variety of strategies in and out of the classroom to capture and continue students' interest in science. Employ diverse instructional approaches to help meet the needs of diverse learners. Encourage and consider giving extra credit to students who take advantage of informal science educational opportunities, such as visiting museums in person or on-line and writing about what they liked about their visits.

Consider students' goal orientations and have your students reflect on their own goal orientations. In the classroom, require students to set their own personal learning goals for science activities and encourage them to do so outside the classroom. Once students have established their goals, help them learn how to monitor their own progress in achieving those goals so that they can be more successful in attaining them and thereby further increase their motivation to learn science.

Precautions and Possible Pitfalls

 Examine and give students feedback on the goals they set for their science activities. If a student's goals tend to emphasize the student's ego/social perceptions (e.g., to impress someone else), the goals are unlikely to have the intended advantage of promoting the student's own interest in learning science. Similarly, if a student's goal is to do the minimum work possible, his or her science motivation is unlikely to be enhanced. Guide your students in setting goals that focus on growth, such as finding out about something that interests them or getting more involved in their work.

BIBLIOGRAPHY

Meece, J. L., Blumenfeld, P. C., & Hoyle, R. H. (1988). Students' goal orientations and cognitive engagement in classroom activities. *Journal of Educational Psychology, 80,* 514-523.

Paris, S., Yambor, K., & Packard, B. (1998). Hands-on biology: A museum-school-university partnership for enhancing students' interest in science. *Elementary School Journal, 98,* 267-287.

THE TIP (3.6)

 Use different motivational strategies for girls and boys.

What the Research Says

 When it comes to motivation, girls tend to be generalists, whereas boys tend to be specialists. Interest, rather than intellect, often lies at the heart of the differences between boys and girls in science achievement. Girls tend to be interested in a wide range of subjects, whereas boys tend to concentrate their interests more narrowly. Pollmer (1991) conducted a study with 457 students, 338 of whom attended special mathematics- and science-oriented schools and 119 of whom attended regular schools but had excellent grades in mathematics, physics, and chemistry. At the beginning of the 2-year study, the students were asked to rate their interest in later studying science. Then, several times over a period of 2 years, teachers were asked to rank their students' interests in science. The rankings of the girls in the sample became worse over time.

In Pollmer's study, girls and boys were asked to rate how much they liked doing a variety of mathematical/physical and linguistic/literary tasks. The mathematical/ physical tasks included finding variations on solutions to problems, solving especially difficult tasks, creating tasks by oneself, doing puzzles, and playing chess. The linguistic/ literary tasks included making puns; following dialogues in literature, drama, or a radio play; having discussions with intellectuals; and finding contradictions or inconsistencies in texts. The girls in the study were interested in a variety of areas and tended to study all subjects equally rather than invest in one area at the expense of the others, as the boys tended to do. Over time, the girls' interests expanded while the boys' interests narrowed.

Classroom Applications

 On average, girls often seem to do less well in science classes than do boys. This phenomenon does not happen because girls have less talent in science than boys, but because girls tend to have greater interests in a wider range of topics than do boys. Consequently, you may more easily motivate your girl students by presenting them with science concepts that touch a wider range of subjects. For example:

1. Relate the structure of the atom or radioactivity to Madame Curie and the women's issues she may have experienced during her life.

2. Relate the scientific method, discovery, and imagination in science to creativity in art.

3. Connect the nervous system and brain function to surrealist painting and the beginnings of psychoanalytical thought and brain research during the same period.

4. Relate famous scientists such as Darwin and Galileo to philosophy and/or history. What role did science play within the social and culture constructs at the times these scientists lived? Have your students work on projects that correspond with their interests and write papers or reports.

Precautions and Possible Pitfalls

Don't be disappointed if your efforts to motivate girls do not produce observable desired effects. For older girls, entrenched identities tend to have been set in the younger grades. Continue to give girls the opportunity to demonstrate their abilities to achieve in science. You might be planting seeds that will blossom in later years!

BIBLIOGRAPHY

Brickhouse, N. W., Lowery, P., & Schultz, K. (2000). What kind of a girl does science? The construction of school science identities. *Journal of Research in Science Teaching, 37,* 441-458.

Pollmer, K. (1991). Was behindert hochbegabte Mädchen, Erfolg im Mathematikunterricht zu erreichen? [What handicaps highly talented girls in being successful in mathematics?] *Psychologie in Erziehung und Unterricht, 38,* 28-36.

THE TIP (3.7)

 If your students have poor science self-concepts, implement a variety of strategies to help them feel they can be successful learners in science.

What the Research Says

An individual's academic self-concept involves his or her feeling of confidence (or lack of confidence) in his or her ability to achieve, the individual's level of self-reliance, and the individual's recognition of his or her own strengths and weaknesses. A positive academic self-concept results from frequent and consistent success experiences in specific subjects that are generalized to overall success in school. With repeated failure experiences, a student develops a widespread, self-defeating pattern of achievement motivation and an avoidance of failure to protect a sense of dignity. A student's academic self-concept affects his or her choice of tasks, willingness to try, persistence, and actual performance. When a student's self-concept of ability is threatened, he or she may show failure-avoidance motivation. Failure-avoidance strategies include not trying, procrastinating, false effort, and even denial of effort. Failure without effort is equated to failure with honor. Self-concept is multidimensional. It has one general facet and several specific ones, for example, in specific subject areas (Brookover, Le Pere, Hamachek, & Erickson, 1965).

Many studies have indicated that there is almost no relationship between students' self-concepts in different subject areas. For example, a student may feel she is a great reader (good reading self-concept) but is bad in science (poor science self-concept). Research suggests that such self-perceptions are formed through internal and external comparison processes. Internal comparison involves comparing one's own performance in different subjects (e.g., "I am better in English than I am in science"). External comparison involves comparing oneself to others ("Most of the students in my class are better in science than I am").

Classroom Applications

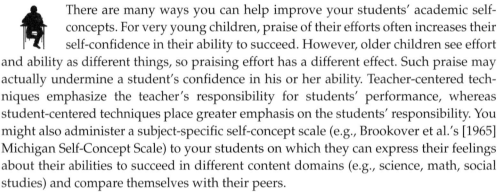

There are many ways you can help improve your students' academic self-concepts. For very young children, praise of their efforts often increases their self-confidence in their ability to succeed. However, older children see effort and ability as different things, so praising effort has a different effect. Such praise may actually undermine a student's confidence in his or her ability. Teacher-centered techniques emphasize the teacher's responsibility for students' performance, whereas student-centered techniques place greater emphasis on the students' responsibility. You might also administer a subject-specific self-concept scale (e.g., Brookover et al.'s [1965] Michigan Self-Concept Scale) to your students on which they can express their feelings about their abilities to succeed in different content domains (e.g., science, math, social studies) and compare themselves with their peers.

Following are some examples of teacher-centered techniques for improving students' academic self-concepts:

1. Convey your positive expectations for students' performance.

2. Provide a cushion of frequent and consistent success experiences by (a) starting with the known/simple and moving gradually to the unknown/complex and (b) helping students break complex problems/tasks into reachable subgoals.

Listen to your students attentively and treat them respectfully. Consider using the following student-centered techniques:

1. Encourage students to have positive expectations of their own performance and not to push themselves too hard or be too easy on themselves.

2. Teach students to direct their self-criticism to their own correctable actions instead of themselves as people. For example, "I studied the wrong material" instead of "I'm just not good in science."

3. Help students learn to recognize their successes and identify their patterns of success and failure.

4. Guide students in developing action plans that will help them to translate failure experiences into strategies for improving their performance.

5. Encourage students to redefine success in terms of exceeding their own past performance in science instead of comparing themselves to others, or comparing themselves in math to a subject in which they feel confident.

Precautions and Possible Pitfalls

 Bear in mind that not all methods work well with all students and not all teachers can implement the techniques suggested above with equal facility and effectiveness. Therefore, you must select those methods that best suit you and best fit your intended population or individuals. It is best not to rely strictly on teacher-centered techniques. You should try to stretch yourself and experiment with the student-centered techniques with which you feel most comfortable. This will help to prevent your students from becoming dependent on you for the development and maintenance of their positive science self-concepts. Teacher-centered techniques, when used at all, are best used in the beginning, to develop students' positive science self-concepts. Then it is best to shift to student-centered techniques.

BIBLIOGRAPHY

Brookover, W., Le Pere, J., Hamachek, T., & Erickson, E. (1965). *Self-concept of ability and school achievement, II* (Final report of Cooperative Research Project No. 1636). East Lansing: Michigan State University.

Marsh, H. (1986). Verbal and math self-concepts: An internal/external frame of reference model. *American Journal of Educational Research, 23*(1), 129-149.

THE TIP (3.8)

 When you consider how your students view themselves as science students, be sensitive to possible gender and ethnic differences as well as to the relationship between ethnicity and gender.

What the Research Says

Historically, girls and members of certain ethnic minority groups have under-achieved in schools. This is especially true in science and math classes. Research suggests that girls and boys may have different science preferences and self-perceptions, depending on the specific area of science. For example, Kahle and Damnjanovic (1994, 1997) found that fourth-grade girls preferred biological science, whereas the boys they studied preferred physical sciences.

Stereotyping may impose obstacles to success for some students inside and outside the classroom. Stereotypes convey explanatory information about specific groups (e.g., blacks are lazy, girls are bad at science and math) that may be used as attributions for children's performance by adults and the children themselves.

Reyna (2000), who examined the underlying attributional structures of all stereo-types, has identified three types:

- Stereotypes that, when used, become internal controllable attributions and expla-nations for controllable behaviors or states of affairs, implying internal, stable, controllable causes (examples: Whites are bigoted. Certain girls are promiscu-ous. Mexicans are lazy.)

- Stereotypes that suggest a trait, attribute, or behavior that is beyond the person's control (examples: Jocks are dumb. Old people are senile. Women are weak. Irish are lucky.)

- Stereotypes that imply external causes that lie outside the individuals being stereotyped and remove responsibility, placing it on factors outside the individ-uals' control (examples: Some groups are underprivileged by a racist society. African Americans and Latinos, as a group, are not as successful as whites because they are lazy or inept.)

Reyna found that each one of these attributional signatures has specific effects on judg-ments of responsibility. Recognizing that stereotypes are vehicles for attribution judg-ments, educators can prepare themselves to deal with the effects that stereotypes may have on students and their own perceptions so that they will be better able to counter-act or diminish them.

Classroom Applications

Classrooms across the United States are increasingly characterized by ethnic diversity, and this trend will become even stronger as the 21st century pro-gresses. Teachers often have unconscious stereotypes of students based on their ethnicity and gender. It is very important that you treat each of your students as an individual and that you tune in to and understand each student's thoughts and feelings about learning science.

Precautions and Possible Pitfalls

 Beware of stereotyping students based on gender or ethnicity. Although there are general trends for girls versus boys (e.g., girls' preferring biology to physics) and for students from different ethnic groups, you should not assume that your students have any predispositions toward particular characteristics.

BIBLIOGRAPHY

Kahle, J. B., & Damnjanovic, A. (1994). The effects of inquiry activities on elementary students' enjoyment, ease and confidence in doing science: An analysis by sex and race. *Journal of Women and Minorities in Science and Engineering, 1*, 17-28.

Kahle, J. B., & Damnjanovic, A. (1997, March 14). How research helps address gender equity. *Research Matters—to the Science Teacher* (no. 9703) [On-line]. Available Internet: http://www.narst.org/research/gender2.htm

Reyna, C. (2000). Lazy, dumb, or industrious: When stereotypes convey attribution information in the classroom. *Educational Psychology Review, 12*(1), 85-110.

THE TIP (3.9)

 Use persuasion (*not* indoctrination) to change your students' attitudes.

What the Research Says

 Extensive studies conducted by science educators have demonstrated persuasion to be an effective method of changing students' attitudes about science. Shrigley and his associates have studied how attitude change is affected by (a) the source of the message, (b) the content of the message, (c) how the message is delivered, and (d) the audience (see Abdel-Gaid, Trublood, & Shrigley, 1986; Shrigley & Kobella, 1987; Thompson & Shrigley, 1986). They distinguish between persuasion and indoctrination, noting that in both cases the goal is to establish certain attitudes and beliefs, but persuasion does so by emphasizing the reasons underlying the beliefs, whereas indoctrination emphasizes only the content of the beliefs. Among the many interesting conclusions from this body of research are the following:

- Students' attitudes about science can be changed through the use of messages less than 30 minutes in length.

- Gains in factual information do not affect attitude change.

- To increase the persuasiveness of a message, one should present both sides of the issue.

- Anecdotes rich in concrete detail are more effective than abstract statistical data in changing attitudes.

- Males tend to have more positive attitudes about science than do females.

- Persistence of attitude change is not affected by the person's ability to recall the message, but it is affected by the person's self-generated thoughts about the message.

- The medium (e.g., videotape, printed material) doesn't matter; the message is the key.

Classroom Applications

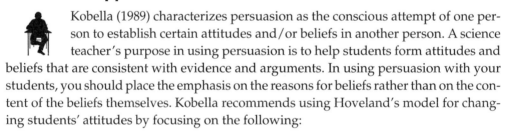
Kobella (1989) characterizes persuasion as the conscious attempt of one person to establish certain attitudes and/or beliefs in another person. A science teacher's purpose in using persuasion is to help students form attitudes and beliefs that are consistent with evidence and arguments. In using persuasion with your students, you should place the emphasis on the reasons for beliefs rather than on the content of the beliefs themselves. Kobella recommends using Hoveland's model for changing students' attitudes by focusing on the following:

- Who says what?
- To whom?
- How is it said?
- What is the effect?

Debating is an excellent way of using the persuasion approach to change students' attitudes. Make sure that the students taking part in debates incorporate good reasons for their positions into their persuasive arguments. Help them to develop their critical thinking skills for this type of activity by teaching them how to evaluate sources and their credibility, including whether their sources' positions might be tainted by special interests or preexisting biases and how to assess how well specific arguments support the general conclusion.

Do your own classroom research on changes in your students' attitudes about science. Both pencil-and-paper and computer-based attitude scales about science are available. Such scales may include items regarding attitudes toward scientific concepts and/or using scientific materials.

Precautions and Possible Pitfalls

Although the research cited above suggests that science attitudes can change in as brief a time as half an hour, other research suggests that attitude change is often a long, slow process. Don't get discouraged if you don't see relatively immediate change in your students' attitudes. You might be planting seeds that will blossom later.

Note that if you have your students debate a controversial topic, such as evolution versus creationism, you should anticipate and be prepared to address the adverse reactions some parents might have.

BIBLIOGRAPHY

Abdel-Gaid, S., Trublood, C. R., & Shrigley, R. L. (1986). A systematic procedure for constructing a valid microcomputer attitude scale. *Journal of Research in Science Teaching, 23,* 823-839.

Kobella, T. R., Jr. (1989, April 1). Changing and measuring attitudes in the science classroom. *Research Matters—to the Science Teacher* (no. 8901) [On-line]. Available Internet: http://www.narst.org/research/attitude.htm

Petty, R. E., & Cacioppo, J. T. (1986). *Communication and persuasion: Central and peripheral routes to attitude change.* New York: Springer-Verlag.

Shrigley, R. L., & Kobella, T. R., Jr. (1987). *Applying a theoretical framework: A decade of attitude research in science education.* University Park: Pennsylvania State University, Department of Curriculum and Instruction.

Thompson, C. L., & Shrigley, R. L. (1986). What research says: Revising the Science Attitude Scale. *School Science and Mathematics, 86,* 331-334.

THE TIP (3.10)

 Motivate your students by helping them to value science and to channel their efforts toward activities that have been found to predict achievement in science.

What the Research Says

Howe (1996) conducted a study of 80 students in an eighth-grade science classroom using questionnaires, observations, and structured interviews of students and teachers. The sample included equal numbers of girls and boys and equal numbers of African Americans and whites. The results showed that most students in all groups valued achievement in science and desired success, and they thought that their parents and teacher did, too. There was a relationship between students' value for science and the efforts they made in science. Interestingly, Howe found a few gender and ethnic differences. Girls of both ethnic groups attributed their successes to effort, and their views of effort appeared to be more passive than the views of boys in both ethnic groups. For the girls, effort was connected with the passive activities of listening, reading, and working on in-class assignments. Conversely, for the boys, success was associated with ability instead of effort, and lack of success was associated not with lack of ability but with lack of effort. For the boys, effort involved more active work with experiments and equipment. The activities that characterized active effort had positive correlations with science achievement, whereas the activities that characterized passive effort were not associated with high achievement in science. According to Howe, the Japanese conception of ability comprehensively includes the traditional talent or intelligence as well as the capacity for persistence and hard work.

Classroom Applications

Howe describes several educational implications of her research. It is especially important for teachers to realize that most students do value science and want to succeed. Teacher recognition of students' individual efforts is an important motivational factor. You can show your recognition of your students' efforts in a variety of ways:

- Praise students' efforts through oral and/or written comments on papers.
- Have your students keep individual logs or progress charts and review them weekly.

- Encourage peers to recognize each other's efforts when doing group work.

- Reward students' efforts.

- Observe students working individually and in cooperative groups and assess their efforts.

- Discuss with the class the issue of passive versus active conceptions of "effort."

- Design classroom activities that emphasize active effort.

- Encourage girls to participate actively in classroom experiments and the use of equipment instead of passively standing around watching boys engage in all the action. It is your responsibility to ensure balanced access to meaningful classroom experiences across gender and ethnic groups.

Precautions and Possible Pitfalls

Not all efforts are equal. Nominal, superficial efforts should be treated differently from serious, meaningful efforts. Don't automatically equate a student's continuing to get wrong answers with lack of effort, however. The student may actually be working harder, spending more time studying than in the past, and thereby showing a greater quantity of effort, but may not be using effective strategies, so the quality of the outcome might be poor. Or the student might have a misconception or gap in prior knowledge that makes it difficult for him or her to comprehend new material.

BIBLIOGRAPHY

Howe, A. C. (1996, December 9). Adolescents' motivation, behavior and achievement in science. *Research Matters—to the Science Teacher* (no. 9603) [On-line]. Available Internet: http://www.narst.org/research/adolescent.htm

CHAPTER FOUR

Social Aspects of Science Classrooms

THE TIP (4.1)

 Make classroom activities and the transitions between them flow smoothly.

What the Research Says

 In a classic study of classroom management, Kounin (1970) compared effective and ineffective teachers. The effective teachers' classes did not have many problems, whereas continual disruption and chaos characterized the ineffective teachers' classes. By observing effective and ineffective teachers, Kounin discovered that the major difference between them was that the effective teachers prevented problems, whereas the ineffective teachers waited until problems arose and then handled them. One way the effective teachers prevented problems was by making sure students were not sitting around waiting for the next activity, but were engaged in meaningful work all the time. The effective teachers made smooth transitions between activities, conducted activities at a flexible and reasonable pace, and employed lessons that involved a variety of activities.

Classroom Applications

 A smooth beginning to a class is quite obviously an important aspect of effective instruction. When you can, have your day's agenda on the board when students arrive, so that they can start immediately on the first activity. This allows you to take care of the obligatory paperwork associated with the beginning of most classes without allowing students to become distracted by their personal and individual issues while the class waits for your attention. Establish a policy of addressing students'

individual issues, such as missed assignments, individual grades, and test scoring questions, before or after school or at another appropriate time that doesn't interfere with the beginning of class.

Once you can give the class your undivided attention, rather than spending time having students copy their homework on the board at the beginning of a lesson, a smooth beginning would have them immediately bring their work to the class's attention by showing it on an overhead projector or video monitor. If students are displaying the results of their homework on overhead transparencies, provide the transparencies ahead of time, so they can prepare them as part of their homework and can present their work without taking class time to copy it onto transparencies.

You can provide smooth transitions between topics during class time by structuring the order of topics to be presented in a logical way, so that one comfortably leads into the next or one situation is an elaboration of its predecessor. Again, have the order of the topics already on the board to help mentally prepare your students. Transitions should be smooth in terms of both topics presented (content) and student activities (process). If you are conscious of the value of making smooth transitions, you greatly increase the likelihood that you will accomplish them.

Precautions and Possible Pitfalls

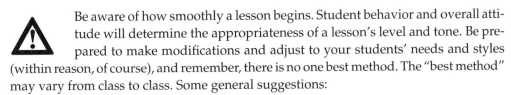 Be aware of how smoothly a lesson begins. Student behavior and overall attitude will determine the appropriateness of a lesson's level and tone. Be prepared to make modifications and adjust to your students' needs and styles (within reason, of course), and remember, there is no one best method. The "best method" may vary from class to class. Some general suggestions:

1. Avoid interrupting students while they are busy working.

2. Avoid returning to activities that have been treated as finished.

3. Avoid starting a new activity before finishing the preceding one.

4. Avoid taking too much time when beginning a new activity. Slowing down can breed trouble.

BIBLIOGRAPHY

Kounin, J. (1970). *Discipline and group management in classrooms.* New York: Holt, Rinehart & Winston.

THE TIP (4.2)

 Structure classroom activities so that students learn to work cooperatively with others, as teamwork is common in scientific endeavors.

What the Research Says

 When students work in cooperation with other students, they often get more out of learning than they do when they work on their own or even when they work with the teacher. When students are isolated from each other and compete with each other, they are less involved in learning, their learning is not as deep, and they have fewer opportunities to improve their thinking. Students who work cooperatively learn more and higher-level subject-area knowledge, and they tend to retain and apply what they have learned when working on difficult tasks more effectively than do students who work individually. In addition, cooperative learning motivates students to learn because learning becomes fun and meaningful, boosts students' self-esteem as they explain content to others, and improves interpersonal relationships among culturally diverse students. Finally, cooperative learning develops students' higher-level thinking skills, such as metacognition, as students compare their own knowledge and strategies with those of others.

Scientists seldom work in isolation; they usually require input and feedback from their peers to extend and refine their own thinking. Often scientific enterprise is undertaken by teams; individuals cooperate with each other on a project, and teams cooperate with other teams.

Classroom Applications

 One kind of activity in which cooperative learning may be beneficial is when students investigate or solve a problem. The following example of such an activity, from an earth science class, is an application of plate tectonics basics with a bit of oceanography and biology thrown in.

Set up groups of two to four students and give the groups latitude and longitude coordinates somewhere in the Atlantic Ocean. The students' job is to design, or hypothesize, what an island might look like if it formed at the given location, based on local geology. Assign the island an age of 60,000 years, and ask the students to describe what the island's life might look like and how life would have gotten there.

Continue to introduce new topics and build the project, having students analyze ocean currents and weather patterns. Have each student take a piece of the island's natural history to study, learn about, and describe. Help the students create a rubric (which they will eventually turn into a table of contents) to help them structure their project. Have the members of each group divide up the tasks to be done, and remind them to keep the communication going among themselves to keep the project components cohesive.

In engaging your class in this activity, you model the thinking you want your students to engage in. Each student has an important piece of the project to complete. The project is very "open-ended," and these amateur naturalists can delve as deep as they like into the content's complexity. They can find climate and weather information on the Internet. They can locate adjacent islands as references. They can dive back into the biology lessons they remember on Darwin and the Galapagos Islands. The central thread is their island, but the range of science concepts they may encounter is huge.

In the end, outcomes of the project can include papers or presentations. With such an activity it is hard for any group members to "fall through the cracks," because each partner has too large a stake in the outcome. This project, with its range of problems, is rich in opportunities for group work.

An excellent resource you might consult in planning cooperative learning activities in elementary and middle school science classrooms is Hassard's *Science Experiences: Cooperative Learning and the Teaching of Science* (1990).

Precautions and Possible Pitfalls

Not all group work is cooperative learning. Students must work together, help each other, and learn from each other in order for real cooperative learning to take place. Be careful that one person doesn't dominate any given group, which often tends to happen. Assigning group roles is one way you may either prevent this or handle it when it does occur. You need to monitor your groups constantly as they are solving problems to make sure the students stay on task and are working in productive ways. Although some teachers have suggested that cooperative learning can be used across the board, most research indicates that careful selection of problems for use in cooperative learning groups is important. Research on the effectiveness of cooperative learning in science indicates that this technique is more suitable for some science problems and skills than for others. For example, easy problems are not particularly appropriate for cooperative learning groups because such problems don't require students to collaborate and help each other to find solutions.

Don't let students form their own groups; working with friends can inhibit learning. Carefully set up student groups in advance to maximize diversity on as many variables as possible, including gender, cultural and linguistic background, achievement, personality, and social characteristics.

Johnson and Johnson (1975) emphasize the importance of training students in cooperative skills, such as giving feedback, asking questions, and listening, before cooperative learning begins to help ensure that the groups function effectively. They also recommend "group processing" at the end of a cooperative learning activity, during which students evaluate their individual performance and that of their group (e.g., Did anyone dominate the discussion? How well did the group stay on task?) and plan for future improvements.

BIBLIOGRAPHY

Hassard, J. (1990). *Science experiences: Cooperative learning and the teaching of science.* Menlo Park, CA: Addison-Wesley.

Johnson, D., & Johnson, R. (1975). *Learning together and alone: Cooperation, competition, and individualization.* Englewood Cliffs, NJ: Prentice Hall.

Slavin, R. (1990). *Cooperative learning: Theory, research and practice.* Englewood Cliffs, NJ: Prentice Hall.

THE TIP (4.3)

Use the jigsaw technique of cooperative learning as an interesting and effective way to help students learn.

What the Research Says

Contrary to some people's belief that cooperative learning has only social benefits, research has shown that the jigsaw technique of cooperative learning helps students to learn and apply academic content as well. Eppler and Huber (1990) conducted an experimental study with seven classes of students in grades 7 and 8. The 141 students in the sample were separated into four experimental classes and three control classes. The experimental classes were taught with the jigsaw technique, and the three control classes received regular instruction through lectures. The experiment lasted about 4 weeks, with one double lesson per week. Eppler and Huber examined the social, personal, and academic benefits of jigsaw and traditional instruction. The social and personal benefits they observed to result from the jigsaw method included growth in students' self-control, self-management, ambition, independence, and social interaction. They also found that the jigsaw technique reduced intimidation in the classroom, which inhibits learning and leads to introverted student behavior. The academic benefits of the jigsaw method that Eppler and Huber found included improvements in students' reading abilities, systematic reproduction of knowledge, and abilities to make conclusions and summarize.

Students in the jigsaw classrooms demonstrated improved knowledge as well as the ability to apply that knowledge when compared with students in traditional classes. They were not afraid to ask questions or to scrutinize presented information when they were able to ask for and get an explanation of something from a peer.

Classroom Applications

 The following example of the use of the jigsaw technique in a physics class displays the six steps the method entails:

1. Separate a new part of the curriculum into five major sections.

2. Split a class of 25 students into five groups of 5 students each. These groups are designated the *base groups*. (The groups should be heterogeneous in terms of gender, cultural background, and achievement levels.)

3. Have every member of each base group select one of the major sections (or assign a section to each). For example, one member might focus on the section on the physics of light, another might focus on the section on energy conversion for photosynthesis, another might focus on the section on vision, neurons, and sight, and so forth. If the number of group members exceeds the number of sections, two students can focus on the same section.

4. Have the base groups temporarily divide up so that each student can join a new group in order to become an "expert" in her or his topic. All the students focusing on the physics of light will be in one group, all the students focusing on energy conversion in photosynthesis will be in another group, and so on. Have the students work together in these temporary groups, called *expert groups*. There they acquire knowledge about their topics and discuss how to teach those topics to students in their base groups.

5. Have students return to their base groups, where each serves as the expert for his or her topic. Have all the students take turns teaching to the members of their base groups what they have learned about their topics in the expert groups.

6. Give a written test to the entire class. In steps 4 and 5, students have the opportunity to discuss and exchange knowledge. In this step you have the opportunity to check the quality of students' work, to see what and how much they have learned from each other.

One of the advantages of the jigsaw method of cooperative learning is that there is always active learning going on; students do not become bored while passively listening to reports from other groups, as sometimes happens with Johnson and Johnson's (1975) "learning together" method.

Precautions and Possible Pitfalls

 As students teach the members of their base groups in step 5 of the jigsaw technique, teachers are frequently tempted to join in the discussions and advise the students regarding the best way to teach their subjects. This type of teacher intervention diminishes the social and intellectual benefits of this technique. Although you need to monitor group work in order to intervene when students make substantial mistakes in understanding academic content, you should not interfere with how students decide to teach this content to their peers.

BIBLIOGRAPHY

Aronson, E., Blaney, N., Stephan, C., Sikes, J., & Snapp, M. (1978). *The jigsaw classroom.* Beverly Hills, CA: Sage.

Eppler, R., & Huber, G. L. (1990). Wissenswert im Team: Empirische Untersuchung von Effekten des Gruppen-Puzzles [Acquisition of knowledge in teams: An empirical study of effects of the jigsaw technique]. *Psychologie in Erziehung und Unterricht, 37,* 172-178.

Johnson, D., & Johnson, R. (1975). *Learning together and alone: Cooperation, competition, and individualization.* Englewood Cliffs, NJ: Prentice Hall.

THE TIP (4.4)

 Make special efforts to encourage girls to study science and be sure that you give girls the same quantity and quality of attention as you give to boys. Be aware of cultural biases that may have steered your female students away from biology, chemistry, and physics in particular and science in general. Many might really enjoy science!

What the Research Says

 Sonnert and Holton (1996) identify two factors that explain gender disparities in science: One is a *deficit model,* which emphasizes how women and men are treated differently; the other is a *difference model,* which emphasizes how women and men act differently. Kahle, Parker, Rennie, and Riley (1993) note that teachers need to take a complex set of sociocultural, personal, and educational factors into account in attempting to increase the achievement levels and numbers of female students in school science. Research also suggests that the issues that affect girls in science are similar across groups and should be addressed at an early age (Kahle & Damnjanovic, 1997). According to Sabina Nawaz and other women who work in science-related fields, cues in early life and social pressures often steer girls away from studying science and reinforce the view of science as a male-dominated discipline and career path (see Urschel, 1996). Girls' interest in science starts decreasing in junior high school and continues to decline in high school as girls see science as less useful than do boys.

In a study involving four middle school African American girls, Brickhouse, Lowery, and Schultz (2000) found that different self-identities affected the ways the girls engaged in school science. They also found that the girls measured their success in science not by their understanding of science but by their grades and class participation. Understanding was not a priority for them, and it appeared to play a marginal role in these female students' constructions of identity. It is not clear how violating gender expectations may make it more difficult for girls to take on school science identities or if boys face the same difficulties. However, it appears that girls who take on easily recognizable social roles for girls and bring with them the usual experiences and talents of girls are also the ones who have the fewest problems in constructing school science identities.

Classroom Applications

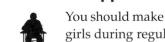 You should make every effort, consciously and conscientiously, to encourage girls during regular classroom instruction. Do not allow boys to select all of the best seats in the classroom or to dominate student responses. Take care not to show gender bias, and attempt to identify famous female scientists from the past and highlight their contributions to the development of science.

Have girls take leadership roles in science activities, such as serving as tutors in the classroom or for students from lower grades. Assign girls to do research papers on women in science. In addition, there are many female scientists who would be pleased to come to a secondary school to give a talk to a class on career options or to give a content talk to a science class. A list of such persons can be obtained from the Association for Women in Science (see the association's Web site at http://www.awis.org).

Further information on women in science is available in the numerous publications of professional science organizations and from commercial publishers. Such sources include Cooney's edited volume *Celebrating Women in Mathematics and Science* (1996) and the Project WISE (Women in Science and Engineering) Web site (http://www.wise.sunysb.edu/index.htm). The commercial Internet site Amazon.com lists a huge number of book selections on the subject of women in science, math, and engineering. Add some of these sources to your library.

Find out what interests your female students and then help them to see and appreciate the science that underlies whatever they care about, whether it is music, sports, clothes, or attracting guys. Providing an authentic context for the sciences is always a good idea. For older girls, this approach can be especially important for gaining their attention and triggering their curiosity. Their interests provide the entrance to learning pathways for girls who would normally be indifferent to "textbook" science content.

Students always seem to want to explore human behavior and the world they personally know. There are many underlying science concepts in everyday occurrences and objects in their lives that can be embedded in curriculum.

Precautions and Possible Pitfalls

 Don't assume you already know what interests your students. Be prepared to listen to them for clues on how to tap into this strategy. You will need to think on your feet and find the connections in a spontaneous way, almost informally. The key here is that you must be able to recognize the opportunities when they are presented to you.

The inclusion of gender issues in science should be a natural part of the instructional program and not merely an add-on—an add-on approach would seem obvious and unnatural, and so would defeat the purpose.

As we have noted, cultural influences often negatively affect girls' attitudes about and their performance in science. If you find a woman scientist who is willing to speak to your class, as suggested above, it is imperative that you interview the potential speaker before the class presentation. This will help you to get to know the visitor and help you to prepare the class for the ensuing presentation. In turn, you can prepare the speaker for the class and any peculiarities (both favorable and unfavorable) about the class that it might be wise for her to be aware of prior to the presentation.

Keep in mind that your students' parents may hold stereotypes about women in science that need to be overcome. Reach out to parents to let them know that girls can be as successful as boys in science, both in their schoolwork and in careers.

BIBLIOGRAPHY

Brickhouse, N. W., Lowery, P., & Schultz, K. (2000). What kind of a girl does science? The construction of school science identities. *Journal of Research in Science Teaching, 37,* 441-458.

Cooney, M. P. (Ed.). (1996). *Celebrating women in mathematics and science.* Reston, VA: National Council of Teachers of Mathematics.

Kahle, J. B., & Damnjanovic, A. (1997, March 14). How research helps address gender equity. *Research Matters—to the Science Teacher* (no. 9703) [On-line]. Available Internet: http://www.narst.org/research/gender2.htm

Kahle, J. B., Parker, L. H., Rennie, L. J., & Riley, D. (1993). Gender differences in science education: Building a model. *Educational Psychologist, 28,* 379-404.

Sonnert, G., & Holton, G. (1996). Career paths of women and men in the sciences. *American Scientist, 84,* 63-71.

Urschel, J. (1996, June 26). Way of teaching math, science puts girls off. *USA Today* [On-line]. Available Internet: http://nmnwse.org/putoff.html

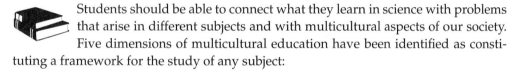

THE TIP (4.5)

Make multicultural connections in science.

What the Research Says

 Students should be able to connect what they learn in science with problems that arise in different subjects and with multicultural aspects of our society. Five dimensions of multicultural education have been identified as constituting a framework for the study of any subject:

- *Integrate content,* reflecting diversity when teaching key points.

- *Construct knowledge* so that students understand how people's points of view within a discipline influence the conclusions they reach in that discipline.

- *Reduce prejudice* so that students develop positive attitudes toward different groups of people.

- *Use instructional techniques* that will promote achievement for diverse groups of students.

- *Modify the school culture* to ensure that people from diverse groups are empowered and have educational equality.

Classroom Applications

In teaching, you need to take into consideration that science is not free of cultural influences, that some science textbooks reflect racial biases, and that the history of science should not be viewed only from a Eurocentric perspective (Pugh, 1990). Following are some examples of how you might apply to science the five multicultural dimensions listed above:

- *Integrate content* so that lessons in the history of science include the contributions of scientists from many cultures and ethnicities. For example, teach students about George Washington Carver, an African American who made major contributions that have influenced botany, agribusiness, and biotechnology.

- *Construct knowledge* so that students see the universal nature of the mathematical components of science: measuring, counting, locating, and designing.

- *Reduce prejudice* by using scientific data to challenge stereotypes. For example, show that there are more whites than blacks on welfare, or teach the economic value of recycling bottles and cans by using the book *The Black Snowman* (Mendez, 1989).

- *Use instructional techniques* that motivate students and demonstrate respect for diverse cultures. For example, group together students from different cultures for cooperative learning activities, encourage all students to participate in extracurricular activities, and have high expectations of success from all students, regardless of cultural backgrounds. Assign African American students to tutor white and/or Asian students.

- *Modify the school culture* by making special efforts to work with minority parents, especially those for whom English is not their native language, on improving their children's learning in science.

Precautions and Possible Pitfalls

 Be sure to avoid any patronizing tone in presenting the multicultural aspects of your lessons. Also, try to be broad in your multicultural focus, so that members of any particular cultural group (e.g., African American, Latino, Asian) don't feel they are being left out.

BIBLIOGRAPHY

Banks, J. A. (1994). Transforming the mainstream curriculum. *Educational Leadership, 51*(8), 4-8.

Bishop, A. (1988). Mathematics education in its cultural context. *Educational Studies in Mathematics, 19*, 179-191.

Gallard, A. J. (1992). Creating a multicultural learning environment in science classrooms. *Research Matters—to the Science Teacher* [On-line]. Available Internet: http://www.narst.org/research/multicultural.htm

Mendez, P. (1989). *The black snowman*. New York: Scholastic.

Moses, R., Kamii, M., Swap, S., & Howard, J. (1989). The Algebra Project: Organizing in the spirit of Ella. *Harvard Educational Review, 59,* 423-443.

Pugh, S. (1990). Introducing multicultural science teaching to a secondary school. *School Science Review, 71*(256), 131-135.

Strutchens, M. (1995). *Multicultural mathematics: A more inclusive mathematics* (ERIC Digest). Columbus, OH: Clearinghouse for Science, Mathematics and Environmental Education.

THE TIP (4.6)

 Train student tutors to specialize in helping students (especially the educationally challenged) through difficult parts of labs.

What the Research Says

 A whole classroom of students helping other students has been found to be an efficient and effective method of enhancing achievement. Fuchs, Fuchs, Mathes, and Simmons (1997) conducted a study in which 20 teachers participated in a study of classwide peer tutoring with 40 classrooms in elementary and middle schools. Half of the schools implemented classwide peer tutoring programs and half did not. Both urban and suburban schools participated, and the students came from diverse backgrounds, both culturally and linguistically. The researchers established three different categories of students: average achievers, low achievers without learning disabilities, and low achievers with learning disabilities. The peer tutoring programs were conducted 3 days a week, 35 minutes a day, for 15 weeks. Stronger students were paired with weaker students, and teachers reviewed each pair to ensure the individuals were socially compatible. In all pairs, students took turns serving in the roles of tutor and tutee. Student pairs worked together for 4 weeks, and then teachers arranged new pairings. The teachers received training on how to train their students to be tutors; this training included teaching students how to correct each other's errors. Achievement tests were administered before and after the peer tutoring program. Regardless of whether students were average achievers or low achievers, and regardless of the presence or absence of learning disabilities, students in the peer tutoring classrooms achieved at higher levels than did those in the classrooms without classwide peer tutoring.

Classroom Applications

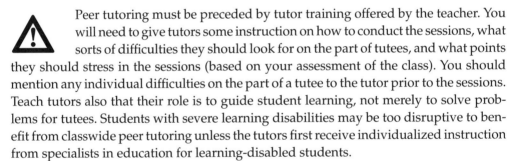

There are many areas in science classes that lend themselves to peer tutoring programs. When there is a skill to be learned and all a student needs is experience with success (i.e., drill with immediate feedback), peer tutoring can provide an efficient way for you to monitor and support the student who is trying to master the skill. Say a student has difficulty identifying an unknown chemical, an anion or cation. Most tests are simple; however, there are many tests. Individual students within groups can specialize as peer tutors in specific chemical tests or flame tests. There are many tests that peer tutors can become expert at and then share their expertise with individual students. A student who has difficulty doing these tests could find the support of a peer tutor to be a genuine asset. Rather than waiting for an opportunity to talk with the teacher, he or she has access to the peer tutor, saving everyone time. In addition, the tutor, in explaining the methodology to the student, has an opportunity to strengthen his or her own understanding of the concept of test reactions (a higher-order thinking skill) and the role of the reaction in chemistry. Thus peer tutoring often results in mutual benefits for the students involved.

Precautions and Possible Pitfalls

Peer tutoring must be preceded by tutor training offered by the teacher. You will need to give tutors some instruction on how to conduct the sessions, what sorts of difficulties they should look for on the part of tutees, and what points they should stress in the sessions (based on your assessment of the class). You should mention any individual difficulties on the part of a tutee to the tutor prior to the sessions. Teach tutors also that their role is to guide student learning, not merely to solve problems for tutees. Students with severe learning disabilities may be too disruptive to benefit from classwide peer tutoring unless the tutors first receive individualized instruction from specialists in education for learning-disabled students.

BIBLIOGRAPHY

Fuchs, D., Fuchs, L., Mathes, P. G., & Simmons, D. (1997). Peer-assisted learning strategies: Making classrooms more responsive to diversity. *American Educational Research Journal, 34*, 174-206.

THE TIP (4.7)

  Reach out to students' parents to form a partnership in educating elementary and high school students.

What the Research Says

Students want their parents to be involved in their education. A high level of parental involvement in children's education generally leads to a high level of academic achievement. Often, parents are involved with their children's education while the children are in elementary school, but stop being involved once the children reach high school. One study involving 748 urban elementary and secondary school students (257 in grade 5, 257 in grade 7, 144 in grade 9, and 90 in grade 11) looked at requests for and attitudes about the students' families' involvement in education. Of these students, 449 were black, 129 were Hispanic, and 121 were white. The study compared high and low achievement in mathematics and English (reading for elementary school students) and examined whether there were ethnic differences in students' feelings about family involvement. Students in all grades requested parental assistance with schoolwork and had positive attitudes about using their parents as educational resources, although the elementary students made more requests and had more positive attitudes than did the secondary school students. Both high- and low-achieving students showed interest in parental involvement. However, at the elementary school level, high-achieving Hispanic students in mathematics had more favorable attitudes than did low-achieving Hispanic students in mathematics. Black and Hispanic students were generally more interested in parental involvement than were white students (Hartman-Haas, 1983).

Classroom Applications

Reach out to your students' parents to enhance their involvement and develop partnerships with them in their children's education. Many parents are unaware that they have the ability to have an impact on their children's education even if they are not well educated themselves. You can explain and illustrate for parents how a parent can function as an educational manager and/or teacher. Give parents some examples of the ways in which a parent can serve as an educational manager:

1. Provide the time, a quiet place, and adequate light for studying. Help the child determine the best time and place to work.

2. Each night, ask the child if there is a homework assignment and ask to see it when it has been completed.

3. Each night, ask the child about what happened in school that day.

4. Have a dictionary accessible and encourage the child to use it.

5. Find out when tests are to be given and make sure the child has a good night's sleep beforehand and breakfast the day of the test.

6. Visit the school to discuss the child's progress and to find out what can be done at home.

7. Communicate positive attitudes and expectations about the child's school performance.

8. Avoid letting a child's household responsibilities assume more importance than schoolwork.

Prepare a handout listing such examples for parents, so they have some idea about what they can do at home to support this partnership.

Precautions and Possible Pitfalls

If a student's parents do not speak English well, they may be reluctant to communicate with a teacher. In such cases, if you cannot speak the parents' language, you may be able to gain access to a community volunteer who can act as a school advocate and resource for the parents, or someone from the school might be able to translate a letter or handout for the parents into the parents' native language.

BIBLIOGRAPHY

Hartman-Haas, H. J. (1983, April). *Family educational interaction: Focus on the child.* Paper presented at the annual meeting of the American Educational Research Association, Montreal.

Hartman-Haas, H. J. (1984). Family involvement tips for teachers. *Division of Research Evaluation and Testing Research Bulletin* (pp. 1-12) Newark, NJ: Board of Education.

THE TIP (4.8)

 Inform your students' parents that they should not let media reports about studies of other children change their views of their own children's abilities to be successful in science.

What the Research Says

 Parents may develop misconceptions about their children's abilities as a result of reports in the media. Jacobs and Eccles (1985) examined the impact on parents of a media report on gifted junior high school students. A report on findings of major gender differences in students' mathematical aptitude had received extensive media coverage, and the researchers compared parents' views about their children's mathematical aptitude before and after exposure to the media coverage. They found that the media coverage changed parents' attitudes about their children's mathematical abilities. Fathers of sons and mothers of daughters developed stronger sex-based stereotyped beliefs after exposure to the media coverage.

Classroom Applications

 Many students find science to be frustrating. Many parents react to their children's frustration by saying that they didn't do well in science themselves, and they tend to accept low achievement from their children. Sometimes it appears to be a sort of "badge of honor" for a person to admit weakness in science and/or mathematics (unlike almost any other subject). Consider offering periodic workshops for your students' parents to keep them informed about what you are teaching, how you are presenting it, and what is expected of their children, both in performance and in results. This sort of workshop experience will also give you an opportunity to communicate with parents regularly and to inform them of their individual child's progress and ability to be successful in science. Then parents will be more prepared to interpret reports from the media and other sources. They will also be less likely to succumb to overgeneralizations and stereotypes that can undermine their children's performance in science.

Precautions and Possible Pitfalls

You need to be extremely patient when working with parents. Recognize that many of them may have been away from a school setting and the concomitant behavior for many years. Be cautious when reporting frequently on a student's progress; leave room for improvement and never "close the door" on an individual student, no matter how frustrating the child's lack of progress may be. Remember that some parents have a tendency to overreact to teachers' comments, and that may have deleterious effects.

BIBLIOGRAPHY

Jacobs, J. E., & Eccles, J. S. (1985). Gender differences in ability: The impact of media reports on parents. *Educational Researcher, 14*(3), 20-25.

THE TIP (4.9)

 Recognize that students' scientific conceptions are strongly affected by their cultural backgrounds.

What the Research Says

 Children's ideas about science are personal and social constructions that are affected by their personal experiences and the culture they live in. Students from the same cultural backgrounds tend to have similar scientific conceptions.

Classroom Applications

Consider the following example of how scientific knowledge and processes can clash with personal and cultural constructions.

The Human Genome Project is often seen as one of the greatest scientific endeavors of all time. A related project, the Human Genome Diversity Project, is seen in a much different light. The premise of the Human Genome Diversity Project is simple: Collect or sample diversity by comparing the genomes of individuals from a variety of cultures and races. One side in the debate that has arisen over this project sees it as an opportunity for more powerful groups to exploit indigenous peoples. Consider the following:

In the previous month (June 1993), 150 members of indigenous groups from 14 United Nations member states developed and tabled with the U.N. the "Mataatua Declaration" [the Mataatua Declaration on Cultural and Intellectual Property Rights of Indigenous People]. This Declaration demanded "an immediate halt to the Human Genome Diversity Project until its moral, ethical, socio-economic, physical and political implications had been thoroughly discussed, understood and approved by indigenous peoples" (Mataatua Declaration 1993). The Mataatua Declaration was followed by several others, including ones from the Maori Congress (representing groups from the North and South Islands of Aotearoa), the National Congress of American Indians, and the Central Australian Aboriginal Congress. In late 1993 the one group, the WCIP, renamed the Project the "Vampire Project." (Juengst, 1996)

The Western scientists on the other side of the debate had not anticipated this response, as they considered the Human Genome Diversity Project just basic science. Some other interesting debates have arisen as information about the project has filtered through various societies, including the following:

1. Scientific debates about the nature and boundaries of racial and cultural groups

2. Technical debates about the ethics and validity of group and individual consent (What obligations do scientists have to inform and educate indigenous peoples or other groups?)

3. Moral and social debates about whether and how Diversity Project subjects should participate in planning and implementing the project (Who will own or control the information?)

As you can see, the Human Genome Diversity Project as science can sound harmless to many people. However, to others, it represents problems well beyond the laboratory. Consider the following questions:

- Will genetic research on these groups lead to increased racism and discrimination?

- Would researchers be required to ask these groups for their consent?

- If so, how would the project determine how to define these groups? How would those involved in the project determine who can legitimately speak for any given group?

- Whose genomes should be represented in genomic science? Who would be included and excluded? Indigenous peoples? African Americans? Caucasians? (If these are valid biological groups at all.)

- What do standards of equity require? If these genomes are considered representative of groups, would the research pose risks to these groups? Should their consent be required to conduct the research, and, if so, how would consent be obtained?

- How would populations be selected, bounded, and sampled?
- What rules would be used to determine who could speak authoritatively for the groups to be studied?
- Some groups have problems with the collection of bodily tissues of any kind. What is the obligation of scientists to help groups and individuals understand Western science? What is the obligation of the researchers to understand these groups' perspectives?
- How does one approach a group elder and ask for tissue samples?

Not all science concepts produce multiple perspectives, but you should be aware of and alert to differences in the ways students, especially students within minority and ethnically diverse populations, might view science and science concepts.

Precautions and Possible Pitfalls

 It is extremely difficult to predict conflicts in the ways students may view science and science concepts. You might use class discussions or surveys to gather information that may help you to predict contrary views. Use any conflicts that do arise as opportunities to explore respectfully the social components within science.

BIBLIOGRAPHY

Driver, R., Squires, A., & Wood-Robinson, V. (1994). *Making sense of secondary science: Research into children's ideas.* London: Routledge.

Juengst, E. (1996). Respecting human subjects in genome research: A preliminary policy agenda. In H. Y. Vanderpool (Ed.), *The ethics of research involving human subjects: Facing the 21st century.* Frederick, MD: University Publishing Group.

Steinberg, D. (1998, January 19). NIH jumps into genetic variation research. *Scientist,* p. 1.

THE TIP (4.10)

 Take a fresh look at how the assignment of homework might present unexpected problems for students and families.

What the Research Says

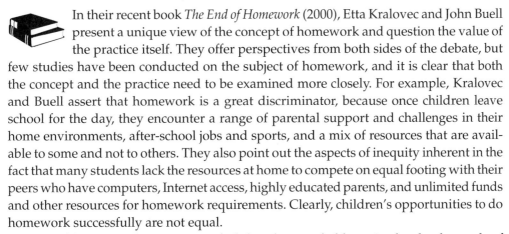 In their recent book *The End of Homework* (2000), Etta Kralovec and John Buell present a unique view of the concept of homework and question the value of the practice itself. They offer perspectives from both sides of the debate, but few studies have been conducted on the subject of homework, and it is clear that both the concept and the practice need to be examined more closely. For example, Kralovec and Buell assert that homework is a great discriminator, because once children leave school for the day, they encounter a range of parental support and challenges in their home environments, after-school jobs and sports, and a mix of resources that are available to some and not to others. They also point out the aspects of inequity inherent in the fact that many students lack the resources at home to compete on equal footing with their peers who have computers, Internet access, highly educated parents, and unlimited funds and other resources for homework requirements. Clearly, children's opportunities to do homework successfully are not equal.

In addition, tired parents may feel that they are held captive by the demands of their children's schoolwork, unable to develop their own priorities for family life. Kralovec and Buell provide examples of communities that have tried to formalize homework policies in attempts to balance the demands of homework with extracurricular activities and the need for family time.

Kralovec and Buell also point out that the practice of assigning homework persists despite the lack of any solid evidence that doing homework achieves any of the practice's much-touted benefits. Homework is one of our most entrenched institutional practices, yet it is one of the least investigated.

The big questions that Kralovec and Buell explore include the following:

- With single-parent households becoming more common, and with both parents working in many two-parent households, is it reasonable to accept the homework concept, as it is now practiced, as useful and valid, considering the trade-offs families need to make?

- How does homework contribute to family dynamics in negative or positive ways?

- Does homework unnecessarily stifle other important opportunities for children or create an uneven or unequal playing field for some students?

Classroom Applications

 Think about the inequalities that may exist within the range of students in your classes regarding their ability to complete homework assignments. Certain students may be excluded from the opportunities for support and other resources that are available to others. Consider the following questions:

- What is homework?
- How much homework is too much?
- What are or should be the purposes of homework?
- Can different assignments be given to different students in the same class?
- Do all your students have an equal opportunity to complete homework successfully?
- Who is responsible for homework, the students or the parents?
- Do all your students have the same capacity to self-regulate?
- How do you factor in other school activities or family-based responsibilities?
- What is the best and most equable way to deal with "overachievers"?
- Is the homework load balanced among teachers?

Precautions and Possible Pitfalls

 Traditionally, homework has been seen as a solution to educational problems rather than the cause. It may take you a little bit of acclimatization time to begin to look at the concept of homework with new eyes. However, the value of homework in providing opportunities for students to deepen their science knowledge should not be ignored. This is especially important for students in the United States, whose achievement lags behind that of students in other countries where school days and years are longer. Beware of the politics involved in any discourse regarding the homework concept.

BIBLIOGRAPHY

Kralovec, E., & Buell, J. (2000). *The end of homework: How homework disrupts families, overburdens children, and limits learning*. Boston: Beacon.

CHAPTER FIVE

Using Technology in Science Teaching

THE TIP (5.1)

When using multimedia techniques to teach science, consider how you present the material to students. The physical proximity of pictures and related text can affect learning.

What the Research Says

 Research suggests that the physical proximity of learning materials to each other as well as the presentation mode affects science learning. Moreno and Mayer (1999) conducted an experiment in which 132 college students viewed computer animations showing lightning. Based on prior research findings indicating that presentation methods affect low-experience learners more than high-experience learners, the researchers included only low-experience learners in the study. They measured experience by using a questionnaire to assess students' prior knowledge of meteorology. Students in one condition were presented with printed text and pictures that were physically separated from each other (text not near animations), whereas students in another condition saw physically integrated text and pictures (text near animations). Moreno and Mayer found that students who saw integrated materials learned about the lightning process better than did students who saw separated materials.

Classroom Applications

It is clear that just "exposing" your students to content offers little insurance that they will absorb the lesson. The way a lesson is delivered means a lot, and clumsy delivery can doom the message. As with any other presentation or communication effort, you have to present your students with a clean and coherent package. Much of the very early educational software suffered with the problem of delivery. It competed with video games, but the pace was often slow and the content didn't amount to much more than drill and practice. Most students today have seen great multimedia presentations as entertainment, and for them many educational multimedia efforts pale in comparison. The competition for your students' attention is great.

Spend as much time focusing on *how* you deliver instruction as you do on *what* you are delivering. Survey and evaluate what is available before you settle on a specific multimedia strategy. Search for multimedia materials that you can preview before purchasing. Whether you purchase, preview, or make multimedia materials yourself, pilot any presentation with a few select students first.

Precautions and Possible Pitfalls

In this era of multiple intelligences, most educational research suggests that a lesson's content and concepts should be presented and experienced in a variety of pedagogical styles. Although multimedia materials can provide your students with rich experiences and activities, such materials should not be their sole contact with the curriculum. Offer a variety of avenues for students to assimilate lessons and come to know the material.

BIBLIOGRAPHY

Moreno, R., & Mayer, R. E. (1999). Cognitive principles of multimedia learning: The role of modality and contiguity. *Journal of Educational Psychology, 91,* 358-368.

THE TIP (5.2)

When adding technological tools and the "learning curves" they involve to science classes, you will need to make comparable reductions in other areas of the course requirements.

What the Research Says

 A traditional undergraduate physics course on math methods was redesigned to incorporate the use of a computerized algebra program during all aspects of the course. The goal of the redesign was to expose beginning students to professional tools currently used by mathematicians and physicists. At the same time, a new "multimedia" physics class sought to integrate math and physics content with other multimedia forms. Runge et al. (1999) used these two classes as research laboratories to begin a qualitative case study, first to describe the courses and then to develop an understanding of the effects that technology had on instruction and learning in the courses. They found that the instructors in both courses made rather substantial changes in their methodology the second time through, based on their early experience.

Runge et al. provide an overview of the issues as follows:

- Students resisted the additional process orientation of adding technology as another layer of course requirements. Computers add another layer of process skills to learn.

- The teachers needed to be better prepared and have their own technological act together.

- The advance workload involved in preparing for such courses was enormous and went unnoticed by the students. To the students, book content represented the curriculum: Reduced use of books resulted in little student-perceived structure.

- The teachers needed to have a means for demonstrating the technology and needed to have backup plans in case of problems.

- The teachers needed to develop clear procedures for students to follow when they encountered problems.

- Whenever students seemed to have strong learning preferences and styles, their expectations about how they "ought to be taught" conflicted with the design of the courses. Expectations needed to be described explicitly and explained for possible conflicting expectations. Problematic conflicts in how and why instruction is implemented needed to be resolved.

- Instructors somewhat underestimated the basic instruction needed. They were challenged to provide guidance and examples without providing "simple" templates that would structure the students' homework with little imagination or editing. Technology used as a professional tool required in-class instruction that modeled real problem-solving modes.

Overall, this research suggests that the necessary transition from traditional instruction to tool-based instruction is dramatic and fraught with difficulty for teachers and students. The researchers note that they find their data to be far less positive or encouraging than they would have liked. As experienced teachers, as technology users, and as scientists foreseeing drastic changes in the kinds of intellectual skills students are likely to bring to the professional world, they see a long developmental role ahead.

Classroom Applications

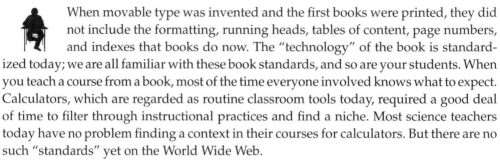 When movable type was invented and the first books were printed, they did not include the formatting, running heads, tables of content, page numbers, and indexes that books do now. The "technology" of the book is standardized today; we are all familiar with these book standards, and so are your students. When you teach a course from a book, most of the time everyone involved knows what to expect. Calculators, which are regarded as routine classroom tools today, required a good deal of time to filter through instructional practices and find a niche. Most science teachers today have no problem finding a context in their courses for calculators. But there are no such "standards" yet on the World Wide Web.

As new technology continues to filter into the classroom, first, teachers await better-trained students from below. Second, teachers need to address the concerns listed in the research and accept a rather steep learning curve for implementing technology for themselves and their students. Runge et al. (1999) found a remarkable similarity in problems and pitfalls between the two independent classes they studied, even though the two used very different technologies. "Real-world" professional tools impose a rather drastic transition for all stakeholders. When you introduce a new technology, become as informed as you can about it, and also be aware of the potential transitional problems you will need to address as a professional educator.

Precautions and Possible Pitfalls

Do not underestimate the huge amount of work, for both you and your students, involved in making technological transitions. Frustrated students can sabotage your best efforts by not authentically engaging in the "new" type of instruction. Students who would do well in traditional classes may need nurturing and assurance when the rules change.

BIBLIOGRAPHY

Runge, A., Spiegel, A., Pytlik Zillig, L. M., Dunbar, S., Fuller, R., Sowell, G., & Brooks, D. (1999). Hands-on computer use in science classrooms: The skeptics are still waiting. *Journal of Science Education and Technology, 8,* 33-44.

THE TIP (5.3)

 When you are planning to teach students to use computer applications, consider their prior knowledge of the content before you decide on the instructional methods you'll use.

What the Research Says

 The effectiveness of instructional methods used to teach students to use computer applications depends on students' prior knowledge of the material being taught. Tuovinen and Sweller (1999) conducted a study with students who were learning to use a database program. Students in one condition were given worked-out examples of how to use the program, whereas students in the other condition explored use of the program in a discovery fashion. Classroom instruction in the computer application preceded the students' participation in the two conditions. The researchers found that the use of worked-out examples was much more efficient with students who had limited prior knowledge, whereas this benefit evaporated for students with more prior knowledge. Students who had prior knowledge were able to activate and use it during discovery learning, thereby enhancing their efficiency.

Classroom Applications

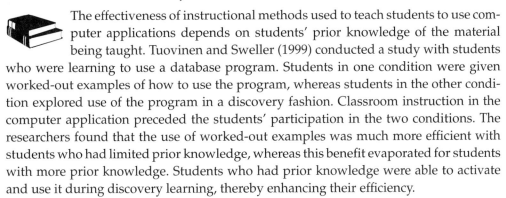 You may want to group students homogeneously for learning to use computer applications based on their prior knowledge, so that more experienced students use discovery learning and less experienced students start with worked-out examples.

You could also group students heterogeneously, having more experienced students work with less experienced students during discovery learning, so that the more experienced students can teach or guide the less experienced students in their discovery learning.

Precautions and Possible Pitfalls

 If you decide to group students homogeneously, don't keep the less experienced students working permanently using worked-out examples. Once they have gained some experience in the content area, encourage them to apply what they have learned through discovery learning.

BIBLIOGRAPHY

Tuovinen, J. E., & Sweller, J. (1999). A comparison of cognitive load associated with discovery learning and worked examples. *Journal of Educational Psychology, 91,* 334-341.

THE TIP (5.4)

 When you are helping students to acquire computer skills, teach them to set goals that focus on the process of learning to use the skills instead of on the product or outcome of learning.

What the Research Says

 It is beneficial to teach students to set different learning goals for different reasons, because different kinds of goals have different effects. Goal setting can affect students' achievement and motivation, as well as how students regulate the use of their thoughts, actions, and feelings. Students can use the goals they set as standards for assessing their own progress. Goals that focus on the learning process emphasize the strategies that students use in acquiring skills or information. In contrast, goals that focus on the product of learning emphasize outcomes or results, such as how much was accomplished and how long it took. In research conducted on goal setting for students who were learning to use the computer, Schunk and Ertmer (1999) found that students who set process goals felt that they learned more effectively than did students who set product goals. Students in the process condition believed that they were more competent in performing hypercard tasks (i.e., they had greater self-efficacy) than did students in the product condition, and achievement results showed that students in the process condition were indeed more successful in performing hypercard tasks than were students in the product condition.

Classroom Applications

 Have your students set process goals on a regular basis when they are acquiring new knowledge or skills. Use a think-aloud procedure and write on the board to model for students how they should set process goals. Have students, individually or in groups, brainstorm process goals they can set for particular computer tasks and write their process goals in their notebooks. Periodically check their notebooks to assess their progress in achieving their goals, and then have them set new goals to replace those they have already accomplished.

Following are some examples that illustrate process goals students may need to master before they can finish a project or activity:

- A student group needed to learn a spreadsheet and graphing program to be able to manage and summarize the data from a laboratory experience. They needed to complete a tutorial and manipulate a few small data sets before looking at their own data.

- A student using a laptop computer with physiology sensing capacity needed to learn the accompanying software to make his experiment and data collection fully functional.

- The members of an earth science group accessing a weather and climate Web site were required to learn the site's specific programs before they could manipulate their temperature and rainfall data.

- Science students from a high school located near a university needed to master the university library's digital library and e-journal access to acquire needed science fair background information.

- A student needed to evaluate the many Internet diet and food analysis sites to assess which were the most accurate and useful.

- A student needed to learn a graphics program in order to develop overheads and slides to be used in a science presentation.

Precautions and Possible Pitfalls

 Don't let students simply copy your process goals for learning to use a computer. Self-generated goals are more personally meaningful to students than teacher-imposed goals.

BIBLIOGRAPHY

Schunk, D., & Ertmer, P. (1999). Self-regulatory processes during computer skill acquisition: Goal and self-evaluative influences. *Journal of Educational Psychology, 91*, 251-260.

THE TIP (5.5)

  Don't overlook the Internet as a source of full, rich scientific inquiry-based curricular alternatives that include not only content but opportunities to engage in the process of doing science or inquiry-based learning.

What the Research Says

Kids as Global Scientists (KGS), characterized as a telecommunication program, is an interactive, integrated, inquiry-based science curriculum project developed by meteorologists and teachers from the University of Michigan and sponsored by the National Science Foundation. It resides on the Internet, which makes it accessible to large numbers of teachers and students. Its current Internet project engages more than 200 schools in interactive investigations. Through KGS, professional weather experts interact with students, answering questions generated by students. The total length of a unit runs 6 to 8 weeks. (For more information, visit the KGS Web site at http://tecfa.unige.ch/edu-comp/success-stories/fiches/f265.html.)

The investigation and interaction that KGS offers are facilitated by the use of specialized interactive software designed specifically for the project. The software provides all "textbook content" and, in addition, connects students to the Internet, simulations, and current imagery collections of weather data and allows them to download data. In one unit, the program suggests that students undertake a final project of building a hurricane-safe house and simulating the force of the hurricane by using a leaf blower.

KGS provides teachers with guides, software, and all other materials needed to empower the project. It develops thematic units within the earth science discipline of atmospheric science and meteorology.

Mistler-Jackson and Songer (2000) conducted a study that centered on the assessment and evaluation of one class participating in one unit or program of KGS. They selected six sixth-grade students representing three motivational levels for intensive study to examine how different students view learning science and the use of technology both before and after a technology-rich program. Mistler-Jackson and Songer analyzed pre- and postassessment scores for the entire class, and the six students' comments from individual interviews provided one example of evidence from each motivational level. Overall, their assessment results indicated significant gains in content knowledge and a high level of motivation with the project. Students usually find the use of the Internet and a telecollaborative environment engaging and motivating.

Classroom Applications

 Treating the Internet as a classroom is an emerging use of available technology. In addition to KGS, the World Wide Web offers many other opportunities for you to engage students in interesting programs. Distance learning is available as an alternative to site-dependent learning. Many colleges and universities and a few high schools now offer participation in digital classrooms. Advanced placement classes are now offered on-line as alternatives for students whose schools don't have the ability to provide such programs.

As an inquiry-based science experience, KGS offers an authentic, guided, safe experience that is not only content rich but also process rich. The technological tools students must use while participating help motivate them to learn. Not all science works this easily in real life, but for a taste of real science, KGS serves the purpose. The Internet educational market is growing, and KGS is a well-packaged, user-friendly project.

A number of Internet sites currently act as repositories of data. For example, climate and weather data are easily available, and the GenBank Web site provides almost unlimited genomic and molecular science data (http://www.ncbi.nlm.nih.gov/genbank/genbankoverview.html). Imaginative, creative, and motivated teachers can develop their own inquiry-based opportunities. Many sites offer free data that teachers can use to answer student questions. There are even digital libraries that offer access to periodicals and other resources. Some information access is limited to subscribers, and some sites can be accessed only through colleges or universities that subscribe to their services. Opportunities for using the Internet in instruction are open-ended in nature and can be as simple or as complex as you desire.

Precautions and Possible Pitfalls

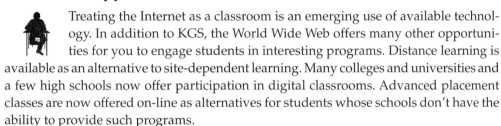 Although Internet technology provides a sexy and often motivating alternative to conventional hands-on experiences, the evaluation and preparation time remains the same. It also takes time to find and survey potentially useful Internet sites to see what they have to offer. Technology has its quirks and breakdowns, and access may not be available on demand or on your class's schedule.

Opportunities are open-ended in nature and can be as complex or simple as you want. There are even digital libraries that offer access to periodicals and other sources.

Appropriate use policies are a necessity, and Web surfing can keep students off track for extended periods of time. In addition, the idea that the Internet can provide serious instruction sometimes requires an adjustment in perception and a context change for both students and parents.

BIBLIOGRAPHY

Mistler-Jackson, M., & Songer, N. B. (2000). Student motivation and Internet technology: Are students empowered to learn science? *Journal of Research in Science Teaching, 37*, 459-479.

THE TIP (5.6)

 You can develop a Web-based curriculum to engage students in the analysis of a diverse range of scientific resources now available on the Internet, but teach students to evaluate critically the sources and information found on the Web.

What the Research Says

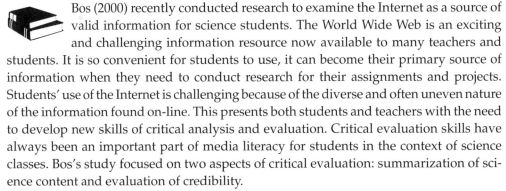 Bos (2000) recently conducted research to examine the Internet as a source of valid information for science students. The World Wide Web is an exciting and challenging information resource now available to many teachers and students. It is so convenient for students to use, it can become their primary source of information when they need to conduct research for their assignments and projects. Students' use of the Internet is challenging because of the diverse and often uneven nature of the information found on-line. This presents both students and teachers with the need to develop new skills of critical analysis and evaluation. Critical evaluation skills have always been an important part of media literacy for students in the context of science classes. Bos's study focused on two aspects of critical evaluation: summarization of science content and evaluation of credibility.

Participants in Bos's study were students in two 11th-grade science sections at an alternative high school in a medium-sized midwestern college town. The classes involved were in the third year of a "Foundations of Science" sequence, an integrated science curriculum that follows the principles of a project-based approach. It also has a heavy technology component. A total of 44 students (27 girls and 17 boys) took part in the study, which centered on answering three questions:

- Can students summarize the scientific resources that they find on the Web?
- Can students identify and evaluate evidence in the scientific resources that they find on the Web?
- Can students identify the sources and potential biases (points of view) of the scientific resources that they find on the Web?

Bos examined 63 student Web reviews published by the students. Content analyses showed that the student summaries were usually accurate. However, the students had problems in assessing how comprehensive and detailed given sites were. When asked to evaluate credibility, the students struggled to identify scientific evidence cited or presented supporting Web site claims. This was a problem because many Web sites do not present evidence as one might find it in a scientific journal format. The students were able to determine publishing sources but were challenged in identifying potential biases among Web publishers.

The findings of Bos's study can provide teachers with a solid grounding for further development of media literacy activities. Technical and pedagogical scaffolding based on site-specific goals and demands can facilitate student acquisition and reinforcement of critical evaluation and assessment skills.

Classroom Applications

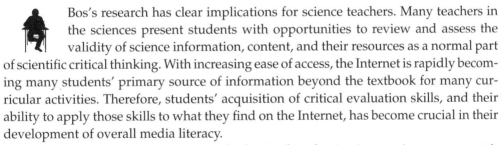 Bos's research has clear implications for science teachers. Many teachers in the sciences present students with opportunities to review and assess the validity of science information, content, and their resources as a normal part of scientific critical thinking. With increasing ease of access, the Internet is rapidly becoming many students' primary source of information beyond the textbook for many curricular activities. Therefore, students' acquisition of critical evaluation skills, and their ability to apply those skills to what they find on the Internet, has become crucial in their development of overall media literacy.

There are many ways you can embed critical evaluation into projects or present it as a separate independent activity. Ideally, experienced students will be able to critique Web site information routinely. However, to get to that point, you may need to begin by scaffolding the activity, first creating prompts or triggers to serve as review categories. This could be as detailed and complex as needed for beginning student researchers. A simple prompt work sheet might look like this:

1. Content

   What is the purpose of this resource? Who is the target audience?

What scientific claims are made? What information/content is available here?

2. Source credibility

Who is publishing this page? Are there any potential biases or conflicts of interest?

How much support or evidence exists for the claims made within the resource? Is it referenced or academically cited to back up the claims or information that goes beyond common knowledge?

3. Overall organization

How well organized is the information? Is there a central page where everything is accessible? Are there links to other relevant Internet sites? How technical is the information?

4. Appearance

Is it a professionally designed resource? Do the graphics support the information and help communicate it? Does the resource "teach" the information?

Again, you can adjust the level of guidance, triggers, and prompts to the class's needs and to the experience of your students.

Precautions and Possible Pitfalls

At its best, the Internet provides students with relatively easy access to valid resources for a variety of curricular activities. However, it can also be a source of biased content and misinformation. Also, text found on Web sites can be copied and pasted into word-processing programs, making the material very easy to plagiarize.

Some students will rely too heavily on the Internet and not utilize other more traditional and less readily accessible resources. You should be careful to make these points clear to your students and should encourage them to plan ahead so that they can use other sources of information.

BIBLIOGRAPHY

Bos, N. (2000). High school students' critical evaluation of scientific resources on the World Wide Web. *Journal of Science Education and Technology, 9,* 161-173.

THE TIP (5.7)

Create new perspectives for educational or instructional television and related Internet multimedia technology as a teaching and learning tool.

What the Research Says

In a survey of the history of broadcast technology and education, King (2000) presents a clear view of the technology's "hits and misses" as an educational tool. Early instructional approaches using television focused on the development and improvement of content knowledge. This was in line with the goals of scientific literacy of the time, to make the process of acquiring knowledge more efficient. As these programs evolved from the 1950s to the 1970s, they began to include a role for problem solving and science process skills, but they still focused on scientific knowledge. The program *3-2-1 Contact* used a problem-solving component to engage students' interest, thus expanding the focus and definition of scientific literacy. Although television has not revolutionized the teaching of science, as early advocates had hoped, it has provided a useful tool for bringing the world into the classroom, much as motion pictures had done in previous generations.

Beakman's World, Watch Mr. Wizard (and later *Mr. Wizard's World*), *Newton's Apple,* and *Bill Nye, the Science Guy* have all presented activities that children can do at home or in school. Often, such programs have used magic tricks to present scientific principles and processes. In contrast, *Nova,* NASA Television (providing real-time coverage), and the Discovery Channel have designed informational programs specifically for classroom use. Many of these bring the natural world into the classroom and examine and survey it in an informal way. Some offer sets of support materials to use in conjunction with programs. Reviewing a variety of such companion resources, King (2000) found that they tend to consist of content review and often miss the opportunity to use content information as a springboard to a deeper level of problem solving.

Classroom Applications

 Science can come alive through the creative use of video, Webcasts, and video-assisted training. Videotapes have, at times, been used as "fillers" or instant curriculum to cover an absence, but they can be placed into a richer curricular paradigm.

There have long been television science shows that have provided curricular solutions. They often bring larger science problems into the classroom or illustrate experiments that are not possible for students to conduct, for a variety of reasons. They can take students to locations and situations that cannot be duplicated any other way. A science story featured on the nightly news or a television magazine program with science content can begin to create for students a relevance and context for science content in the real world. It can also be a beginning to a new unit, featured concept, or investigation. Well-presented television programs can examine science issues and processes from a variety of perspectives not otherwise available in the classroom or school. Most science teachers already make use of this technology.

So what's new? Creative teachers still use the wide range of science programs available on network and cable television. What is new is the range of video programming, sometimes interactive, available on the Internet. There are educational Web sites that present science concepts in multimedia formats ranging from short clips to longer "live" Webcasts, bringing a range of worldwide science events to viewers. Type "video curriculum" or related words into an Internet search engine, and you will find a huge range of multimedia curricular sites and support. The beauty of this is that much of it can be viewed at any time. You no longer need to edit out commercials or be home at just the right time to tape a show. You survey the available Web sites, choose the most appropriate and reliable sites, and integrate the content into your curriculum. Students can experience the content on their own computers, on their own schedules, or as a class in the school's computer room.

Precautions and Possible Pitfalls

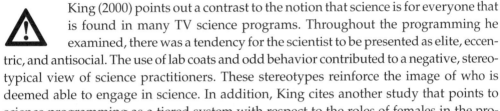

King (2000) points out a contrast to the notion that science is for everyone that is found in many TV science programs. Throughout the programming he examined, there was a tendency for the scientist to be presented as elite, eccentric, and antisocial. The use of lab coats and odd behavior contributed to a negative, stereotypical view of science practitioners. These stereotypes reinforce the image of who is deemed able to engage in science. In addition, King cites another study that points to science programming as a tiered system with respect to the roles of females in the programs. That study found that only 35% of the scientists on television programs were female. The entire proportion of females on the programs was 52% of the cast. The nonscientist female characters had subservient roles, such as apprentices and lab assistants. Overall, the children's science educational programs profiled were helpful in bringing content knowledge and presenting science in action but perpetuated a number of sex role stereotypes and presented scientists as eccentric or odd. Once aware of these shortcomings, you can use these observations as triggers to other interesting curricular pathways.

Looking to the Internet, the biggest problem is the uneven quality of what is available. Previewing all of the media available is time-consuming. Do not underestimate the work you will need to do to integrate this new, more interactive version of the old video standby. In addition, students come with a wide range of computer and Internet literacy; you may need to integrate information about the use of these tools into your lessons.

BIBLIOGRAPHY

Bos, N. (2000). High school students' critical evaluation of scientific resources on the World Wide Web. *Journal of Science Education and Technology, 9,* 161-173.

King, K. P. (2000). Educational television: "Let's explore science." *Journal of Science Education and Technology, 9,* 227-245.

THE TIP (5.8)

 Visit http://www.thinkquest.org—the ThinkQuest Web site with your students and encourage them to participate in this challenging international educational technology competition.

What the Research Says

Research shows that students need challenging tasks with a moderate amount of risk to motivate them to perform at high levels (Clifford, 1990). Most students enjoy working with other students in groups on complex projects more than they do working alone, and cooperative learning facilitates content mastery, encourages development of higher-level cognitive skills, and improves social relationships among students from culturally diverse backgrounds (Slavin, 1990). Teachers at the 1999 ThinkQuest conference whose students participated in ThinkQuest projects observed that on several occasions students who had been bored in class and those who had been labeled "slow learners" made spectacular efforts and created highly sophisticated Web sites when they worked on international collaborative projects that interested them. It was also reported at this conference that one of the student projects on cloning sheep was so good that NASA put the material on its Web site.

ThinkQuest offers an Internet-based educational program for virtually all subjects and grade levels. Each year, thousands of teachers and students from around the world work to create content-rich Web sites, competing for more than $2 million in cash awards and scholarships (Lightner, 1999).

ThinkQuest began in the United States in 1996 and has grown to involve 49 other countries. The organization reports that since 1996, almost 50,000 students and educators from 100 countries have participated in ThinkQuest competitions, bringing together young people from diverse cultural and linguistic backgrounds with widely varying socioeconomic statuses and levels of technology.

ThinkQuest is based on the assumption that the Internet and related technologies are powerful new learning tools that young people everywhere can use. Its focus is on engaging students around the world as program participants who learn to assimilate, organize, and share their knowledge with others.

Classroom Applications

 ThinkQuest involves students in designing Web sites, so although some of the work may actually occur in the classroom, much of it will not. Contestants work in teams, with coaches (usually teachers) who help them develop Web sites that serve as educational resources for others.

Visit this fascinating project Web site first by yourself and then with your students. ThinkQuest enables students to participate in carrying out relatively long-term, complex projects that tap students' individual interests, stimulate their creativity, develop their problem-solving skills, and help them learn to work effectively in collaboration with others, much as scientists do in the real world. There are three different levels of participation:

1. *ThinkQuest Internet Challenge:* This is the original international competition on which ThinkQuest was originally founded. It involves junior high and high school students, ages 12-19.

2. *ThinkQuest Junior:* This is a U.S. competition for students in grades 4-6.

3. *ThinkQuest for Tomorrow's Teachers (T3):* This effort focuses on teachers and involves collaboration between student teachers and college and university faculty.

In addition to its extremely stimulating Web site, where many student projects are available for examination, ThinkQuest produces CD-ROMs that enable classes without Internet access to view the student projects. Many of the student-designed Web sites are in multiple languages, because of the international scope of the competition.

On a recent visit to the ThinkQuest Web site, we found numerous fascinating projects in the sciences, with titles that included the following:

Unraveling Genetics	Your Physical Life
Weather Wiz	Math Applications for Science
The Theory of Special Relativity	Artificial Neural Networks
The Last Jungles of the World	We Grow Body Parts
Where Is Earth Standing?	The Heart of the Rainforest

In addition to projects from the current competition, the ThinkQuest Web site's library provides links to sites from previous years' competitions (with finalists identified) and provides brief descriptions. These Web sites include the following:

- *The Sciences Explorer:* This site is intended as a resource for scientists of all ages and was a finalist in the 1997 Internet Challenge. It contains high-quality interactive materials in chemistry, physics, biology, and mathematics. Activities include crossword puzzles, 3-D tours, calculator programs, and conversion tables. The site is available in English, Spanish, French, German, and Italian.

- *Scholarfish: The Science Opportunity Finder:* This is characterized as a site students can use to find opportunities in science, such as research, scholarships, and content on both local and national levels. The site was developed for the 1998 Internet Challenge.

- *Super Science:* This site is intended to help students do their science homework without giving them the answers and by making learning fun. It was developed by a fifth-grade class for the 1999 ThinkQuest Junior competition. It includes tables comparing the U.S. measurement system with the metric system, information on the Hale-Bopp comet, and students' own periodic table of elements.

There are 22 subcategories within ThinkQuest's science competition. In addition, students can create interdisciplinary projects, such as "Earthquakes and Psychological Effects" and "Ecology and Citizenship."

Precautions and Possible Pitfalls

Beware of making assumptions about which students are likely to participate in such a complex project. Some of your weakest students may surprise you (and themselves) with newly awakened interests and strengths.

BIBLIOGRAPHY

Clifford, M. M. (1990). Students need challenge, not easy success. *Educational Leadership, 48*(1), 22-26.

Lightner, B. (1999). ThinkQuest: Learning that is teamwork-driven. *MultiMedia Schools, 6*(5), 19-22.

Slavin, R. (1990). *Cooperative learning research: Theory and practice.* Englewood Cliffs, NJ: Prentice Hall.

THE TIP (5.9)

 Critically review science software and try using or recommending to your students some of the rare good software available for learning science.

What the Research Says

Computers can be effective learning tools, and course or subject-area software abounds in virtually all the sciences. Unfortunately, much of it is at the level of drill and practice or rote memorization of facts. The other end of the software continuum involves students in exploring scientific concepts more actively, meaningfully, and deeply through learning from their own experiences, thereby enhancing learning. Many teachers have not been trained in software evaluation and should consult software reviews and the literature to identify potential problems, such as graphics that are more distracting than educational and unclear menus or directions for students. Teachers need to evaluate software for selection purposes before they use it and should judge its effectiveness after they have used it. Selection judgments require teachers to consider the characteristics of their students, how their students will interact with the software, and how the software fits into other curricular materials, activities, and assessments. Effectiveness judgments require teachers to assess the extent to which the software succeeds in achieving the identified academic goals.

Classroom Applications

Interactive Physics is a high school-level application that can be used to introduce students to the history of physics as well as basic physics concepts. One especially attractive feature of this software is an exploration area where students actually do simulated experiments to develop and test their understanding by applying concepts to solve physics problems.

The FreshPond Education Web site provides reviews of educational software. FreshPond uses the following criteria in making such evaluations (http://www.freshpond.net/treasures/technology/softreviews/softeval.htm):

- Resource requirements and support

    What are the hardware requirements for this software?

    Can this software be networked?

    Is it easy to use?

Does it have a teacher's guide?

Does it provide telephone or electronic support?

- Connections to curriculum

    How could the software help to support the implementation of curriculum standards or frameworks?

    Which content and/or performance standards does it address?

    How might it help students in their learning?

    What will it help students know and be able to do?

- Added value

    How might the software add value to the curriculum?

    What does it offer that could not otherwise be achieved?

    How do the resources take advantage of the medium?

- Appropriateness for audience

    Is the content developmentally appropriate for the intended audience?

    Is there any material that might be objectionable for the target age group?

    Is the reading level accessible?

- Effectiveness of organization and design

    How engaging and easy to use is the software?

    Is it designed for maximum clarity and effectiveness in the context of your busy work life?

    Is the software flexible enough to accommodate various learning styles?

    How is the software designed to be implemented in a classroom? (as a tool? a tutorial? an interactive activity? an exploration?)

Precautions and Possible Pitfalls

Software should supplement, not supplant, the regular instructional program. Make sure that you actually try using the software as you expect your students to use it, so that you can anticipate and address potential problems before they arise.

BIBLIOGRAPHY

Cohen, S., Chechile, R., Smith, G., Tsai, F., & Burns, G. (1994). A method of evaluating the effectiveness of educational software. *Behavior Research Methods, Instruments, & Computers, 26,* 236-241.

Duncan, N. C. (1993). Evaluation of instructional software: Design considerations and recommendations. *Behavior Research Methods, Instruments, & Computers, 25,* 223-227.

McDougal, A., & Squires, D. (1995). A critical examination of the checklist approach in software selection. *Journal of Educational Computing Research, 12,* 263-274.

THE TIP (5.10)

Apply the standards of the International Society for Technology in Education (ISTE) to your own teaching and to students' learning. Use the Research, Analysis, and Communication (RAC) Model™ to integrate these standards into your instruction.

What the Research Says

International standards for technology in education were first established by the ISTE in 1993. The standards are for all subject areas and grade levels, for students ages 5-18. Specified as standards for *all* teachers, the first edition included 13 performance indicators. In the second edition of the standards (1997) the number of indicators grew to 18; these were divided into three categories:

1. Basic computer/technology operations and concepts

2. Personal and professional use of technology

3. Application of technology to instruction

Currently the *ISTE National Educational Technology Standards for Teachers* (2000) are in their third edition and consist of 23 performance indicators, which are grouped into six categories:

1. Technology operations and concepts

2. Planning and designing learning environments and experiences

3. Teaching, learning, and curriculum

4. Assessment and evaluation

5. Productivity and professional practice

6. Social, ethical, legal, and human issues

Not only is technology here to stay, but its influence is exploding exponentially in education and all other aspects of life. Teachers need to integrate technology into their instruction now or their students will be left behind in the future.

The RAC Model (Bowens, 2000) is an instructional framework for integrating technology into the curriculum through lesson planning and assessment across subjects and grade levels. Research shows that teachers have identified the following benefits of RAC lessons:

1. The lessons encourage more student-centered learning.

2. Students engage in more critical thinking.

3. Material can be integrated across subject areas.

4. The lessons are easily incorporated into performance-based classrooms.

5. Students are required to apply important skills in a meaningful context.

6. The lessons provide teachers with opportunities to evaluate students' work.

Classroom Applications

 To plan your use of technology to meet the national standards both for teachers and for students, visit the ISTE Web site (http://www.iste.org/) and download or view the standards. The Web site also has numerous instructional resources to help you integrate technology into your instruction in virtually all grades and subjects. Resources include a database of lessons that you can search for lesson plans that integrate technology into science teaching, specifying the particular topic and grade level for your needs. The site also contains resources that have been developed for multidisciplinary units and allows you to enter your own lesson plans. According to the ISTE Web site:

Multidisciplinary Unit Resources section includes resource units designed to provide powerful themes around which multidisciplinary learning activities can be built. Each unit addresses the theme with a variety of activities, related technology, and thematically relevant information, tools, and resources. Each activity is designed to address content standards from two or more subject areas while also addressing the National Educational Technology Standards (NETS) for Students performance indicators. Units for each grade-range provide developmentally appropriate themes, tools, and resources from which teachers can choose when developing specific learning experiences.

Implementing the RAC Model involves three phases:

1. *Research:* Students gather information from various resources, not just paper and pencil. For example, they go to various Internet sites to acquire information on what DNA is, where it is found, and how it is used to help solve crimes.

2. *Analysis:* Data analysis depends upon the results of the research. Students must think critically and use the information they have gathered. For example, students are asked to take a position about whether or not DNA should be used to determine a suspect's guilt or innocence, and they are required to justify their position with evidence from their research.

3. *Communication:* Students prepare products to share their results. For example, students write an essay stating and justifying a position about using DNA results to convict someone. In the essay, they must include an explanation of what DNA is and where it can be found.

Precautions and Possible Pitfalls

Don't expect yourself or your students to meet all 23 performance indicator standards the first or second time around. You and your students may need more time and experience to assimilate new information and develop new skills. Use the standards as longer-term goals and to establish performance criteria for assessment purposes.

BIBLIOGRAPHY

Bowens, E. M. (2000). Research, analysis, communication: Meeting standards with technology. *Learning & Leading with Technology, 27*(8), 6-9, 17.

International Society for Technology in Education. (2000). *National educational technology standards for teachers* (3rd ed.). Eugene, OR: Author.

THE TIP (5.11)

Use video-based instruction that anchors science concepts and skill learning to interesting topics embedded in meaningful problem-solving contexts.

What the Research Says

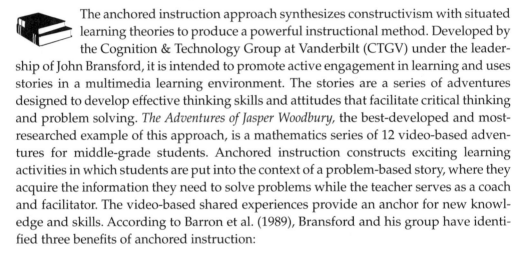

The anchored instruction approach synthesizes constructivism with situated learning theories to produce a powerful instructional method. Developed by the Cognition & Technology Group at Vanderbilt (CTGV) under the leadership of John Bransford, it is intended to promote active engagement in learning and uses stories in a multimedia learning environment. The stories are a series of adventures designed to develop effective thinking skills and attitudes that facilitate critical thinking and problem solving. *The Adventures of Jasper Woodbury*, the best-developed and most-researched example of this approach, is a mathematics series of 12 video-based adventures for middle-grade students. Anchored instruction constructs exciting learning activities in which students are put into the context of a problem-based story, where they acquire the information they need to solve problems while the teacher serves as a coach and facilitator. The video-based shared experiences provide an anchor for new knowledge and skills. According to Barron et al. (1989), Bransford and his group have identified three benefits of anchored instruction:

- Students receive rich information sources, including input of relevant issues, inherent problems, sensory images, and dynamic features.

- Students have the opportunity to form rich mental models more easily as they perceive dynamic events. This advantage has been found to be especially useful for students with low interest and low achievement in science.

- Students develop pattern recognition skills from auditory and visual cues they encounter in the adventures.

Classroom Applications

 A two-part science series created by the Bank Street College of Education, "The Voyage of Mimi" and "Mimi Ports of Call," teaches students about whales and develops science and mathematics skills as the students, as research assistants, become part of the crew of a ship that is on a whale study voyage. Students must learn and apply scientific principles, including navigation and map reading, in order to complete the first voyage. The second voyage of Mimi is especially recommended for ethnically diverse classes that include Hispanic students, because the voyage involves a trip to Mexico. The distributor, Sunburst, provides supplemental materials, including a whale database, wall charts, posters, and teaching tips for implementing the series. (For further information, go to http://www.sunburstonline.com.)

Additional sources of support for implementing anchored instruction approaches are available through the World Wide Web. Instead of purchasing adventures, teachers can use anchored instruction through Internet trips, such as virtual tours, field trips, and simulations, to provide problem-solving contexts that will anchor new knowledge and skills. Students can also use the Web to research solutions to the problems they are solving. (Visit http://www.ed.psu.edu/nasa/achrtxt.html for more information.)

Precautions and Possible Pitfalls

 Especially when you are using entertaining instructional materials such as those described here, it is vital that you remember that technology is the medium, not the message. Science content and skills should not be lost as the focus of the adventures.

BIBLIOGRAPHY

Barron, L., et al. (1989). *Enhancing learning in at-risk students: Applications of video technology* (ERIC Digest). Syracuse, NY: ERIC Clearinghouse on Information Resources. Available Internet: http://ericae.net/ericdb/ed318464.htm

THE TIP (5.12)

 Keep up with the development of 3-D science simulations that can virtually immerse students in the phenomena they are learning about, whether these are science process skills or specific scientific concepts.

What the Research Says

This tip reflects an emerging dimension of science teaching that resides primarily in research laboratories at present, but is probably not too far from broader implementation. Internet 2, which will enable simulations and virtual experiences, is on the horizon. Interdisciplinary teams are developing genuine science learning experiences that seem almost to border on science fiction in their dramatically realistic quality. Dede, Salzman, Loftin, and Ash (2000) have developed three-dimensional immersive environments of guided inquiry into such scientific concepts as motion, mass, force, energy, molecular structure, and chemical bonding. These virtual reality environments are called NewtonWorld, MaxwellWorld, and PaulingWorld. In these environments, students can directly confront and overcome strongly held misconceptions (based on invalid generalizations from their own experiences) that they bring with them when they enter science courses and that persist when they leave traditional science instruction. The immersive environment succeeds where the traditional environment fails because

> we rely on sensorial immersion to enhance the saliency of important factors and relationships and to provide experiential referents against which learners can compare their intuitions. Learners can be "inside" moving objects; this three-dimensional, egocentric frame of reference centers attention on velocity as a variable. Multisensory cues are used to further heighten the saliency of crucial factors such as force, energy and velocity. (Salzman, Dede, Loftin, & Chen, 1999)

> In NewtonWorld, users experience laws of motion from multiple points of view. In this world of neither gravity nor friction, balls hover above the ground. Users can become a ball; see, hear and feel its collisions; and experience the ensuing motion. (Dede, Salzman, Loftin, & Ash, 2000)

Research that involved immersing high school students in NewtonWorld has examined the features of virtual reality and the learning processes and outcomes, the students' learning experiences, and the nature of the interaction experiences. The results suggest that being able to observe the phenomena from a multiplicity of perspectives was vital to the students' understanding. Even more important was the use of visual, auditory, and tactile cues to help students focus on important information.

Science learning spaces are envisioned to provide rich and engaging experiences for students learning science process skills (Koedinger, Suthers, & Forbus, 1999). Three independent software systems are combined to produce a science learning space, or SLS:

1. Simulated experiments are conducted and data are collected.

2. Representations of construction tools are used for visualizing and evaluating conceptual models and for analyzing data.

3. Intelligent tutors observe the learner's work and provide targeted assistance for developing higher-order science process skills, such as developing an experimental strategy, choosing representation tools, speculating, and arguing.

Classroom Applications

 As we have mentioned, these technologies are currently emerging, but what is on the horizon includes immersing students in virtual worlds, including Newtonian physics, electrostatics, and quantum-mechanical bonding. The envisioned SLSs involve immersing students in simulated experiments where they conduct research and analyze the results.

The following are some of the differences between conventional science classes and SLS learning environments:

1. Typical science classes are characterized by content that consists of lecture on fixed topics with a uniform pace for the class and an emphasis on learning facts, whereas in SLS there are vast options in the topics and methods of presentation of content, pace is based on the individual student, and the emphasis is on concepts and process skills.

2. Inquiry in traditional classrooms can be obstructed by long waits and boring procedures, whereas SLS simulations allow students to use time much more efficiently.

3. Conventional classroom tools are pencils and paper; SLS requires students to use data representation and model construction software.

4. Teachers in traditional classes are limited in how much individual attention and assistance they can provide to each of their students, but in SLS student support is individualized by an intelligent tutor that is available as needed.

As a classroom teacher without the goggles and other expensive equipment you would need to immerse students in virtual reality, try to direct your creative juices toward

- The availability of calculators does not eliminate the need for students to learn algorithms.

Precautions and Possible Pitfalls

Although the research supports the use of the calculator as an instructional tool, remember that it is not a cure-all. Traditional instruction can also be successful and should include the "basics" behind calculator use. Calculators can become a management problem or a source of unequal access to instructional tools in some schools that lack the funding to provide class sets. Some students may not be able to provide their own or may not have access to calculators at home.

BIBLIOGRAPHY

Tarr, J. E., Mittage, K. C., Uekawa, K., & Lennex, L. (2000). A comparison of calculator use in eighth-grade mathematics classrooms in the United States, Japan, and Portugal: Results from the Third International Mathematics and Science Study. *School Science and Mathematics, 100,* 139-150.

CHAPTER SIX

Informal Science Learning

THE TIP (6.1)

 Provide your motivated students with the opportunities and information they need to participate in research apprenticeship programs.

What the Research Says

 Kurth and Richmond (1999) studied 27 10th- and 11th-grade students (14 girls and 13 boys) from across the United States who participated in a 7-week residential summer science research program. The investigation centered on how their experiences as research apprentices shaped the students' views of the culture and the practice of science. The researchers focused on two questions:

- What is it that is compelling to young apprentices about the dimensions of scientific culture and practice?

- Once identified, how do these features influence what they learn, and where does this learning take place?

In this program, students were provided the opportunity to play a variety of roles and to access a variety of resources to aid them in developing a more accurate and complex picture of scientific culture and practice.

The three "communities" defined as contributing to the students' science literacy began with the laboratory-centered community, which focused primarily on students' participation in their labs. The contacts available to the students included the faculty mentor, postdoctoral students, graduate or undergraduate students, and technicians. Next, a program-centered community provided students with guest speakers, field trips, and other site personnel not associated with specific labs. Finally, a peer-centered community provided students with opportunities to reflect on, compare, and contrast their experiences and acquired knowledge.

Kurth and Richmond found that the apprenticeship program was a natural extension of what good teachers of science or any other subject try to do for their students as they help them to learn. However, in this program, students were apprenticed to individuals who were active players in the scientific community and embodied its values. The apprentices were more active, and their participation in the culture of science contributed to their development of "powerful literacy." Such literacy is characterized by students' ability to use, think, and reflect on the contributions of learning and knowledge acquisition to their understanding of science, to use the tools provided and to reflect on their use, thus enhancing their understanding of the discipline. Exit assessments showed that the overall change in the students' understanding of the world of science over the 7-week period was dramatic.

Classroom Applications

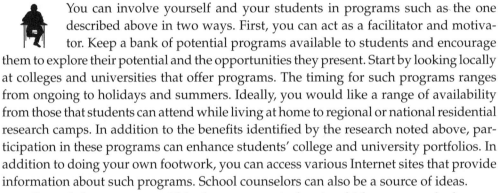

You can involve yourself and your students in programs such as the one described above in two ways. First, you can act as a facilitator and motivator. Keep a bank of potential programs available to students and encourage them to explore their potential and the opportunities they present. Start by looking locally at colleges and universities that offer programs. The timing for such programs ranges from ongoing to holidays and summers. Ideally, you would like a range of availability from those that students can attend while living at home to regional or national residential research camps. In addition to the benefits identified by the research noted above, participation in these programs can enhance students' college and university portfolios. In addition to doing your own footwork, you can access various Internet sites that provide information about such programs. School counselors can also be a source of ideas.

Second, there are areas within classroom curriculum in which you can embed opportunities for the deeper insights into scientific practice found in apprenticeship programs. Kurth and Richmond identify four such areas:

1. Structure investigations so that they problematize data collection and analysis, and help students to understand that ambiguity is not necessarily the result of mistakes they commit, but rather may be inherent in the problem itself.

2. Orchestrate work so that expertise can be distributed across group members, paralleling the distribution of expertise in scientific communities.

3. Scaffold the building of understanding so that scientific terminology supports the construction rather than inhibits the process or is isolated from it. Use the language of science in context within an application.

4. Have students engage in longer-term, connected investigations in which what they learn in earlier phases serves as foundation knowledge for tasks they undertake later.

The experiences that students encounter during apprenticeship programs or mentored relationships cannot be completely transported into a science classroom. However, creative educators can build or simulate some apprenticeship experiences into instructional practice.

Precautions and Possible Pitfalls

 Providing opportunities and encouraging students to enter programs such as those described above can add to responsibility overload. You can share the burden by involving the counseling department or the librarian, or maybe a parent volunteer. Schools or departments that provide and encourage participation in these types of programs usually are held in high esteem by parents and communities.

BIBLIOGRAPHY

Kurth, L. A., & Richmond, G. (1999). Moving from outside to inside: High school students' use of apprenticeship as a vehicle for entering the culture and practice of science. *Journal of Research in Science Teaching, 36,* 677-697.

THE TIP (6.2)

 Support and foster in your students more outgoing, risk-taking exploratory behavior within your curricular paradigm.

What the Research Says

 What are the traits and elements that foster development of scientific inquiry and later science career choice? Does science experienced informally have more influence than the science classroom on students' science attitudes? Joyce and Farenga (1999) studied the attitudes toward and interest in science of 111 high-ability students between the ages of 9 and 16. A contrasting study group within another investigation of 64 eminent scientists attempted to identify life experiences related to the scientist's career choice (Roe, 1952). Based on that study, for which the sample consisted of 20 biologists, 22 physicists, and 22 social scientists, the researcher established a global picture of particular early characteristics of the scientist. This and numerous other studies established the benchmark early personality traits that Joyce and Farenga used in assessing the young gifted students in their sample. Scientists have been shown to exhibit early preferences for solitary activities, independence of thought, self-acceptance, strong achievement motivation, curiosity about causality in relationships between natural phenomena, and involvement in investigations. Using this information, Joyce and Farenga examined the links among the early science-related experiences, attitudes toward science, future interest in science, and gender of young high-ability students.

The results of their study suggest that children develop the perception of science as an appropriate or inappropriate field of study before the age of 9. The researchers found that in the physical sciences, extracurricular or informal interests in mechanical construction sets, activities with electricity, working with physical gadgets, and tinkering with objects related to a later career choice in science. Connections between the life sciences and these interests were less apparent, but still suspected. Joyce and Farenga also found that socialization processes for young girls foster the development of psychological attributes that hinder science achievement. Young girls are often encouraged to conform to compliant rather than exploratory styles of behavior.

The potential for science achievement of gifted learning-disabled students, disinterested students, and underachieving students may go unrecognized. Biographical studies indicate that future scientists may not always be identified in their early academic years by reading and mathematics scores on standardized tests. Joyce and Farenga conclude that educators need to be mindful that special abilities in science are indicated in subtler ways and at younger ages.

Classroom Applications

From a curricular standpoint, informal creative science-related experiences can help to facilitate greater interest in science as well as foster and maintain ongoing curiosity. Traditional science education was once very content oriented, but there has been a systematic shift in recent years toward a process orientation. The "balance of power"—if that term expresses the essence of this issue—is more and more toward the process end. The teaching of science more as a process than as a compendium of facts can aid in the development of characteristics in children that have been described by researchers as important for science achievement.

Design and include in a formal way more open-ended activities with fewer "right" answers. For example, a set of LEGO blocks can be turned into an imaginary organism with an environment suited to its created characteristics. Or you can give students an environment and have them create a "new" LEGO organism adapted to the environment. Such activities can contribute to more motivating and interesting "school science" environments. This is especially important in the younger grades: Create a more "inquiry-based" pedagogy for students at a young age.

Given that early informal or extracurricular interests appear to relate directly to later career interest, you need to provide opportunities that will create curiosity in your students. Help students practice "thinking" more like scientists and less like students interested only in their grades. In addition, parents and teachers are in the position to discourage dependent behaviors that require external feedback and rely on external rewards. Encourage girls to work independently in addition to collaboratively. Research also indicates that differences in early socialization processes in young people appear to favor young boys when it comes to achievement, interest, and attitudes toward science. Encourage and expect participation in activities in which girls can experience an exploratory style of behavior. The implication for the classroom is that young students—male or female, high ability or not—need to learn self-directed behaviors and to work with less external approval.

All of these activities should foster and facilitate behaviors that have been identified as key in the development of future scientists and science career choices. And, maybe more important, these qualities are interdisciplinary in nature—they are valuable in any discipline.

Precautions and Possible Pitfalls

Students' "success" or mastery within the types of curricular goals described above is not easy to assess, evaluate, and measure. The curricular objectives, goals, and outcomes are often seen as too nebulous and ambiguous. Student mastery can be exhibited with display boards, oral presentations, and demonstrations. Reflective essays are also a good way for students to communicate knowledge of inquiry-based processes. Each of these assessment tools could be further defined with a rubric.

Examine your own gender biases and how they could enter the classroom environment. This can be difficult, as biases can be subconscious in nature. Ongoing dialogue and reflection with colleagues can help. Also, students, as peers, can come with the same subconscious biases and influence the classroom's gender issues. Occasional and timely class discussions can illuminate some of them.

BIBLIOGRAPHY

Joyce, B. A., & Farenga, S. J. (1999). Informal science experience, attitudes, future interest in science, and gender of high-ability students: An exploratory study. *School Science and Mathematics, 99*, 431-437.

Roe, A. (1952). *The making of a scientist.* Westport, CT: Greenwood.

THE TIP (6.3)

 Consider alternative assessment styles and instruments when evaluating the outcome of an informal science activity.

What the Research Says

Research in this area begins by pointing to Frank Oppenheimer, the originator of the Exploratorium in San Francisco, who argued against formal assessment in science centers and moved on from there. Oppenheimer saw the inherent value of informal learning in promoting science education and science and opposed the dominant, narrow view of science education taken in traditional, in-school science. Because learning is not graded, no one "flunks" an informal encounter with science. Some researchers believe that the many informal experiences are so individual and multifaceted that they cannot be assessed with letter grades or scores. Some see the lack of evaluation as an obvious strength in engaging science in a more social, open-ended, learner-directed and -centered, less planned and sequenced, and nonevaluative contact with science. Trying to evaluate so many potential unintended outcomes is just not fair to students.

Among four relevant research papers examining out-of-school informal science activities (Korpan, Bisanz, Bisanz, Boehme, & Lynch, 1997; Kurth & Richmond, 1999; Ramey-Gassert, 1997; Revital & Yehudit, 2000), all used students' written reflections (some used a rubric to guide students' responses) to survey the students' perceptions of how much they learned and the quality of what they learned.

Classroom Applications

The assessment instruments identified in the research cited above were not designed to yield scores or grades. They were designed to measure the overall effectiveness of informal science encounters. This information could then be used to modify the encounters themselves, not to rate the students' success or failure.

One study featured assessment that was produced by parents who interacted with their children (Korpan et al., 1997). The children were stimulated by their parents' involvement and felt comfortable with their parents. The researchers found this type of assessment to suffer from low reliability and validity, but it had its advantages. The collaborative, nonthreatening nature of the informal project fostered active and meaningful learning and integrated school, home, and community.

It is clear that traditional content assessment may miss the point of the out-of-school experience. A wider range of attributes and facets needs to be measured, and a content test would send the wrong message to students about what is important. Extending the experience by expanding it with a related performance-based project or writing activity or other application would be a better gauge of mastery than a traditional test. The researchers conclude that projects, with appropriate scoring rubrics, in which students combine science content from the classroom and the informal experience are the best way for students to demonstrate this type of learning. Ultimately, you want to facilitate the growth of enthusiasm and motivation.

Precautions and Possible Pitfalls

Consider a student who usually performs poorly in the traditional classroom yet exhibits enthusiasm and interest in more hands-on activities and participation in out-of-school learning experiences. Such a situation presents you with a dilemma: How do you encourage this student and not penalize him or her with the narrow range of traditional classroom assessment devices? Don't turn the student's enthusiasm off. Balancing opportunities for successful assessment and evaluation gives the student more than one pathway to follow in finding and demonstrating success. Oral presentations, project display boards, and other instructional outcomes can help this kind of student find success.

BIBLIOGRAPHY

Korpan, C. A., Bisanz, G. L., Bisanz, J., Boehme, C., & Lynch, M. A. (1997). What did you learn outside of school today? Using structured interviews to document home and community activities related to science and technology. *Science Education, 81,* 651-662.

Kurth, L. A., & Richmond, G. (1999). Moving from outside to inside: High school students' use of apprenticeship as a vehicle for entering the culture and practice of science. *Journal of Research in Science Teaching, 36,* 677-697.

Ramey-Gassert, L. (1997). Learning science beyond the classroom. *Elementary School Journal, 97,* 433-450.

Revital, T. T., & Yehudit, D. J. (2000). Formal and informal collaborative projects: engaging in industry with environmental awareness. *Science Education, 84,* 95-113.

THE TIP (6.4)

 As an alternative activity, facilitate class or individual students' involvement, as nonscientists, in scientific investigations through projects in which a range of individuals gather data for use by scientists to investigate questions of research importance.

What the Research Says

In an examination of a citizen-science project, Trumbull, Bonney, Bascom, and Cabral (2000) surveyed 700 participants regarding their experiences in a project concerning birdseed preference conducted by the Cornell Laboratory of Ornithology. In surveying postactivity reflective letters, the researchers found that 80% revealed that participants had engaged in thinking processes similar to those that are part of scientific investigations.

Citizen-science projects are based on the assumption that participants can increase their understanding about the process of science through engagement in authentic science, in contrast to traditional, tightly scripted school laboratory investigations. The results of the research support this assumption. For example, based on their research, Trumbull et al. couldn't say that their subjects' participation in the citizen-science project caused this thinking, but they could say that participation provided these individuals a forum in which they engaged in these habits of thought. The researchers note their hope that younger people and those less educated than their sample group also would experience benefits from participation in projects with scientists.

Classroom Applications

A quick Internet search will turn up a number of citizen-science project opportunities, including that sponsored by the very Cornell group featured in the research mentioned above. A little local searching of college or university science departments will provide you with potential projects or suggestions on how to create your own. Environmental issues often produce opportunities to conduct science and place it in a larger interdisciplinary context. There are many ways to integrate this idea into the formal curriculum:

- Involve both your students and their parents in the project.
- Reward individual participation with extra credit.
- Provide a citizen-science project as a science fair option.

- Bring in an outside expert to mentor such a project.
- Make it a long-term class project.

Precautions and Possible Pitfalls

 Be aware that teaching this way usually involves more work. Organization, resource collection, and assessment can be messy. Some students who have been successful in the traditional curriculum and pedagogy may not want to become more active learners. If you undertake the work as a class project, there are inherent problems of responsibility and degree of buy-in and engagement. The rewards of participation in citizen-science projects can be great, but you need to be aware of the potential pitfalls and frustrations.

BIBLIOGRAPHY

Trumbull, D. J., Bonney, R., Bascom, D., & Cabral, A. (2000). Thinking scientifically during participation in a citizen-science project. *Science Education, 84*, 265-275.

THE TIP (6.5)

 Consider carefully designed informal science experiences as intervention strategies for combating disinterest among underserved and/or underrepresented minority students.

What the Research Says

Research conducted by Jones (1997) has found support for the idea that an informal approach to science education can be an effective strategy for reaching out to underserved or underrepresented minority students. Participants in the Young Scholars Program at Ohio State University, which was 6 years old at the time of Jones's study, served as the sample for this research. The Young Scholars Program is a precollege intervention program designed to prepare academically talented, economically disadvantaged minority students for college education. The students range in grade levels from 7th to 12th grade. Jones's data were derived from specific content coding (content categories included learning, enjoyment, and displeasure) of open-ended written dialogue. A total of 521 essays were collected from 630 students. Jones surveyed and focused on the program's efforts to increase the students' agricultural science literacy and to entice students to consider the possibility of collegiate study in agricultural fields. This would increase the racial/ethnic diversity of the student population in the College of Food, Agriculture, and Environmental Sciences.

Past strategies used within the Young Scholars Program to increase interest in participation in these areas of science were ineffectual and had been met with disinterest by the students. As a result, the program was restructured, and it then met with much more success. The program used a very deliberately structured field-trip format to challenge the students' existing notions and change their perceptions of the science fields featured.

When the academic context was relaxed, the students seemed to interpret the demonstrations and exhibitions in more meaningful ways. The project emphasized both science literacy and career issues in science education. Quantitative analysis of the reactions of program participants, both students and scientists, revealed much more positive interactions with each other and more positive content of the interactions than were found in previous attempts. Functional educational innovation was examined after the fact for the generation of insights into educational practices. The results showed growth and improvement of content knowledge and conceptual understanding as well as positive changes in impressions.

Classroom Applications

Jones started with the idea that science, specifically university or college science, presents a rigid, impersonal educational style that does not appeal to many students of color. Science presentations can seem excessively formal and unfriendly to people who come from strong communities where human contact is valued. To add to the perception, most presentations and programs are facilitated and presented by individuals from traditionally represented ethnic and racial populations.

In the program Jones studied, whenever possible, efforts were made to use nontraditional scientists (all women and men of color) to break down the stereotypical notion that all scientists are white males. Abstract basic science concepts and projects were de-emphasized in favor of the presentation of concrete applied science applications. The students could identify with the science content and concepts within a concrete and more authentic context. This idea represents elements of a constructivist theory approach designed to connect to the students' previous knowledge and experience base and expand upon and modify it.

What does this mean for the classroom teacher with similar student demographics? It means that informal contact with the disciplines of science may be a more effective and valid pathway for presenting the nature of science and capturing the interest of underserved students. It also means that, whenever possible, you should make an effort to use nontraditional scientists or other people from the field of science to deliver the message. In this way, informal science experiences can influence and cultivate the students' interest, opening the doors of science to historically underrepresented people. Look at field trips and other informal contacts with science from a new perspective.

Precautions and Possible Pitfalls

 Access to science through informal pathways has not been the focus of much research, so you may not find much help in the professional and academic literature. This is one small effort to make science education more inclusive. You should not look on this effort as a perfect alternative. There is always the question of the wisdom of replacing more traditional curriculum with alternative strategies, especially if the students are expected to take standardized tests. For those who make the effort to modify their own informal and formal practices based on the research in this area, success or change in attitudes might be hard to measure or observe. You will need to measure the success or progress of your methods or program approach one student at a time and over a long period.

BIBLIOGRAPHY

Jones, L. (1997). Opening doors with informal science: Exposure and access for our underserved students. *Science Education, 81,* 663-677.

THE TIP (6.6)

 Explore the range of informal science opportunities available to you.

What the Research Says

 Ramey-Gassert (1997) has elaborated on the differences between learning that occurs in the classroom and learning that takes place outside the classroom:

> In-school learning tends to be solitary, based on symbols and the abstract, and divorced from real-world experiences, with little or no connection to the objects and events represented. In contrast, out of school learning more commonly involves the accomplishment of an intellectual or physical task by a group that is interacting using real elements, which allow learning to take on greater meaning. (p. 433)

She goes on to point out that "enjoyment should be recognized as a precursor to learning. Students must be engaged by the learning task and actively involved in enjoyable, stimulating learning tasks to sustain the motivation needed to understand and assimilate new information." Ramey-Gassert's research took the form of an informal survey and reflection on the potential benefits that nontraditional science activities offer. Her emphasis was on longer-term experiences rather than the single field trip.

Classroom Applications

 The range of informal relationships (as opposed to one-shot visits) that science classrooms can engage is wide. Here is a limited list to help you generate ideas (many of the places named here as examples have Internet sites):

- *Museums:* Many museums offer a number of activities to choose from. They provide traditional access to museum exhibits, behind-the-scenes visits, pre- and postvisit activities, and, for those with transportation or budget problems, outreach programs. Many also offer internships, opportunities for students to serve as counselors to younger students, and specialized programs for more motivated and interested individual students. They can offer suggestions on how best to utilize their resources. Examples of museums that have such programs include Philadelphia's Franklin Institute Science Museum and the Cranbrook Institute of Science in Detroit.

- *Informal science centers:* Most, if not all, science centers have outreach programs. Like museums, many science centers not only provide student programs but also offer teachers opportunities for professional enhancement. They teach teachers how to interact with the content of the science centers or with local environments near their schools. They connect teachers to resources their schools can't provide. Some of these facilities offer opportunities for principals and administrators also. Research has shown that the key to innovations and success of staff development is administrative support. Teachers can call these programs to the attention of their administrators. Great examples of such educational centers include San Francisco's Exploratorium, Berkeley's Lawrence Hall of Science, and the New York Hall of Science.

- *Business and industry:* Many science-related businesses and industries mandate community and school educational interaction. They offer programs, many with corporate and government funding, that focus on a variety of important topics, such as gender equity (e.g., Project WISE [Women in Science and Engineering]). The focuses of particular industry programs can be very specialized. Many industries have found that being part of the fabric of their communities through education is good business. Innovative teachers can often take a leadership role in the creation of programs that link classrooms with the educational resources business and industry have to offer. Providing businesses with user-friendly strategies can foster valuable relationships and new resources.

- *Government agencies:* Many local, state, and national government agencies offer programs and are mandated and funded to provide them. From park docents to junior rangers, programs offer a range of educational potential. Many government-sponsored activities and even junior lifeguard programs include science components in their curricular planning. Health departments, the National Weather Service, the U.S. Geological Survey, and many other science-related agencies offer instruction-rich opportunities. Students can access most weather data on the Internet, without ever having to leave the classroom.

- *Private foundations, clubs, and civic organizations:* Trout Unlimited, the Sierra Club, and the Wilderness Society are all private organizations that include and emphasize educational components in their goals and objectives. They offer a range of both student- and teacher-centered educational opportunities. For example, Trout Unlimited offers "Salmon in the Classroom" programs, and the Wilderness Society provides teacher outdoor leadership training.

Type the phrase "informal science" or "informal science education" into an Internet search engine (we suggest you try MetaCrawler, at http://www.metacrawler.com, which surveys a range of other search engines). With these terms, we got 68 hits, or leads to Internet sites that contain those terms. This is a good place to start. The range of opportunities is so great, you cannot hope to cover it totally, or even in significant part. Start to view your neighborhood as a source of resources and begin to ask around. Survey your students' parents for contacts. There is no one right way to search for or utilize these resources.

Precautions and Possible Pitfalls

 As we have noted, the range of opportunities is great, and utilizing the resources available to you takes time and energy. Managing contacts, students, parents, and resources is going above and beyond traditional teaching responsibilities. Schools and teachers that make these connections are seen in a much more favorable light than are those that do not.

Many connections can affect your daily curriculum and instructional practices, and others remain outside the classroom and are not integrated. Some can be utilized within a full class of students and others should be made available only to the most interested and motivated. There is no one right way to include the informal educational realm in your instructional practices, but if you can include it, you will greatly enrich your professional growth and the lives of your students.

BIBLIOGRAPHY

Ramey-Gassert, L. (1997). Learning science beyond the classroom. *Elementary School Journal, 97*, 433-450.

THE TIP (6.7)

 Explore how the unique learning opportunities in out-of-school learning environments can contribute to a more intrinsically motivating science classroom environment.

What the Research Says

 Learning outside of school (informal education) plays a vital role in the development of competence in language, reading, mathematics, and a variety of other school-related domains. The research suggests that we can assume that such learning also contributes to science classroom education and attitudes. Informal learning experiences help preschool children acquire a wide range of early literacy before they begin attending school. They learn a language, usually before they enter a classroom!

Korpan, Bisanz, Bisanz, Boehme, and Lynch (1997) conducted structured interviews with parents of elementary school children to examine the nature and scope of children's science-related activities outside of school. They found a remarkable level of participation in extracurricular science-related activities, such as watching both science nonfiction and science fiction television shows, reading activities, computer use, community activities (such as going to zoos), home observations and simple science experiments, questioning and discussion, and household interest in and familiarity with science. The researchers found that, often, time and interaction within science-related activities outside of the formal science classroom exceeded time within it.

According to Woollard (1998), zoos have always served educational functions, going back more than 3,000 years to the Chinese "gardens of intelligence." The Internet is currently providing the newest ways in which zoos are being used for educational purposes. One Web site, goodzoos.com (http://www.goodzoos.com), makes available information about and reviews of zoos from all over the world as well as information on many different types of animals.

Classroom Applications

The research makes it clear that learning outside of school should not be ignored and can be a new source of motivating instructional strategies. If science students are required to spend only a few hours a week in science instruction, the overall role that schooling plays in developing science literacy is questionable. How can you use this fact? In planning more formalized science instruction, you need to take into account the influence of students' home and community environments.

Simple structured interviews or questionnaires can yield insights and characterize the development of scientific thinking. This knowledge can lead to a perspective on common experiences (e.g., exhibits at a museum) that can facilitate discussions, aid in the interpretation of phenomena, and frame classroom lessons and activities. This information could also serve to highlight the range of motivations and competencies among students and help you to identify areas in which student "experts" could make a contribution to classroom learning, science fair projects, or other activities. It also can help you to identify influential allies at home who can reinforce your efforts with individual students or act as broader class resources.

Students bring to your class their experiences with a full range of informal science-related activities. Although students' participation in such informal activities may diminish or change as students get older, much of their backgrounds and attitudes are based on this informal education. By being cognizant of the influence that home and community environments have on overall science literacy, you can begin to incorporate this information into your instructional practices. Creative teachers can explore, enhance, and develop a range of curricular connections to students' informal science backgrounds.

Consider establishing school-museum and/or school-zoo partnerships to make the most of informal science learning opportunities in your area. Many museums and schools have their own education departments and might be interested in your outreach efforts. Through the institutionalization of such relationships, many teachers and students will be able to benefit from informal science learning. Perhaps students (and teachers) can serve as museum or zoo volunteers as part of such partnership agreements.

Precautions and Possible Pitfalls

 "School" science is often seen as less enjoyable and sometimes more threatening than the informal variety that students encounter outside the classroom. Don't make the mistake of presuming that the classroom science experience provides the best or only way to understand science.

Much of the science students experience outside the classroom can be classified as "edutainment." Integrating the two realms is challenging but very doable. Research into the connections is just beginning to illuminate the instructional relationships and doesn't yet offer a wide range of "tested" curricula that utilize the knowledge. Don't let the lack of formal connections discourage you! Create your own strategies to integrate the two paradigms within your instructional objectives and comfort zone.

BIBLIOGRAPHY

Korpan, C. A., Bisanz, G. L., Bisanz, J., Boehme, C., & Lynch, M. A. (1997). What did you learn outside of school today? Using structured interviews to document home and community activities related to science and technology. *Science Education, 81*, 651-662.

Ramey-Gassert, L. (1997). Learning science beyond the classroom. *Elementary School Journal, 97*, 433-450.

Woollard, S. P. (1998). The development of zoo education. *International Zoo News, 45*, 422-426.

THE TIP (6.8)

Optimize your students' opportunities to learn in museum and science-center environments by fine-tuning your pre- and postvisit preparation.

What the Research Says

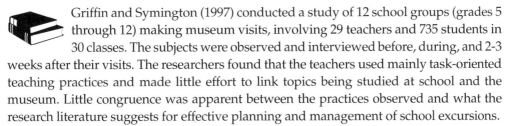

Griffin and Symington (1997) conducted a study of 12 school groups (grades 5 through 12) making museum visits, involving 29 teachers and 735 students in 30 classes. The subjects were observed and interviewed before, during, and 2-3 weeks after their visits. The researchers found that the teachers used mainly task-oriented teaching practices and made little effort to link topics being studied at school and the museum. Little congruence was apparent between the practices observed and what the research literature suggests for effective planning and management of school excursions.

Griffin and Symington suggest a framework that teachers might use in planning learning-oriented museum visits. The framework is based on knowledge of natural learning behaviors exhibited by family groups combined with constructivist theories of learning. Teachers can combine these factors with strategies that have been noted in the research literature (and confirmed by Griffin and Symington's study) to facilitate learning on school excursions to museums.

Classroom Applications

Most science teachers have not been trained to maximize learning opportunities for students and classes outside the confines of the school and classroom. Based on their investigation, Griffin and Symington offer six guidelines that they believe teachers will find useful in gaining a new perspective on field-trip pedagogy and curriculum:

1. Integrate the museum visit with a classroom-based unit. The museum often provides resources the school can't. Use this to your advantage. Use the resources to begin, end, or reinforce classroom instruction.

2. Use a learner-centered approach in which the students are finding answers to their own questions rather than your questions or the museum's questions.

3. Encourage students to compile new questions from their own observations during the visit. Use the trip to stimulate interest and encourage self-motivation.

4. Begin to utilize natural learning methods and behaviors used by informal groups. How do families utilize the exhibits and other opportunities? How do they choose which exhibits to visit and how much time to spend at each exhibit? Spend less time at each exhibit as the day goes on.

5. Utilize cooperative learning strategies and social interactions. Breaking a class up into smaller groups accompanied by parent volunteers is a strategy that may reduce initial confusion.

6. Be aware that once they are in a new learning environment, students and teachers will need to adapt to the new setting. Consider planning for an orientation period, or have guides from the relevant institution help you fine-tune the visit.

Griffin and Symington also suggest that teachers communicate with museum staff about collaborative strategies they might develop and more purposeful and linked preparation and postvisit activities. Some science museums provide free handouts for parents and teachers to help them make the most of their visits. The list below is an adapted version of some "tips for visiting a science center" published on the "tryscience" Web site (www.tryscience.org/astc_tipsforvisiting.html), as presented by the Association of Science-Technology Centers:

1. Plan ahead. Request a brochure and review it with your students. Get tickets for special shows in advance.

2. Visit the museum more than once. You—and your students—have limits for what can be learned in one day.

3. Visit often. You'll find something new and exciting each time.

4. Bringing a group of children? Share child-watching responsibilities with other adults (e.g., parent volunteers).

5. Big-screen movies are "awesome," but use discretion. Very young or sensitive children may reach sensory overload and get scared.

6. Check out the museum's store for kits, books, and other materials that can extend the educational experience. Your school may have a budget for such curriculum supplements.

7. Encourage your children to ask questions like these: What does this remind you of? What do you think will happen if . . . ?

8. Help students relate museum displays and experiences to their own prior knowledge and/or personal experience.

9. Encourage your students to ask questions to stimulate their curiosity and expand their learning process.

10. Can't answer a student's question? Simply say something like "I don't know. Let's find out." No one is expected to know everything.

11. Respect your students' ideas. Enjoy their perceptions of what they see, hear, and feel. Remember, scientific breakthroughs start when somebody sees the world differently.

The Association of Science-Technology Centers provides members with discovery rooms for young children, family fun events, classes, demonstrations, camp-ins, science fairs, career days, summer science camp opportunities, and large-format films, among other benefits. Consequently, some science teachers might enjoy membership as both teachers and parents. Local science museums can provide additional information.

Precautions and Possible Pitfalls

 Not all field-trip destinations are staffed by people who read the academic literature and research. Don't rely on them to provide the majority of curriculum, pedagogy, and learning relevance. Some are more in tune with classroom science education than others.

Visiting a site in advance can help you to gain some control over the learning and social environment you will be encountering. Pay special attention to the timing within the visit. Students should not be rushed or left on their own too long.

Students and classes sometimes behave very differently when they encounter new settings. Having parents along can make a big difference in managing students' behavior.

Many teachers are fearful of the management challenges that field trips present. As with many other instructional techniques, experience can be the best teacher. Research concerning teaching and learning within informal settings is rare, but this area is a growing target for science education.

BIBLIOGRAPHY

Griffin, J., & Symington, D. (1997). Moving from task-oriented to learning-oriented strategies on school excursions to museums. *Science Education, 81,* 763-779.

CHAPTER SEVEN

Assessment in the Science Classroom

THE TIP (7.1)

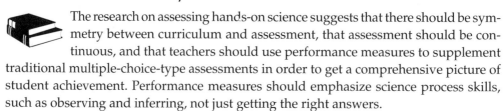

Use a combination of assessment strategies to evaluate student performance, making sure that your evaluations reflect what students were expected to learn in your course.

What the Research Says

The research on assessing hands-on science suggests that there should be symmetry between curriculum and assessment, that assessment should be continuous, and that teachers should use performance measures to supplement traditional multiple-choice-type assessments in order to get a comprehensive picture of student achievement. Performance measures should emphasize science process skills, such as observing and inferring, not just getting the right answers.

In addition to measuring students' performance, additional types of measures teachers might use to create a multifaceted assessment system are written student responses and teacher-involved responses. A multifaceted assessment strategy that includes alternative forms of assessment is now recommended for science teachers (Reynolds, Doran, Allers, & Agruso, 1996).

Classroom Applications

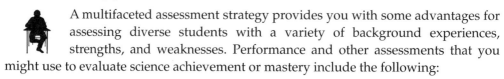

A multifaceted assessment strategy provides you with some advantages for assessing diverse students with a variety of background experiences, strengths, and weaknesses. Performance and other assessments that you might use to evaluate science achievement or mastery include the following:

1. Lab notebooks or journals in which students record procedures and conclusions

2. Computer simulations of hands-on investigations

3. Short-answer paper-and-pencil problems in planning, analyzing, and/or interpreting experiments

4. Multiple-choice and other types of test items (e.g., essay, short answer) developed from observations of students conducting hands-on investigations

5. Projects such as student-produced articles, books, or Internet sites

6. Concept maps or other graphic organizers

7. Interviews about long-term investigations

8. Portfolios and presentations demonstrating student work

9. Manipulative skills, such as focusing a microscope on a slide to identify the contents

10. Lab performance, such as thoughtfulness and carefulness in executing procedures

Precautions and Possible Pitfalls

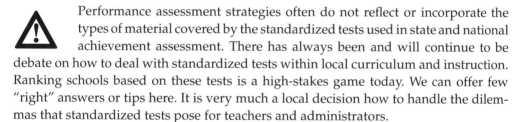

Performance assessment strategies often do not reflect or incorporate the types of material covered by the standardized tests used in state and national achievement assessment. There has always been and will continue to be debate on how to deal with standardized tests within local curriculum and instruction. Ranking schools based on these tests is a high-stakes game today. We can offer few "right" answers or tips here. It is very much a local decision how to handle the dilemmas that standardized tests pose for teachers and administrators.

BIBLIOGRAPHY

Reynolds, D. S., Doran, R. L., Allers, R. H., & Agruso, S. A. (1996). *Alternative assessment in science: A teacher's guide.* Buffalo: State University of New York at Buffalo, Education Department.

Shavelson, R. J., & Baxter, G. P. (1992). What have we learned about assessing hands-on science? *Educational Leadership, 49*(8), 20-25.

THE TIP (7.2)

 Refine your assessment procedures by repeatedly testing items and procedures and then making revisions based on these experiences.

What the Research Says

 Effective science achievement performance assessment requires multiple iterations. Taking shortcuts in this process often leads to poor assessment and low-quality classroom instruction (Shavelson & Baxter, 1992).

Classroom Applications

 Try out test items and procedures on students before you incorporate them into your assessment program. Get students' comments about the items and procedures, and use this feedback to revise or eliminate problematic items and procedures. Ask questions such as the following, suggested by Shavelson and Baxter (1992), about your assessments:

1. Do they provide reliable measures?

2. Are they consistent with the instructional experiences your students have had?

3. Do the performance measures provide information that supplements traditional pencil-and-paper methods (e.g., multiple-choice)?

4. Are the performance and traditional measures interchangeable?

Precautions and Possible Pitfalls

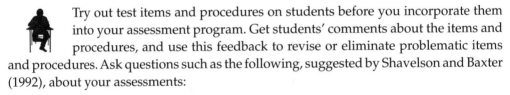 In science education today, there has been a shift from a content-dominated curriculum to a more process-driven curriculum. Some assessment techniques work well in one of these areas and fail in the other. Some researchers have suggested that there can be little or no overlap: Objective tests measure content achievement well, and performance assessments measure process achievement well. Others feel that objective tests can be written to assess process skills. Be aware of the distinction between the two arenas, and learn all you can about the ongoing assessment debate and how the information applies to your classes.

BIBLIOGRAPHY

Shavelson, R. J., & Baxter, G. P. (1992). What have we learned about assessing hands-on science? *Educational Leadership, 49*(8), 20-25.

THE TIP (7.3)

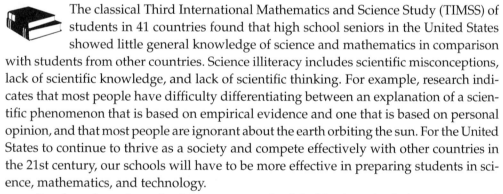

Use benchmarks and standards to determine science literacy levels.

What the Research Says

 The classical Third International Mathematics and Science Study (TIMSS) of students in 41 countries found that high school seniors in the United States showed little general knowledge of science and mathematics in comparison with students from other countries. Science illiteracy includes scientific misconceptions, lack of scientific knowledge, and lack of scientific thinking. For example, research indicates that most people have difficulty differentiating between an explanation of a scientific phenomenon that is based on empirical evidence and one that is based on personal opinion, and that most people are ignorant about the earth orbiting the sun. For the United States to continue to thrive as a society and compete effectively with other countries in the 21st century, our schools will have to be more effective in preparing students in science, mathematics, and technology.

Benchmarks and standards serve as meaningful, objective criteria for assessing and comparing students' progress in science. Lemons and Griswold (n.d.) have successfully used benchmarks to help improve students' mastery of college biology as part of a comprehensive curriculum development, implementation, and assessment plan. Components of their approach are presented below.

Classroom Applications

 Make scientific literacy one of your highest priorities. Focus instruction on developing a body of interconnected knowledge of important scientific content, including concepts, facts, and theories. Also work to develop students'

scientific thinking and reasoning skills, so that they learn to think like scientists. Design in-class and out-of-class activities to help students connect what they are learning about science with real-life examples, issues, and events.

To ensure that your students acquire, understand, and can use important scientific concepts and skills, streamline the curriculum. Ted Sizer is well-known for promoting the idea that in teaching, "less = more"; that is, less coverage across topics means greater depth within important topics. Make sure your assessment strategies are aligned with your curriculum and pedagogy. If your state has standards for science learning, you can use those as your benchmarks.

Lemons and Griswold (n.d.) define performance benchmarks as "specific student outcomes which operationally define student achievement" and serve as a framework for the design and/or selection of learning and assessment activities. They identify three benchmark levels, with the lowest requiring the recall of factual information and the highest requiring prediction and analytic thinking. They provide these examples, from their cardiac unit, of what students should be able to do at the different levels:

- *Identify* the macroscopic features and locations of the key regions of the heart, including the chambers, valves, tributary vessels, and vascular supply (Level I).
- *Predict and calculate* how SV and ejection fraction (EF) vary, based on changes in end diastolic volume (EDV) and/or end systolic volume (ESV) (Level III).
- *Measure* intervals and use them to calculate heart rate (Skills Benchmark).

Lemons and Griswold list the following examples of learning activities to address these cardiac benchmarks:

- Studying the parts of the heart using a model
- Explorations with a hands-on model of the heart to test predictions about output under various conditions
- Analyzing a recording of frog heart contractions

In this approach, once you have established benchmarks, you can plan corresponding learning and assessment activities. (For more information, see Lemons & Griswold, n.d.)

Precautions and Possible Pitfalls

 Benchmarks and standards should be applied to *all* students, including girls and members of minority groups. They also should be used with special education students and bilingual or ESL students. Many of these students may need to develop feelings of self-efficacy in science as a precursor to attaining scientific literacy. It is likely that you will find it easier to help your students achieve scientific literacy if you have the support of other science teachers, their immediate supervisors, your principal, your district science curriculum coordinator, your superintendent, your students' parents, and the local community. The effort should be districtwide.

BIBLIOGRAPHY

Lemons, D., & Griswold, J. (n.d.). *The human A&P benchmarks curriculum* [On-line]. Available Internet: http://harold.sci.ccny.cuny.edu/hfp_home.htm

Nelson, G. D. (1999). Science literacy for all in the 21st century. *Educational Leadership, 57*(2), 14-17.

Schmidt, W. H., McKnight, C. C., & Raizen, S. A. (1997). *Splintered vision: An investigation of U.S. mathematics and science education.* Norwell, MA: Kluwer Academic.

THE TIP (7.4)

 Provide students with explicit, detailed feedback about their performance.

What the Research Says

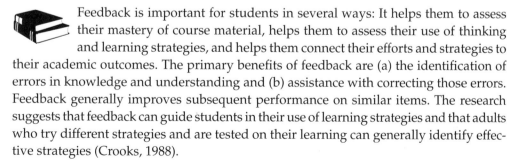 Feedback is important for students in several ways: It helps them to assess their mastery of course material, helps them to assess their use of thinking and learning strategies, and helps them connect their efforts and strategies to their academic outcomes. The primary benefits of feedback are (a) the identification of errors in knowledge and understanding and (b) assistance with correcting those errors. Feedback generally improves subsequent performance on similar items. The research suggests that feedback can guide students in their use of learning strategies and that adults who try different strategies and are tested on their learning can generally identify effective strategies (Crooks, 1988).

Classroom Applications

 Go beyond simply marking items right or wrong and giving students scores on tests, so that students can have better ideas about how they went wrong. Make comments that will stimulate students to think about their errors.

Precautions and Possible Pitfalls

Teachers spend many hours grading papers, writing comments, and giving feedback. However, there is always doubt as to how much of their teachers' comments students read and internalize after they see their scores. Many students are not concerned with really knowing the content and scientific concepts on which they've been tested. As an alternative, try to structure class time during activities or quiet assignments so that you can give individual students verbal feedback rather than written feedback. You will receive feedback yourself and get to know your students better.

BIBLIOGRAPHY

Crooks, T. (1988). Impact of classroom evaluation practices on students. *Review of Educational Research, 58,* 438-481.

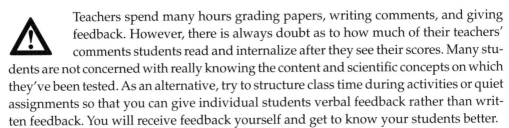

THE TIP (7.5)

 Try having students pose problems as an assessment method.

What the Research Says

Mestre (1994) found that problem posing, when followed by an interview, is a powerful assessment strategy for evaluating the development and understanding of physics concepts in high-performing university physics students. "Good novices" in Mestre's study were able to pose appropriate, solvable problems when responding to a problem situation or concept scenario, but they also had major flaws in their conceptual understanding. The flaws suggested the students were deficient in how their knowledge was organized in memory and how it was connected with procedures and problems.

Classroom Applications

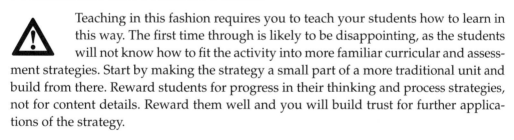 In a classic strategy now becoming popular in some medical schools, problem-based or "case-based" learning scenarios are used to train medical students. Small groups of students tackle ill-structured problems or cases by posing related and appropriate problems and concerns regarding the cases. An instructor mentors each group as the students identify what they know and, more important, what they do not know and need to know. In this way the students take a good deal of the responsibility for their own learning. These types of thinking strategies and habits of mind reflect how professionals need to continue to learn once they leave school.

You can employ the same kind of self-assessment strategy in your science classes, as a vehicle to help your students acquire needed content and useful and important thinking strategies. For example, after a traditional unit on the structure and function of blood, ask your students to evaluate the cause of a young woman's anemia. The causes and reasons for anemia can be complex and varied. Have the students create a detailed list of all the specific questions they should ask and information they might need to form a hypothesized explanation. Once they have done this, convert the "interview" into a class discussion, structuring the collective understanding of anemia and its relationship to blood. The details become integrated into other body systems and diet. Before long, anemia becomes an integrated and interdisciplinary activity.

Precautions and Possible Pitfalls

Teaching in this fashion requires you to teach your students how to learn in this way. The first time through is likely to be disappointing, as the students will not know how to fit the activity into more familiar curricular and assessment strategies. Start by making the strategy a small part of a more traditional unit and build from there. Reward students for progress in their thinking and process strategies, not for content details. Reward them well and you will build trust for further applications of the strategy.

BIBLIOGRAPHY

Mestre, J. (1994, April). *Problem posing as a tool for probing conceptual development and understanding in physics.* Paper presented at the annual meeting of the American Educational Research Association, New Orleans.

THE TIP (7.6)

 Give students the kind of feedback that will most help them improve their future performance.

What the Research Says

Teachers often give students less-than-useful information about their performance. Studies have shown that students benefit more from learning about when they have been wrong than from knowing when they have been right. In addition, for students to improve their future performance, they need to know why something they have done is wrong. Research shows that teachers often fail to provide students with this kind of information about their performance. When students understand why something is wrong, they are more likely to learn appropriate strategies to eliminate their errors (Bangert-Drowns, Kulik, Kulik, & Morgan, 1991).

Classroom Applications

Science instruction, in general, affords students many opportunities to give right answers or wrong answers. By merely indicating the right answer or noting that a student's response is wrong, you do little to aim students in the right direction. Analyze incorrect responses to see if the errors are in reasoning, incorrect interpretations of major concepts, faulty work with details, or somewhere else. Such analysis can often be time-consuming, but it is extremely worthwhile, for it is the discovery of the error (resulting from this error analysis) that can be the key to helping a student sort out his or her science difficulties.

Several types of errors occur in the normal science classroom. First, there are the errors that are common to a large portion of the class. These can be attributable to misunderstandings in class or to some prior learning (common to most of the class) that causes students to react similarly and incorrectly to a specific situation. When you notice this sort of thing, a general remark and clarification to the entire class is appropriate. The misconception may be one of not understanding the mathematical relationships behind a concept, for instance. Understanding of the math leads to mastery of the concept. Analysis of errors in thinking and quick and instant feedback can turn potential drudgery into pride of understanding.

For example, as Stanhope (1994) notes, an understanding of the overall concept of evolution depends on knowledge and application of population genetics:

> One of the more difficult concepts to understand when studying population genetics is Hardy-Weinberg Equilibrium [biology with its underlying mathematics]. Since it is abstract and quantitative, students often feel threatened and quickly shy away from it. They frequently ask, "Why do we have to know this? Of what value is it?"

For this reason, many biology teachers simply avoid the math and focus on the concept. Stanhope continues: "Why do students need to know Hardy-Weinberg Equilibrium, and how do we, as teachers, convey the principle to them?" She notes that understanding the underlying mathematical relationships can help students understand and answer the following questions, which she credits to Merten (1992):

1. How can type O be the most common of the blood types if it is a recessive trait?

2. If Huntington's disease is a dominant trait, shouldn't three-fourths of the population have Huntington's while one-fourth have the normal phenotype? What about the Punnett Square outcome?

3. Shouldn't recessive traits be gradually selected against and gradually disappear from the population?

Stanhope continues:

> These questions reflect the common misconception that the dominant allele of a trait will always have the highest frequency in a population and the recessive allele will always have the lowest frequency. On the contrary, as G. H. Hardy stated in 1908, "There is not the slightest foundation for the idea that a dominant trait should show a tendency to spread over a whole population, or that a recessive trait should die out." Gene frequencies can be high or low no matter how the allele is expressed, and can change, depending on the conditions that exist. It is the changes in gene frequencies over time that result in evolution. The Hardy-Weinberg Principle provides a baseline to determine whether or not gene frequencies have changed in a population and thus whether evolution has occurred.

It is very common for biology students to struggle with the Hardy-Weinberg Equilibrium. There are two threads to teaching this activity: the biological concepts and the mathematical relationships. Early in the instructional unit, errors in thinking about biological concepts and the related math applications can be common and hard for students to deal with. Wrong answers and misconceptions provide "teachable moments" and opportunities for quick feedback. In this case, rapid feedback is important in your effort to help students avoid frustration that turns them off. Most of them have had the math, but not within an authentic context.

Precautions and Possible Pitfalls

It is possible that an error analysis of a student's work may turn up several errors. However, pointing out too many faults at one time may confound the student and consequently have a counterproductive effect. In such a case, arrange the discovered errors in order of importance and discuss them successively with the student, one by one, going on to the next only after successful completion of the preceding one. Follow up to see if students follow their error correction plans successfully and rectify previous errors, especially recurring errors.

BIBLIOGRAPHY

Bangert-Drowns, R. L., Kulik, C. C., Kulik, J. A., & Morgan, M. (1991). The instructional effect of feedback in test-like events. *Review of Educational Research, 61,* 213-238.

Hardy, G. H. (1908). Mendelian proportions in a mixed population. *Science, 28,* 49-50.

Merten, T. R. (1992). Introducing students to population genetics and the Hardy-Weinberg principle. *American Biology Teacher, 54*(2), 103-107.

Stanhope, J. (1994). Introduction. In *Hardy-Weinberg equilibrium* [On-line]. Princeton, NJ: Woodrow Wilson National Fellowship Foundation. Available Internet: http://www.woodrow.org/teachers/bi/1994/hwintro.html

THE TIP (7.7)

Promptly give students information or feedback about their performance.

What the Research Says

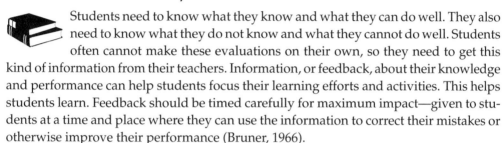

Students need to know what they know and what they can do well. They also need to know what they do not know and what they cannot do well. Students often cannot make these evaluations on their own, so they need to get this kind of information from their teachers. Information, or feedback, about their knowledge and performance can help students focus their learning efforts and activities. This helps students learn. Feedback should be timed carefully for maximum impact—given to students at a time and place where they can use the information to correct their mistakes or otherwise improve their performance (Bruner, 1966).

Classroom Applications

In an inquiry or hands-on science classroom, ask students to set their homework out on their desks while they continue with an activity. Buy a few interesting rubber stamps to use for marking completed or successful work, and circle the room checking homework during the hands-on activity. Look over the homework while you guide and support the ongoing activity. You don't have to correct the homework, and you have the chance to give each student instant verbal feedback! The work can then become part of the students' notebooks. This way you save your prep period or "at-home" time for grading work that requires more of your attention. Keep in mind that it is very tempting to spot-check homework by inspecting it to see if the right answers are offered without looking at the methods used to reach the answers. Whenever possible, you should thoroughly examine your students' homework answers and methods, and then give students information about the quality of their performance. With practice, you will learn to recognize problems with assignments more quickly and easily. Within a class, it is common to find that the same problems pop up as problematic for a number of students.

Precautions and Possible Pitfalls

Make sure that students are in an appropriate frame of mind for receiving feedback—not when in a state of "high drive" or anxiety (Bruner, 1966). If your class is too large for you to do a thorough check of all the homework daily, you can select different subgroups from within the class each day, picking their homework from the collected class set. You may select such subgroups either randomly or by design. In any case, the mode of selection should not be predictable by your students. Otherwise, those who anticipate homework inspection will do a better job, and those who don't, won't. If you do not provide feedback in a timely fashion, it will be of limited usefulness to your students.

Giving students' homework assignments your undivided attention can be difficult within a noisy and active class, and you may need practice to become effective. Your assessment and feedback must be authentic; if students feel you are just "rubber-stamping" their work as completed, you run a risk of devaluing their effort and work.

BIBLIOGRAPHY

Bruner, J. (1966). *Toward a theory of instruction.* New York: W. W. Norton.

Chickering, A. W., & Gamson, Z. F. (1987). Seven principles for good practice in undergraduate education. *Wingspread Journal, 9*(2), special insert.

THE TIP (7.8)

 Specific feedback on practice is essential for improving student performance.

What the Research Says

 Studies have shown that improved student performance results from the amount of feedback given to students. Students need to receive specific feedback on the results of their practice in order for learning to be effective. Practice with specific feedback results in more successful and more efficient learning.

Classroom Applications

 Within science instructional practices, there are usually many opportunities for students to practice the skills presented. By pairing students and having them read each other's work, or by having students compare their work to model solutions, you can create opportunities for regular feedback without a great expense of time. You might also systematically review a small and different sampling of student papers each day, and from this small number of collected papers provide some meaningful feedback to the students. For example, suppose that in your classroom the students are situated in rows. You may "at random" call for the papers of everyone sitting in the first seat of each row, or the students sitting on the diagonal, or everyone in the third row. If you want to check on a particular student's paper a second day, perhaps because you have some serious questions about the student's work, you can include that student again in the group from which you collect papers by calling on a set that also describes the student's seat. For instance, if you called on the third row the first day, and the target student is sitting in the last seat of the third row, on the second day you can call for the papers from all students sitting in the last seat of a row, and so "inadvertently" include the target student a second time.

Because it is unreasonable for you to expect to be able to do a thorough reading of all students' papers every day, you might employ some alternative ways of getting feedback to students on their homework. You might search for parent volunteers and/or retired teachers who may like to take on some part-time work in reading and reacting (in writing) to student work. You might also try to engage some older and more advanced students in undertaking similar activity, using a "cross-age" tutoring approach. This would serve the older students as well, as they can benefit by looking back over previously learned material from a more advanced standpoint.

Precautions and Possible Pitfalls

Teachers often do not have sufficient resources to allow them to provide individual feedback to each student. If you have students give each other feedback, you should be aware that this feedback will be of a different nature from, and is certainly not a replacement for, the kind of feedback you would provide as a teacher. You must monitor student feedback to avoid the perpetuation of students' flawed ideas or misconceptions. The same holds true for feedback provided by teachers' aides, parent volunteers, and retirees assisting in the classroom.

BIBLIOGRAPHY

Benjamin, L. T., & Lowman, K. D. (Eds.). (1981). *Activities handbook for the teaching of psychology.* Washington, DC: American Psychological Association.

THE TIP (7.9)

 Don't emphasize grades in a course or subject too near the beginning of its study.

What the Research Says

Giving grades early stimulates students to participate actively in their lessons, but may undermine achievement in the long run. Research provides evidence that students learn because of anxiety over grades or because they get good grades with a minimum of effort. Giving grades early is especially beneficial for students who require more time to understand things. They tend to be afraid of saying something wrong and of getting bad grades. Students do not tend to view early grading as judgmental about their knowledge; rather, they view it more as informative.

Lechner, Brehm, and Zbigniew (1996) examined the effects of giving grades at an early stage of knowledge acquisition in four ninth-grade classes. The researchers separated the four classes into two groups; students in both groups received computer-aided instruction and got a grade after every step. Students in one group did not get to know about their grades, whereas those in the other group were informed about their grades. Lechner et al. compared the achievements of the two groups on the basis of the grade after every step and on a final test. Students who knew their marks did slightly better on the interim tests. Their learning was apparently enhanced by their awareness of their grades. In contrast, on the final test, students who did not know their interim grades did noticeably better. They were not pushed by the pressure of marks. These students used additional work to develop their feelings of self-control. In this way, they dealt with the issue of their learning needs, understood their needs profoundly, and achieved at higher levels.

Classroom Applications

Give students specific feedback to improve their performance, but avoid giving grades at an early stage of learning. Early marks can easily frustrate students, especially those who are not very interested in a particular topic or even the whole subject—their motivation can sink even further. On the other hand, early grades can promote rapid success. However, in some cases this leads to students' resting on their laurels. During the period when students are acquiring new knowledge, give feedback on the use of their knowledge and skills, but use grades sparingly. More and more, the process of learning and putting together a product is seen as more important than the finished product itself. Simply checking off a step as completed before moving on to the next may be enough incentive (with feedback) to keep instruction (and learning) moving!

Precautions and Possible Pitfalls

 Do not stop all assessment during the early stage. First of all, students need assessment to evaluate or at least estimate their own achievement. In addition, you will always find that some students are entirely motivated by grades. Therefore, during the early learning phase, you should use oral or nonverbal assessment techniques.

BIBLIOGRAPHY

Lechner, H. J., Brehm, R. I., & Zbigniew, M. (1996). Zensierung und ihr Einfluß auf die Leistung der Schüler [Influence of marks on student achievements]. *Pädagogik und Schulalltag, 51*, 371-379.

THE TIP (7.10)

 Make sure your students pay attention to the feedback you give them.

What the Research Says

 Students' paying attention to feedback on items they have gotten incorrect is related to achievement. Two factors affect students' paying attention to teacher feedback: (a) whether they perceive that they can understand the feedback and (b) whether they focus on the negative feelings that arise from making mistakes. In a study of 38 high school students in two classes, Gagne et al. (1987) observed how students processed feedback during computer programming lessons while the teacher discussed the results of a recent test. The researchers categorized their observations into 10 "on-task behaviors" (e.g., looking at the teacher or writing on the test) and 9 "off-task behaviors" (e.g., looking out the window or writing on irrelevant material). Gagne et al. randomly selected 13 low- and high-achieving students for interviews in order to get more detailed information on how they processed feedback. One distinct pattern that emerged frequently was students' judgment that they could not understand the teacher's feedback. When students do understand the feedback, they listen to what the teacher is saying and try to figure out what they did wrong. When they do not understand the feedback, they tune out. The other, less common, pattern that emerged was students' getting upset about making errors. When this occurred, instead of focusing on the problem, the students tended to focus on their negative feelings.

Classroom Applications

 Try giving students an option of two due dates for an assignment. Tell them that if they finish an assignment and turn it in for your feedback on the first date, you will guarantee them a certain number of points or a particular grade. Then, if they sincerely work to incorporate your feedback and turn the assignment in again, you will reward them with a higher grade. For those students who turn their assignments in only on the second due date, evaluate the work in a more traditional way. When teachers use this strategy in academic science classes, it is common for 50% of the students to take advantage of the first due date.

Alternatively, you might evaluate your students' work once and then give them feedback, with no grades. Give them grades only if they incorporate your feedback suggestions into the assignment.

Whether you provide feedback to your students by using these strategies, modifying them, or making up your own, you will begin to feel how your feedback has real value to your students!

Precautions and Possible Pitfalls

 Be aware of the fact that some of your feedback to students, whether given individually or to the class, may be ignored or simply forgotten. Simple awareness of the importance of students' retaining teacher feedback is already one big step in making this aspect of the instructional program effective. Journal entries and/or written error analyses can become tedious and should take various forms. For example, a student might see such an additional written assignment as a form of punishment. If you sense this, you should find an alternative way of reaching the same objective. For instance, you might have the student who received your feedback explain the problem and your proposed resolution to a classmate.

BIBLIOGRAPHY

Gagne, E. D., Crutcher, R. J., Anzelc, J., Geisman, C., Hoffman, V., Schutz, P., & Lizcano, L. (1987). The role of student processing of feedback in classroom achievement. *Cognition and Instruction, 4*(3), 167-186.

THE TIP (7.11)

 Use graphic organizers such as concept maps to assess students' science learning.

What the Research Says

 Novak's research group developed the graphic organizer known as a concept map as an evaluation tool; concept maps allow teachers to assess changes in students' conceptual understanding easily and precisely (see Novak, 1998). Research comparing student-generated concept maps to clinical interviews with students found that the former were as effective as the latter in revealing students' knowledge structures (Edwards & Fraser, 1983). The advantage of this particular type of graphic organizer is that it involves the use of linking words between the represented concepts. Novak and his colleagues have been using concept maps in research and studying their effectiveness in teaching and learning in various settings, including schools and corporations. In 1990, the *Journal of Research in Science Teaching* published a special issue on the use of concept maps, and many more articles on their use in science teaching have been published since then. The Internet can help you find numerous resources on many types of graphic organizers and their wide-ranging educational applications, including some ideas from the Schreyer Institute for Innovation in Learning's on-line *Concept Map Module* (see Zimmaro & Cawley, 1998).

Classroom Applications

 In his own teaching, Novak has used concept maps as assessment tools for many years. He gives students a list of 20 to 30 concepts and asks them to map the concepts, adding 10 to 20 concepts of their own choice. Novak describes this activity as demanding and often makes it a homework assignment.

When you evaluate your students by examining their self-constructed graphic organizers, look for how they organize their knowledge as well as the understanding they show through the relationships demonstrated by their linking lines and concepts. You should also be able to identify creative selection of additional concepts and creative connections between concepts, as well as misconceptions about concepts and their relationships. Graphic organizers can be either hierarchical or nonhierarchical. See Figure 7.1 for an example of a concept map quiz on sedimentary rocks, which was adapted from the National Research Council's *Science Teaching Reconsidered* (1997).

Figure 7.1.   Concept Map-Based Quiz

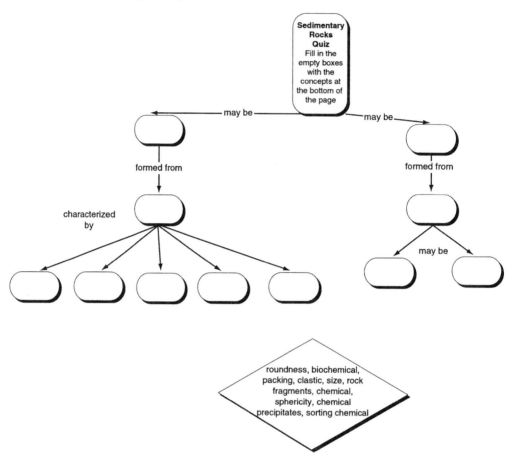

Zimmaro and Cawley (1998) describe two ways that concept maps provide feedback to students and teachers: (a) Teachers can check and students can self-check understanding to see if any connections are missing, and (b) a student's concept map can help the teacher identify student misconceptions and trends in misconceptions across students, which might signal a need for reteaching to clarify understanding. Zimmaro and Cawley also recommend using concept maps to evaluate student learning. The following suggestions are adapted from Zimmaro and Cawley's recommendations:

- For assessing students' prior knowledge, including misconceptions, administer concept maps at the beginning of the course. Such knowledge facilitates instructional planning.

- For formative assessment, use concept maps to evaluate changes in learning and to examine the effects of instruction. Such knowledge facilitates making changes as needed—changes in studying for students and changes in instruction for teachers.

- For summative assessment, use concept maps to evaluate end-of-course knowledge and the effects of instruction. Such knowledge helps you decide on possible revisions in curriculum and instruction for future teaching.

The prereading and postreading organizers illustrated in Chapter 1 show how teachers can use graphic organizers to assess what students have learned, understand, and remember from their reading.

Inspiration Software for graphic organizer construction is an excellent, flexible, easy-to-use tool for teachers and students constructing graphic organizers, including concept maps. The developers claim that use of graphic organizers clarifies thinking, increases retention, taps creativity, develops organizational skills, and deepens understanding of concepts (see the company's Web site at http://www.inspiration.com).

Novak and Gowin (1984) have developed various scoring algorithms for concept maps that provide numeric scores that can be analyzed with statistical tests. Ruiz-Primo and Shavelson (1996) report that it takes only 3 to 10 minutes to score a concept map, depending on the complexity, once scoring criteria have been established.

Precautions and Possible Pitfalls

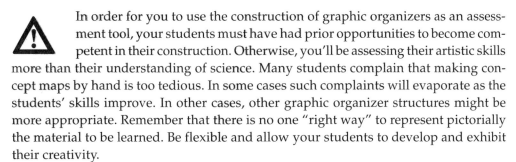

In order for you to use the construction of graphic organizers as an assessment tool, your students must have had prior opportunities to become competent in their construction. Otherwise, you'll be assessing their artistic skills more than their understanding of science. Many students complain that making concept maps by hand is too tedious. In some cases such complaints will evaporate as the students' skills improve. In other cases, other graphic organizer structures might be more appropriate. Remember that there is no one "right way" to represent pictorially the material to be learned. Be flexible and allow your students to develop and exhibit their creativity.

BIBLIOGRAPHY

Edwards, J., & Fraser, K. (1983). Concept maps as reflectors of conceptual understanding. *Research in Science Education, 13,* 19-26.

National Research Council. (1997). *Science teaching reconsidered.* Washington, DC: National Academy Press.

Novak, J. D. (1998). *Learning, creating and using knowledge: Concept maps as facilitative tools in schools and corporations.* Mahwah, NJ: Lawrence Erlbaum.

Novak, J. D., & Gowin, D. B. (1984). *Learning how to learn.* New York: Cambridge University Press.

Ruiz-Primo, M. A., & Shavelson, R. J. (1996). Problems and issues in the use of concept maps in science assessment. *Journal of Research in Science Teaching, 33,* 569-576.

Zimmaro, D. M., & Cawley, J. M. (1998). *Concept map module.* University Park: Pennsylvania State University, Schreyer Institute for Innovation in Learning. Available Internet: http://www.inov8.psu.edu/faculty/cmap.htm

THE TIP (7.12)

☑ Use tests and other assessments of students as teaching and learning opportunities.

What the Research Says

 Research shows that teachers can use tests and other assessment devices to improve as well as to evaluate students' learning of content. One study compared the test performance of students who took an initial test with that of students who did not take an initial test. The researchers found that students who took the initial test did better than those who did not, indicating that they actually learned from the test experience itself (Foos & Fisher, 1988).

Assessment is most effective when it includes students' self-monitoring and self-evaluating, so that students can regulate or manage their own learning. One way of promoting students' ability to self-assess their performance is through error analysis (Hartman, 2001). Research on teaching students to use such strategies demonstrates that students need to be able to answer the following self-questions before they can use the strategies effectively in a variety of situations and for a variety of tasks (Schunk, 2000).

1. *What is error analysis?* Error analysis is a systematic approach for using feedback metacognitively to improve one's future performance. It involves obtaining strategic metacognitive knowledge about one's mistakes and recycling that knowledge for self-improvement.

2. *When and why is it used?* Error analysis has several potential benefits. First, it gives students a second opportunity to master important material. Second, it develops students' metacognition, both strategic knowledge and executive management, as students evaluate their test performance, identify errors and possible

error patterns, and plan for the future. For example, it can help students antici-pate their specific likely errors and self-correct them before turning in a test. Third, it helps internalize students' attributions, so that they recognize that their edu-cational outcomes (grades) are a result of their own efforts, actions, and strate-gies—factors within their control—rather than attribute their performance to external factors outside their control, such as the teacher or bad luck. This could improve students' feelings of self-efficacy and their academic self-concept in the specific subject area, and may perhaps transfer to their general academic self-concept. Thus error analysis improves the critical thinking abilities of self-monitoring and self-evaluating one's own performance, and can improve students' feelings about their ability to succeed in science.

3. *How is an error analysis performed?* Error analysis requires a student to identify what the correct information/answer/approach is, as well as to identify what errors, omissions, and so on were made, determine why they occurred, and plan how to prevent them in the future. When doing error analyses, students are required to (a) identify what their wrong answer was and what the correct answer is (declar-ative knowledge), (b) determine specifically why they got the answer wrong (con-textual knowledge), and (c) formulate an action plan on how they have now learned and understood the material and how they will remember this informa-tion (procedural knowledge).

Error Analysis Model

1. What answer I had AND what the answer really was. OR

   WHAT I did wrong AND what I should have done.

2. WHY did I choose the wrong answer? OR

   Why did I do it wrong?

3. HOW will I remember what I now know is the correct answer? OR

   How will I make sure I don't make the same mistake again?

In all three steps, the student must focus on the specific content involved in the errors rather than on general causes of errors.

Pelley and Dalley's (1997) "question analysis" is intended to help students make a broader analysis of test questions than just a literal interpretation, because a narrower, more literal interpretation can constrain their studying and limit learning. Their proce-dure has four steps: identifying topics, understanding the correct answer, understand-ing wrong answers, and rephrasing the question. Pelley and Dalley encourage students to ask questions such as "How would I have had to study to know that the correct answer was right?" and "How would I have had to study to know that each wrong answer was wrong?" Focusing on the topic rather than the question helps students understand mate-rial more deeply, so they understand how ideas are interrelated and therefore are able to answer more and different questions correctly.

Classroom Applications

 The following are some examples of error analyses on a biology multiple-choice test item and on a research report (Hartman, 2001).

Multiple-Choice Item

Question

Which of the following is correct for the resting membrane potential of a typical neuron?

    a. It is negative outside compared to inside.

    b. It depends on high permeability of the membrane to sodium and potassium ions.

    c. It carries impulses from one region to another.

    d. It results from the unequal distribution of ions across the membrane.

Error Analysis of Item

1. What I got wrong and what the right answer is

   I thought the answer was *b*, but now I know the answer is *d*.

2. Why I got it wrong

   I know there was high permeability to potassium but I forgot it was impermeable to sodium.

3. How I will remember this and prevent future similar mistakes

   I'll remember that the resting potential of a neuron depends on the imbalance. The unequal distribution of ions results from the difference in permeability between sodium and potassium. The membrane is highly permeable to potassium, but it is impermeable to sodium. This causes it to be negative inside compared to the outside.

   I'll also try to use the process of elimination more so I can rule out some of the answer choices.

Error Analysis of a Research Report

1. What I got wrong and what I should have done

   I lost credit because I did not properly cite all of the sources of my information in the text and in the reference list at the end. I should have put the authors' last names and publication years in the body of the report where I discussed them in addition to placing their names on the list at the end of the report. All names have to be in both places; I had some in one place but not the other.

2. Why I did this wrong

> In junior high school we didn't have to do this so I didn't know it was the correct procedure. I didn't understand "plagiarism." I also didn't read the assignment sheet carefully enough to see that this was required. I just read it to get a general idea of what was expected and missed some of the details.

3. How I will prevent similar mistakes in the future

> I'll remember to cite my sources in the text because I'll think about how I would feel if someone took my ideas and didn't give me credit for them. I'll also read my assignment sheets more carefully, looking for specific details instead of general ideas. Finally, I'll use a checklist to make sure I really do everything I plan to do. The checklist will have two sections for each thing I have to do. One section will be to track my progress; the other will be to rate the quality of the work I've done.

Precautions and Possible Pitfalls

 Students typically have differing degrees of difficulty with the three parts of an error analysis. The first part, naming what they got wrong and what the right answer is, tends to be relatively easy for most students. The second part, requiring them to explain why they erred, is moderately difficult, especially when it comes to specifics. Students try to get away with general excuses, such as "I didn't study enough," instead of making specific analyses of why their lack of sufficient studying caused them to make the particular errors they made. The third part of the analysis, about how they will use what they have learned to improve their future performance, is the most difficult for students. Developing retention strategies and learning improvement plans requires hard and sustained thinking.

BIBLIOGRAPHY

Foos, P. W., & Fisher, R. P. (1988). Using Tests as Learning Opportunities. *Journal of Educational Psychology, 80*(2), 179-183.

Hartman, H. J. (2001). Developing students' metacognitive knowledge and strategies. In H. J. Hartman (Ed.), *Metacognition in learning and instruction: Theory, research and practice.* Dordrecht, the Netherlands: Kluwer Academic.

Pelley, J. W., & Dalley, B. K. (1997). *Successful types for medical students.* Lubbock: Texas Tech University, Extended Learning.

Schunk, D. (2000). *Learning theories: An educational perspective* (3rd ed.). Upper Saddle River, NJ: Merrill.

THE TIP (7.13)

 Use portfolios to collect more substantive evidence of your curriculum and teaching initiatives to contrast with and counteract narrowly defined test scores.

What the Research Says

 Hebert (1998) discusses teachers' reflections over a 10-year period concerning the many teaching and learning experiences involved in portfolio assessment. She found that timely evaluation painted a clear picture of what portfolios are and what they are not. Influenced by Howard Gardner's multiple intelligences, the faculty of Crow Island School in Winnetka, Illinois, evaluated their 10-year journey and the evolution of their portfolio "thinking." Overall, they found that portfolios fulfilled the promises portfolios held when they began. The staff defined and refined the roles of all stakeholders in the portfolio concept and today continue to gain a more in-depth view of their students as learners through the use of their full-site-based student-centered portfolio vision.

Classroom Applications

 Following are some points you should consider when thinking about portfolios:

- Portfolios in education, by most definitions, are created to tell a story. Don't be too rigid when deciding what goes into one. Consider allowing and helping your students to decide what goes into the "story" of their learning and growth. Are the portfolios going to be teacher-centered or student-centered? Who decides what goes into one?

- Decide what work will go home and what should stay in the portfolio. Are you presenting parents a "chapter" at a time or are you presenting a more temporal view within the portfolio paradigm?

- Whose portfolio is it? Should you assume the role of a portfolio manager and let students decide what will counterbalance test scores and enter the portfolio? If you decide to do it this way, help the students in their decisions. You are developing competent and thoughtful storytellers. When students are first discovering what a portfolio is, they require a scaffolding strategy.

- Attaching a letter grade to a portfolio seems to run contrary to the nature of the concept. Give it some thought.

- Select a time frame for the history of the learning a portfolio might represent. Is a portfolio a year's worth of work?

- For some students, "telling" a long-term story is too abstract. Defining an audience for the work contributes to a more concrete picture.

- Attach meaning to each piece in a portfolio by asking the student to write a short reason for its inclusion in the story. *Reflection tag* is the term used in the research literature for such reasons. This contributes to the student's metacognitive growth and attaches further value and meaning to the individual content.

- Deliberately teach parents about the value of student portfolios: what they mean to you, the curriculum, and the students.

Precautions and Possible Pitfalls

On the surface, portfolios sound like a simple concept. Do not underestimate the learning curve for teachers, students, and parents if the concept is to function at its best. Expect some frustration during the implementation and transition to portfolio adoption.

BIBLIOGRAPHY

Hebert, E. (1998). Lessons learned about student portfolios. *Phi Delta Kappan, 79,* 583-585.

THE TIP (7.14)

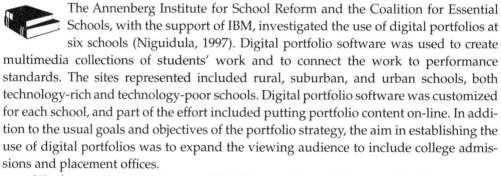

Consider "electronic file cabinets" or "digital portfolios" as assessment alternatives.

What the Research Says

 The Annenberg Institute for School Reform and the Coalition for Essential Schools, with the support of IBM, investigated the use of digital portfolios at six schools (Niguidula, 1997). Digital portfolio software was used to create multimedia collections of students' work and to connect the work to performance standards. The sites represented included rural, suburban, and urban schools, both technology-rich and technology-poor schools. Digital portfolio software was customized for each school, and part of the effort included putting portfolio content on-line. In addition to the usual goals and objectives of the portfolio strategy, the aim in establishing the use of digital portfolios was to expand the viewing audience to include college admissions and placement offices.

Word processing, scanning, and digitizing audio and video provided the means of entry into the multimedia portfolios. Researchers found that there was a need for the targeted schools to support a schoolwide vision on how technology, and digital portfolios in particular, corresponds with the schools' other systems. The main benefit of digital portfolios, in contrast to their paper counterparts, seems to be the ability to make them available to a wider audience. In addition, technology can add a few extra process steps that provide students greater opportunity to reflect on and polish their presentations.

Classroom Applications

 Although a schoolwide digital portfolio requirement might not be realistic or feasible at your school, a digital portfolio option may be just the right thing for specific classes or students. Consider the following ideas:

- Motivated and interested students could have the option of creating digital portfolios.

- Student artists or photographers could benefit by digitizing all of their work, along with appropriate reflections and written content.

- Students interested in technology as a career could benefit by recording their progress in the field as well as fulfilling a specific class portfolio requirement.

- Students could produce digital job résumés in portfolio form.

- The teacher could create a "class" portfolio and turn it into a class Web page, making it available to a much wider audience.

- Parents could be included as collaborators and viewers in the use of digital technology.

Digital media provide another vehicle for communication of student work. Because the idea of digital portfolios is relatively new, the limits of the technology have not been reached. Creative students and teachers can experiment with more innovative uses for the digital portfolio as it finds its niche among other instructional strategies.

Precautions and Possible Pitfalls

 The research points to time as the major instructional concern in the use of digital portfolios. The technological learning curve has a huge time component, and the time needs to come from somewhere. Do not just add new requirements on top of your curricular goals and objectives. Try to estimate realistically the amount of time your students will require to learn any new technology, and be prepared to let go of some other parts of your curriculum or instructional activities.

BIBLIOGRAPHY

Niguidula, D. (1997). Picturing performance with digital portfolios. *Educational Leadership, 55*(3), 26-29.

THE TIP (7.15)

 Create a portfolio format based on a syllabus or on rubric-style goals and objectives for instruction. These serve as "points of reflection."

What the Research Says

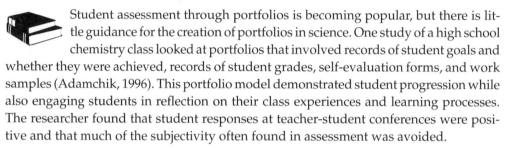 Student assessment through portfolios is becoming popular, but there is little guidance for the creation of portfolios in science. One study of a high school chemistry class looked at portfolios that involved records of student goals and whether they were achieved, records of student grades, self-evaluation forms, and work samples (Adamchik, 1996). This portfolio model demonstrated student progression while also engaging students in reflection on their class experiences and learning processes. The researcher found that student responses at teacher-student conferences were positive and that much of the subjectivity often found in assessment was avoided.

Classroom Applications

A portfolio of the type described above seems like a logical extension of the rubric or class syllabus philosophy. The main issue here is how you can develop a balance between a teacher-centered and a student-centered approach to the creation of goals and objectives. Who develops student goals and objectives? Consider the creation of class-designed portfolios, facilitated and managed collaboratively. Teachers have certain content and process requirements based on school, state, and national expectations for performance. The major goals of constructing portfolios of this type are to illustrate and communicate clearly the goals of instruction and to engage students in the role of self-assessment.

Ideally, the students' goals will be combined with the teacher-mandated goals. Student goals might include class-generated, more personal goals that form student-centered "working" guidelines shared by all stakeholders. These might consider and include the academic side as well as a more metacognitive side.

Once agreed on, the portfolio (rubric or syllabus format) document becomes a meter-stick that students, teachers, and parents can relate to, visit, and revisit as needed to discover where they are on the educational map within the class.

Precautions and Possible Pitfalls

 A document such as that described above has a way of becoming obsolete as class conditions change. Be prepared to revisit the portfolio framework as needed. Adjustments will need to be made; be prepared to share the responsibility for this. Goals and objectives that seemed feasible early on may need to be mediated. As you gain experience, the process will evolve, and your comfort level with this assessment tool will rise.

BIBLIOGRAPHY

Adamchik, C. (1996). The design and assessment of chemistry portfolios. *Journal of Chemical Education, 73,* 528-530.

Hebert, E. (1998). Lessons learned about student portfolios. *Phi Delta Kappan, 79,* 583-585.

THE TIP (7.16)

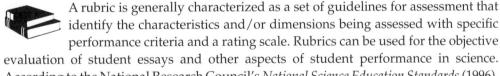 Use rubrics for your science assessments.

What the Research Says

A rubric is generally characterized as a set of guidelines for assessment that identify the characteristics and/or dimensions being assessed with specific performance criteria and a rating scale. Rubrics can be used for the objective evaluation of student essays and other aspects of student performance in science. According to the National Research Council's *National Science Education Standards* (1996), it is especially important that rubric scoring criteria be developed for the specific students to which they will be applied; teachers should not impose preestablished rubrics that were designed for other students. Tables 7.1 and 7.2 illustrate two kinds of rubrics: holistic and analytic.

Classroom Applications

There are various procedures for developing rubrics in science. The Scott Foresman publishing company's science division makes some science rubrics for specific science topics and activities in grades K-6 available on-line (http://www.sfscience.com). Another resource for the use of rubrics in science can be found in the "Teachers' Lounge" section of a Web site established by Sackville High School in Nova Scotia, on a page headed "Rubrics to Evaluate Students' Work in Science" (http://www.sackville.ednet.ns.ca/teacherl/sciencerubrics.htm). This site contains specific guidelines for developing both holistic and analytic rubrics for science learning. Tables 7.1 and 7.2 are adapted from this site, which also offers several other useful resources for science teachers interested in using rubrics as assessment tools.

Constructs are very dependent upon the contexts of their use. Transfer of one rubric to another teacher and class simply will not work most of the time, but examining rubrics from other classes is an important developmental activity and can aid professional growth.

Table 7.1   Holistic Rubric for Science Projects

Proficient (3 points)	The student has a generated a hypothesis, conducted a procedure, collected data, and analyzed results. The student's work is thorough and the results and conclusions are consistent with the data collected. Any minor errors do not affect the quality of the project.
Adequate (2 points)	The project may have a hypothesis, a procedure, collected data, and analyzed results. The project is not as thorough as it could be; there are a few overlooked areas. A few errors affect the project's quality.
Limited (1 point)	The project may have a hypothesis, a procedure, collected data, and analyzed results. The project has several errors that affect its quality.

Table 7.2 Analytic Rubric for Science Projects

Criteria	4 Points	3 Points	2 Points	1 Point
Has a plan for investigation	Thorough plan	Plan lacks a few details	Plan lacks major details	Plan is incomplete and limited
Use of materials	Manages all materials responsibly	Usually uses materials responsibly	Mishandles some materials	Fails to handle materials properly
Collects the data	Thorough data collection	Most data collected	Major portions of data are missing	Data collection consists of a few points

One good suggestion for a construction of a science rubric starts with the writing of the performance standards for a scientifically literate person. This description is then analyzed and divided into different components and complexity levels. The complexity and rigor of the rubric will depend on the experience and ability level of the students and the teacher's goals.

The development of rubrics can come from three perspectives: holistic, analytic, or a combination of both. Holistic rubrics are instruments that contain different levels of performance that describe both the quantity and quality of the task. The instructor determines the best fit for aspects of the lesson for the students. Analytic rubrics are constructs that consist of criteria that are further subdivided into different levels of performance. One starts with the criteria to be assessed and moves on to different levels of performance for the criteria. Analytic rubrics tend to be more precise and concise than holistic rubrics, which contain broader descriptions about levels of performance.

If you type the word *rubric* into an Internet search engine, you will find many good Web sites that can get you started or further refine and develop your rubric philosophy. Whichever style you synthesize as your own, the rubric should try to involve students in patterns of observation, reflection, thinking, and problem solving that reflect the standards of the scientific community as reflected in various standards for content and scientific processes.

Precautions and Possible Pitfalls

 Keep in mind that a major long-term goal of instruction is to have students be able to decide, on their own, what they need to know, how they need to know it, and when they need to know it. Rubrics can create dependence; they will not foster "learning how to learn" unless you deliberately build this goal into your strategy and work to reduce your students' dependence on them. At some point, try having students collaborate with you in the development of mutually agreed-upon rubrics. This exercise serves as guided practice in transferring some responsibility to the students for their own learning.

BIBLIOGRAPHY

Luft, J. A. (1999). Rubrics: Design and use in science teacher education. *Journal of Science Teacher Education, 10,* 107-121.

National Research Council. (1996). *National science education standards.* Washington, DC: National Academy Press.

THE TIP (7.17)

 Be aware of the findings of the Third International Mathematics and Science Study (TIMSS), and don't settle for a single perspective on those findings.

What the Research Says

 The Third International Mathematics and Science Study is big—the most comprehensive worldwide study of student achievement to date. A total of some 500,000 students from five different grade levels in more than 40 countries were tested on a variety of topics; the study produced huge amounts of test data. The testing took place in the mid-1990s, and the results of the study were released a few years later.

A search of scholarly journals for mention of the TIMSS, conducted in the summer of 2000 at the University of California, San Diego, produced some 70 articles in many different types of journals. *Science, Congressional Digest, NSTA's Science Teacher, Phi Delta Kappan, American Enterprise, Scientific American,* and *Issues in Science and Technology* only begin the list of journals that have weighed in on the highly controversial results of the TIMSS (you may have guessed by now that U.S. students, as a whole, didn't do very well in the study). Different authors, reading the same results, have produced unique explanations, offered different solutions, or expressed indifference.

Some have attacked the testing methodology as suspect, saying the cross-country, societal, demographic, and educational institutional differences among the subjects make the data questionable at best. Others have compared the TIMSS results with more favorable increases in SAT scores among U.S. students and better performance on the National Assessment of Educational Progress. Even authors of different articles within the same journals have displayed different stances.

Some have accepted the TIMSS results as a call to arms and have begun placing blame on teachers, textbooks, curricula, not enough homework, and many other facets of the educational system. Each has put his or her own spin on the meaning of the results, with little consensus emerging. In a guest editorial in *Phi Delta Kappan* on-line, Lowell Rose (1998) has provided the following list of suggested changes, should the improvement of U.S. student scores on studies such as the TIMSS become a priority:

1. Forget local control of education, and establish a national curriculum so that the federal government can control what students study and when they study it.

2. Require that all students study algebra, starting no later than the middle grades.

3. Require that every student study calculus before the end of high school.

4. Increase the time students spend in school, and use the added time for more instruction in math and physics.

5. Decrease the time students spend on art, music, and vocational subjects, and devote the time saved to more instruction in math and physics.

6. Decrease the time students spend on extracurricular activities, including sports, and use the time saved for increased instruction in math and physics.

What does all this research and reflection mean? It means that the TIMSS results have spawned a huge range of opinion and discussion with no consensus. Science and math types call for more science classes and better teacher training. More global thinkers and generalists do not want to sacrifice the richness of curricular offerings just to improve U.S. students' performance on a questionable test. Each author's individual spin on the results reflects that person's own stance and agenda.

Classroom Applications

 Like other big studies, the TIMSS has found its way from the academic journals into the mainstream media. As a mathematics or science teacher, you may be asked—by your students' parents, by your school administrators, or others—to comment on or discuss the study and its results. That is one big reason you should become literate in the scope of interpretation of the study. Another reason you should reflect on the results of the TIMSS is that this will provide you with an opportunity to examine your own stance on the results and the opinions that have been stated. There is no lack of opinions or perspectives!

If you are not able to do library literature searches on the TIMSS, try the Internet. Many Web sites offer information and opinions on the subject.

Precautions and Possible Pitfalls

 There is little consensus on the meaning of the TIMSS results, and that can be confusing for you as you form your own opinions, and can make it difficult for you to have discussions with others about the results. Gaining a working literacy in the range of issues involved in the TIMSS can support you in establishing a clear vision of your commitment to professional growth and responsibility that others will recognize. It pays to be aware of this study.

BIBLIOGRAPHY

Bracey, G. W. (1998). Are U.S. students behind? *American Prospect, 9*(37), 64-70.

Hettinger, J. (1999, February). Tackling the TIMSS (Third International Mathematics and Science Study). *Techniques,* pp. 30-32.

Hiraoka, L. (1998, May). The international test scores are in . . . *NEA Today Online.* Available Internet: http://www.nea.org/neatoday/9805/scoop.html

Rose, L. C. (1998). Who cares? And so what? *Phi Delta Kappan, 79* [On-line]. Available Internet: http://www.pdkintl.org/kappan/kros9806.htm

Index

CORWIN
PRESS

The Corwin Press logo—a raven striding across an open book—represents the happy union of courage and learning. We are a professional-level publisher of books and journals for K-12 educators, and we are committed to creating and providing resources that embody these qualities. Corwin's motto is "Success for All Learners."